T0398487

'Lavinia Bifulco presents a rich and subtle analysis of the changing fortunes of the social dimensions of Europe. She combines attention to the complex trajectories of social welfare, in their variations across place and time, with a clear grasp of the forces that have been subordinating the social to the economic.'

*– John Clarke, The Open University, UK*

# Social Policies and Public Action

The concept of public action is a magnifying lens for shedding light on the plurality of institutional and social actors interacting in policies. Taking into account a changing social world that is redefining the State and its instruments, it is well suited for picking out transformations that have been affecting European social policies for some twenty years or so now: the territorial reorganization of powers; the spread of a public-private mix in the provision of services; the rise of new forms of collaborative governance; the institutionalization of the European agenda on social investment.

This book examines social policies as normative and cognitive devices that contribute to organizing social life and are themselves moulded and redefined by it. The perspective of public action is located where it is possible to observe how these devices come into action, the powers and interests they help mobilize and the dynamics they generate. Policies thus appear as a tangle of rather diverse processes in which the erosion of the 'social' coexists with the emergence of innovative forms of social organization.

Public action is the key tool that helps to deal with this tangle by posing the following questions. What vocabularies, significances and practices are set in motion by the 'social' today? What are the resources that fuel it? What powers are deployed in it?

**Lavinia Bifulco** is Professor of Sociology at the University of Milan-Bicocca in Italy.

# Routledge Advances in Health and Social Policy

New titles

**International Perspectives on Elder Abuse**
*Amanda Phelan*

**Mental Health Services for Vulnerable Children and Young People**
Supporting children who are, or have been, in foster care
*Michael Tarren-Sweeney and Arlene Vetere*

**Providing Compassionate Health Care**
Challenges in Policy and Practice
*Edited by Sue Shea, Robin Wynyard and Christos Lionis*

**Teen Pregnancy and Parenting**
Rethinking the Myths and Misperceptions
*Keri Weed, Jody S. Nicholson and Jaelyn R. Farris*

**The Invisible Work of Nurses**
Hospitals, Organisation and Healthcare
*Davina Allen*

**Domestic Violence in Diverse Contexts**
A Re-examination of Gender
*Sarah Wendt and Lana Zannettino*

**Maternity Services and Policy in an International Context**
Risk, Citizenship and Welfare Regimes
*Edited by Patricia Kennedy and Naonori Kodate*

**Innovation in Social Welfare and Human Services**
*Rolf Rønning and Marcus Knutagård*

**Social Development and Social Work Perspectives on Social Protection**
*Edited by Julie Drolet*

Forthcoming titles

**M-Health in Developing Countries**
Design and Implementation Perspectives on Using Mobiles in Healthcare
*Arul Chib*

**Alcohol Policy in Europe**
Delivering the WHO Ideal?
*Shane Butler, Karen Elmeland, Betsy Thom and James Nicholls*

# Social Policies and Public Action

## Lavinia Bifulco

Routledge
Taylor & Francis Group

LONDON AND NEW YORK

First published 2017
by Routledge
2 Park Square, Milton Park, Abingdon, Oxon OX14 4RN

and by Routledge
711 Third Avenue, New York, NY 10017

*Routledge is an imprint of the Taylor & Francis Group, an informa business*

© 2017 Lavinia Bifulco

*British Library Cataloguing in Publication Data*
A catalogue record for this book is available from the British Library

*Library of Congress Cataloging-in-Publication Data*
Names: Bifulco, Lavinia, author.
Title: Social policies and public action / Lavinia Bifulco.
Description: 1 Edition. | New York : Routledge, 2017. | Series: Routledge advances in health and social policy | Includes bibliographical references and index.
Identifiers: LCCN 2016022079 | ISBN 9781472420886 (hardback) | ISBN 9781315609577 (ebook)
Subjects: LCSH: Social policy. | Public welfare. | Charities. | Europe--Social policy.
Classification: LCC HN18.3 .B54 2017 | DDC 306--dc23
LC record available at https://lccn.loc.gov/2016022079

ISBN: 978-1-4724-2088-6 (hbk)
ISBN: 978-1-315-60957-7 (ebk)

Typeset in Times New Roman
by Taylor & Francis Books

To Danilo

# Contents

# Tables

# Introduction

## Social policies and public action: What is the 'social'?

Never, since it first came into being, has social Europe so keenly experienced the iron grip of increasing social problems. According to Eurostat, in 2014 almost 122 million people – about 24 per cent of the EU-28 population – were at risk of poverty or social exclusion, 8 million more compared to 2009 (EU-27). Those most affected are women, children, people living in single-parent households, young people, the less-educated and migrants.

This book starts out from the conviction that we need adequate conceptual and interpretative keys for dealing with the present context of the crisis. The fact is that the crisis takes shape not only in the form of a dramatic increase in social problems, but also as a need for reflection on the categories, values and schemes of significance that have constituted the basis of European systems of social protection. In other words, we have to bring into focus the normative and cognitive dimensions of social policies, and gain an understanding of the cracks, the fault lines and the evolutionary directions in them.

Public action is the key tool I use to gain access to these dimensions. The main question I ask myself can be summed up as follows: 'What is the 'social' in social policies today?'

### Public action

The concept of public action focuses on the intersections between the sphere of government and that of society or, as Lascoumes and Le Galès (2007) argue, on the way political regulation and social regulation interact. It refers to a process-based research perspective, bringing together a number of approaches such as, for example, the policy network and the advocacy coalition approach. In reality there is broad agreement amongst researchers on the fact that policy-making does not coincide with rational decision-making and formal rules but is interwoven with negotiation, dynamics of framing and reframing, conflict and agreement building, so that adaptations and changes are all part of it, in the same way as incoherence and unpredictability.

Thus, public action is a magnifying lens for shedding light on the interactive fabric that characterizes policies after the restructuring of State in Europe, the fruit of a complicated mingling of isomorphic mechanisms and specific national circumstances (Pollitt and Bouckaert, 2000). In France, a country with a deeply rooted republican and Jacobin tradition, what has been at stake has been the sort of modernization capable of paring down the State and rendering it less overwhelming. In the United Kingdom, reorganization gained strength at the same time as reforms of a neoliberal nature. In Mediterranean Europe the leitmotif has been the reduction of inefficiency and waste. Whatever the case, a common phenomenon has been the proliferation of policy instruments aiming at activating and incentivizing individual citizens and local communities, or based on communication, on the production and spread of knowledge or the elaboration of standards (Lascoumes and Le Galès, 2007). The spread of these tools rather than those of a more traditional nature – based on command and control – clearly reveals a stronger focus on processes and interaction.

In this way, the notion of public action takes into account a changing social world that has redefined the State, its instruments and its administrative organization. It brings into focus the ways in which problems and solutions are defined and negotiated in arenas that are very different, due to the greater involvement of society and social actors in the networks of governance. Moreover, it highlights the interplay between three features of policy processes: ambiguity, which is a resource for processes of negotiation and translation; changeability, which can imply both shifts and transformations; and contingency, which means the possibility of alternative options.

As already stated, different approaches to research converge in delineating a process-based perspective of this nature. My objective, then, is not to introduce a new approach but to refine the conceptual and analytical tools already in existence and take advantage of their specific added value in the domain of social policies.

My analytical scheme is based on the following basic points.

First, it conceives of social policies as processes characterized by a high interdependency between actors, levels (supranational, central and local) and phases, leaving behind once and for all the monolithic character and monopoly role of the State and taking into account the shift from government to governance.

A process-based perspective is well suited for picking out essential features of the active or enabling welfare state, the model that has been redesigning European systems of social protection for some twenty years or so now. The very idea of activation, ambiguous though it is, establishes with assuredly evocative power two converging axes of change, both of which are process-oriented: the promotion of agency on the part of the citizens, and acknowledgement of the capacity for self-organization on the part of local communities and social actors. In a nutshell, it could be said that in post-Keynesian welfare what is at stake is a shift from states to processes, which, as well as forms of governing, also affect the relationship between the beneficiaries and the institutions of social protection. The strategies of individualization and personalization of intervention that have taken root since the 1990s have revisited or re-elaborated Marshall's concept of social citizenship as a status, bringing to the foreground the ability of citizens to participate jointly and responsibly in producing their own well-being. As we shall see, this can result in a range of rather diverse situations and in particularly intricate mixtures of empowerment and greater insecurity on the part of individuals. Similarly, the way social rights have shifted from a statute of legitimate entitlements to that of benefits that are the object of negotiations to establish the conditions on which they may be enjoyed, on the one hand responds to a growing demand for individual freedom and autonomy and, on the other, implies that social protection is subordinate to the respect of strict obligations for the beneficiaries, giving rise to paradoxical forms of encouragement to become independent. As regards the territorial bearings of social citizenship, the growing importance of local or urban space responds to demands for a diversification of responses and active involvement of citizens, whilst at the same time revealing a risk of greater territorial inequalities.

A series of changes in social policies, either consolidated or ongoing, can thus be observed together with all their ambiguities when seen from the perspective of processes. This concerns the tools of intervention as well. A significant case is that of the spread of participatory devices in interventions of social inclusion aiming at the active involvement of the 'excluded'. Other examples are the instruments of negotiation used in the realm of public–private partnerships, which stress the need not to refer to pre-established objectives but to pursue reciprocal agreements and re-adjustment. In both cases the potentially innovative effects coexist with a high degree of contingency and limited range. The very close association between the spread of process-based approaches and local scale should also be pointed out. Indeed, localization and the connected questioning of some aspects of standardization and uniformity typical of national space is an essential element in this picture, as is particularly evident in programmes dealing with deprived urban contexts which insist on the construction of cooperative networks between actors, the valorization of local resources and the spread of knowledge in the community, as well as on institution building and social innovation.

Second, my scheme highlights generative or constructive implications of social policies. The concept of public action places the emphasis on something that is in the process of becoming, is mobile and constitutes the subject and object of creation. Echoes are thus to be heard in it of sociological approaches that insist on the 'constructed' nature of social reality. This does not, however, entail a conciliatory conception of policies. As I have said, focusing on public action is significant because it can shed light on the ambiguities and contradictions in processes. It thus brings to light conflict, opportunistic moves, practices of dominion and power relations, inequalities in access to opportunities, conservative and self-reproductive organizational dynamics. It is not a question of pessimism or optimism. The point is to assume an analytical stance that reveals the generative implications of social policies without taking their virtues for granted. From this point of view, the case of social innovation is a good example. In national and local programming in Europe, a repertory of strategies has formed around this issue that stresses the need to come up with new responses to social needs and at the same time generates new social relationships. In an age of institutional uncertainty and seriously dwindling public resources, there is a high possibility that this will nurture quite powerful and persuasive rhetoric as to the intrinsic social qualities of the community, the third sector and civil society, fuelling over-simplified and trivial concepts of what social is (Chapter 10). The point of view of public action helps us deal with this: far from sticking to rhetoric and justifications mobilized in the policy field, it places under observation the dynamics and interaction through which rhetoric and justifications feed – or fail to feed – social innovation.

Third, this leads us to the relationship between ideas and policies, which is a central analytical axis in order to understand the constructive implications of social policies. Since ideas cannot be separated from the social contexts in which they gain strength, the intention is to come to an understanding of how social policies contribute to organizing social life and, vice-versa, how different social materials make their mark on policies giving rise to the issues at stake, the strategies and the perspectives. Actually, we need to acknowledge that the process-oriented trend in welfare and policies is suited to the social and institutional climate of today: the spirit of new capitalism, whose network-based organization values individuals that are permanently active, mobile and capable of initiative and networking (Boltanski and Chiapello, 1999).

Focusing on the relationship between ideas and policies also entails investigating the way these social materials turn into black boxes. The metaphor of black boxes, which I use repeatedly throughout the book, refers to the dynamics by which the social and political categorizations, premises and options shaping and directing decisions are concealed under the guise of technical issues or transformed into necessities. Since they are not a given reality but the fruit of processes – such as the reification of certain ways of setting up problems and solutions, or the naturalization of social issues – these boxes can in theory be unlocked.

Fourth, I also conceive the 'public' in terms of processes of 'publicization'. 'Public' is not a point of departure but, if anything, the result of something that has been constructed and is artificial and contingent. Public does not mean the State. The paths by which this meaning acquired the characteristics of something taken for granted coincide with the development of the institutional architectures of welfare that shaped the societies of Western Europe during much of the twentieth century. The pillar sustaining the solid and complex structure of values, norms, and institutional and social practices causing the public and the State to coincide is precisely the central nature of State authority that has earmarked the construction of these same architectures with both positive and negative consequences. On the positive side, this pillar has enabled the unfolding of processes that are fundamental to the organization of a public domain in social life, beyond the political and administrative context: such processes include the institutionalization of resources and of the right to participate in 'social heritage' (Marshall, 1950) and the democratization of politics and the reinforcement of modern democracy (Crouch, 1999). On the negative side, we witness the well-known baggage of lack of clarity, paternalism and standardization which, together with other factors, have contributed to delegitimizing this authority and to devaluing both the concept of the public and the vocabulary used to discuss it (Clarke, 2004). Be that as it may, the equivalence of the public and the State no longer holds (Clarke, 2004; de Leonardis, 1998). This implies distancing oneself from the opposition between public and private, which has long served as an analytical key within studies of welfare and social policies, and shifting attention from the 'public' understood as the characteristics of actors and organizations to the processes of becoming – or not becoming – public (de Leonardis, 1997; Bifulco and de Leonardis, 2005; Bifulco, 2011c).

## Dimensions of analysis

As is evident from what has been said up to now, my analytical scheme does not examine social policies as answers to the social needs and risks institutionalized in contexts of different national regimes, but as devices that contribute to organizing social life and are themselves moulded and redefined by it. The perspective of public action is located where it is possible to observe how these normative and cognitive devices come into action, the powers and interests they help activate and the effects they generate. Thus, it comprises two complementary points of view: these concentrate, respectively, on the normative options that are incorporated and take concrete shape, not always visibly, in these devices; and on the tangle of rather diverse phenomena that are set off by them, in which, for example, local experiments on new forms of citizenship, which breathe new life into the social realm, coexist alongside very subtle dynamics of social exclusion.

In applying this analytical scheme, the book jointly considers three main dimensions: the types of agency by which actors mobilize, interact and clash within a policy field; the institutional dynamics which delimit and support them; and the mechanisms by which scales of power are defined and redefined.

As regards the first dimension, I assume that the changes at stake in reorganizations of European welfare states have greatly increased the range of actors, and that interests, powers and strategic capacities are not an exclusive prerogative of the decision-makers and street-level bureaucracy but potentially an element defining the role of citizens and users, too. In other words, I consider that the issue of the empowerment of recipients, beyond the rhetoric, requires methods of enquiry capable of unravelling the many knots that empirically entangle questions of individual autonomy and freedom/agency. And this is one of the reasons why I shall refer significantly to Amartya Sen's capabilities approach. As Kremakova (2014, p. 401) observes, an excellent reason for using it as a theoretical and analytical framework is that Sen's concept of capabilities as substantive freedoms 'allows space for human agency as the basis for achieving flourishing and well-being'. One point that should be made clear is that when reasoning on capabilities as a form of freedom, Sen highlights the close and complicated relationship that exists between individual agency and the normative fabric of society, finding strong support here for the anti-utilitarian tendency that inspires his work. Thus, one of the objectives his work accomplishes is that of denying the conception of liberty on which theoretical justification for the new capitalism has been founded.

Coherently with this framework, agency is seen as socially embedded, at the same time sustained and conditioned by institutional contexts. In fact, institutions count a great deal in my analytical scheme. Much of the literature has attempted the task of defining what institutions are and how they influence social action and interaction. My analysis accords special attention to institutions in the sociological meaning of the term, concentrating on the relationship between ideas and institutions. This is in keeping with my concern to bring the normative and cognitive 'stuff' of social policies into the foreground.

The third dimension is connected to the 'spatial turn' that took place in the social sciences during the 1980s. As Mayer (2008, p. 414) puts it, this was when it was discovered that social interactions could be better understood as societally produced in historically specific social spaces – spaces that are no longer considered inert, or a container, but the fruit of active production. In particular, space is decisive for placing social policies in the multi-scale dynamics that constitute them, to varying degrees. Turning the limelight mostly on Europe and the local dimension, I take into account the new configurations of power relations which, for some decades now, have been restructuring the national space of welfare in the post-Keynesian age and to which multilevel governance and the role of cities as the protagonists of the season of social innovation are linked.

## What is the 'social' in social policies?

Applying the analytical scheme outlined above, in the following chapters I take into consideration some of the tendencies towards change that have affected European welfare states over the past few years, in particular the territorial reorganization of powers, the European agenda on social investment, the spread of a public–private mix in the provision of services and the rise of new forms of collaborative governance.

Yet neither the questions I pose, nor the instruments I make use of to answer them, are those that are traditionally found in a comparative analysis of welfare systems and I do not intend them to be so. I analyse transformations of public actions in order to understand how they affect the social realm, i.e. the realm that the welfare state has 'invented' (Donzelot, 1984) by means of a broad and shifting range of devices. This realm includes processes of social reproduction and the connected ones of the production of well-being; the problems, needs and risks that these processes have to deal with; the interventions and forms of solidarity, whether from the institutions or not, that are activated to meet them; the normative horizons of social justice that these interventions take as their points of reference and the entitlements they rest upon; the dynamics of social integration that result from them or, in other words, social bonds and social cohesion. Though brief, this catalogue makes it possible to grasp the often multi-layered depth of the history that the social bears on its shoulders, so to say, in the realm of welfare.

Of course, what affects the social sphere in the context of welfare (starting from social Europe) is to be seen against the background of what Streeck (2011) has defined 'democratic capitalism' and should be placed in connection with its involutions and contradictions, as well as the reorganization of the relations between the economic, political and social spheres taking place on a global scale. As Rose has pointed out (1996, p. 337), mutations in the social are linked to reshaping strategies for governing economics and decoupling relations between social welfare and economic growth. In addition, the social dominion activated by the welfare state is to be found in a precise spatial dimension, i.e. in a single, integrated space, 'territorialized across a nation' (ibid., p. 333), which rescaling processes have transformed in depth. It is therefore evident that the social realm in terms of the social compromise of the mid 1900s (Crouch, 1999) no longer exists.

What significance, logic and practices are set in motion by the social today? What are the resources that fuel it? What powers are deployed in it? What vocabulary is used to define and redefine it?

In dealing with these questions, I attempt to understand the areas of tension in which dynamics of desocialization coexist with the emergence of innovative forms of social relations and aggregation. I start out from the fact that two closely connected dynamics are in operation: on the one hand, the social realm is expanding, extending well beyond its traditional borders; on the other hand, the resources, significances and regulatory structures that have historically constituted it in the context of the welfare state are being worn away. As we shall see in the coming chapters, the development of mechanisms that tend to commodify the social, the adoption of measures that see the social as an investment, the spread of a community register in the mobilization of civil society and the emergence of practices of social innovation coexist alongside one another as modes of reorganizing traditional welfare states.

The focus on public action helps to identify and examine this weft, as it allows us to identify and examine the processual nature of the social, in what way it is the fruit of dynamics – of creation, transformation and erosion – that involve many different actors and levels.

Thus, my analysis also attempts to give an account of the relationship between the dynamics of depoliticization and dynamics of desocialization. A wide-ranging debate has highlighted the modes in which depoliticization may come about: delegation, i.e. the transfer of an issue from governmental arenas towards extra-governmental organizations; privatization, which involves an issue becoming a matter of private choice; denial, which consists in placing issues within the realm of necessity, denying the dimensions of contingency and choice (Burnham, 2014; Hay, 2014). In connection with these dynamics, we should recall the techniques of 'governing by numbers' (Supiot, 2015) by which New Public Management is carried out (auditing, monitoring techniques, etc.) and which tend to objectivize political choices and options in the form of data and facts that are considered 'indisputable' or 'inevitable'. In a way, desocialization and depoliticization proceed in harmony with one another. A crystal-clear example of the mutual reinforcement occurring between the neutralization of political significance and the erosion of the social dimension can be found in policies dealing with the lack of employment, relegating the latter exclusively to the sphere of individual responsibility.

As for the methodology, looking at the interaction between social regulation and political regulation means questioning the confines that traditionally separate a number of scientific fields, mainly, but not only, sociology and the analysis of public policies. I make an effort to take up the tools of the sociology of public action – systematically identified by Lascoumes and Le Galès (2007) supplementing them with analytical categories and inspirations taken from the study of public administration and welfare, the theories of social justice, political geography and urban theory.

Within the range of different positions and arguments that animate the debate on the welfare state, one point that is quite widely accepted is the shift from a quantitative approach to a more qualitative one. As Evers and Guillemard (eds, 2013) observe, issues of limiting spending and reducing budgets and public services, which animated the debate up to the end of the last millennium, have made way for the issue of new social risks and needs, which have called into question the modes of response and institutionalized logic of the welfare state. In line with this perspective, my empirical investigation will give priority to qualitative methods and techniques suitable for dealing with the questions posed, such as if and how notions of social citizenship are being re-worked; what premises and categories issues such as social investment and social cohesion are grounded upon; how knowledge enters into decisions and the information they are based on; how power relations and agency gain strength and how they change.

Opting for a qualitative approach is also consistent with the attention devoted to the beneficiaries of policies who, as already mentioned, offer a privileged perspective for observation. I therefore make use of the capabilities approach framework to explore what their acknowledged role is, what agency they can put into practice, what consequences the measures implemented by public and non-public organizations have on them, what sort of well-being and what sort of freedom they derive from it.

## The structure

The structure of the book reflects my earlier arguments.

In the first part, I present the essential tools I use in my analysis and outline the context, launching the question that runs through the entire book: what is the social? In order to bring into focus the importance of the normative/cognitive dimension of policies, I suggest a tool that places ideas, institutions and agency in relation to one another and combines a cultural study of policies and neo-institutional theory with Amartya Sen's capabilities approach. Subsequently, I use this tool to examine the controversial vicissitudes of social Europe and tackle two questions that are deeply implicated in the entire discussion: the tension between the market and social dimensions in the EU and the current waning of the latter. I pay particular attention to today's uncertainties but start out by recalling the nucleus of values and norms of the welfare states as expressed in some of its key components: equality, rights, social justice and democracy. This nucleus is crucial for understanding the particular project of social organization that forged the European social model and identifying the uncertainties that are clouding its horizons.

In the second part, I investigate the tendencies and dynamics that most clearly reveal the processual declination of social policies in Europe: territorialization, activation, participation, contractualization and the public–private mix. This is a rather specific selection and does not directly take in many mainstream issues in European social policy, though these are dealt with indirectly. Thus, my choice is linked to the perspective I have taken and my consequent interest in highlighting the process-based shifts in the welfare state and their ambivalent implications for the social realm. The picture that emerges is a jigsaw: the development of participatory forms of governance is increasingly accompanied by growing mechanisms of marketization; possibilities for agency coexist alongside strategies for activation policies that burden the individual with excessive responsibility; the expansion of social business accentuates the combination of logics of support and market interests.

Taking as a basis comparative research and case studies, the third part is devoted to the discussion of three specific policy fields on which my empirical investigation has concentrated over the past ten years: school-to-work transitions, care, social inclusion in cities. The fields selected are a crucial terrain for observing the ways in which changes in public action are connected with changes in the social domain.

In addition, these fields are significant because:

- they are centrally linked to new social risks or new ways of facing traditional social risks;
- they evoke recipients who, for various reasons, are those most left in the shadows by the traditional welfare state: young people, families/women, the inhabitants of disadvantaged urban areas;
- since they call into question at one and the same time the differences and the similarities between techniques of intervention, they make it possible to understand how and why common (but not fully agreed upon) tools are brought into play differently in specific contexts, and with what effects.

In the last part, I conclude by bringing together the various threads that run through the study, linking them to the thesis of the loss of consistency of the social dimension in the EU and attempt to answer the questions: what are the meaning and places of the social realm in social policies today?

I am indebted to many people in producing the present volume. I certainly owe many, many thanks to the students who have put me to the test over the past few years with their comments and questions – all the more productive, the more unexpected they were; to the group *Laboratorio Sui Generis* of the Università di Milano-Bicocca, with which I have shared many of the lines of research examined here, with particular thanks to Ota de Leonardis, for the precious and never banal perspectives and paths opened up for collective investigation; to John Clarke, Patrick le Galès and Janet Newman, who discussed earlier versions of some chapters. Lastly, thanks to Patricia Hampton for her competence and patience in dealing with my uncertain English, and to the editors Claire Jervis and Lianne Sherlock for their interest in my work.

# Part I

# The framework

# 1    Concepts and issues

Analysing social policies means tackling questions of values and choices regarding justice, as de Leonardis (2002) maintains. Welfare practices and policies incorporate world views, principles, categorization and criteria for judging what is held to be just, opportune and desirable and what is not. Even giving a definition of welfare is an operation with considerable normative implications, which is anything but neutral.

This initial chapter, which presents the conceptual and analytical instruments used in the volume, begins with a discussion of the approaches that have brought into focus the cognitive and normative dimension of policies.[1] For those who refer to sociological neo-institutionalism, ideas and institutions are overlapping dimensions, even though they do not coincide. It is from this perspective that some coordinates of institutional analyses are referred to later. Focusing on the institutional value of ideas or on the cognitive/normative dimension of institutions means bringing the social and political mix that constitutes social policies to the centre of attention. However, ideas count but so do the tools and mechanisms of coordination by which rights and mutual obligations are instituted (Streeck and Thelen, eds, 2005). Thus, in the following chapters, when referring to institutions I shall privilege the practice of combination and not separation: as well as ideas, I shall take into account the formal arrangements and instruments that regulate and mediate social and public life. This points to the embeddedness of individual agency: the powers and freedoms of actors have to be analysed with reference to social and institutional aspects and not just the individual rationality (Blakeley and Evans, 2009). I shall not, therefore, dwell on interests, taking for granted both their role in the vocabulary of motives and the fact that their very interpretation is filtered through institutional elements and contexts. Instead, I shall discuss agency by taking as my starting point Amartya Sen's (1992, 1999) capabilities approach, which has gained a leading position in discourse and the public agenda as a perspective for re-thinking citizenship and re-designing welfare. The most important point affecting the issues we are about to analyse is that this approach helps tackle the question of what kind of agency is involved in social policies.

## The ideas

The debate on public policies has paid attention to ideas and their performative effects in various ways. Briefly put, ideas count, as do the effects they have on tracing the course of implementation and defining the interpretative schemes of problems and solutions, and either inducing change or holding it back.

According to Muller (1995, 2000), policies are ideas in action. More precisely, policies 'are spaces (a forum) in which the different actors build up and express a relationship with the world that refers to the way they perceive reality, their place in the world and what the world should be' (Muller 2000, p. 195). This involves the process of creating a reality in which the cognitive and normative dimensions are inextricably connected. Indeed:

> public policies serve both to build interpretations of reality (Why does unemployment persist? How to analyze changes in the system of inter-national relations? Is the level of food safety declining?), and to define normative models of action (work needs to be made more flexible, the democratization of eastern European countries should be supported, health controls need to be reinforced)
>
> (ibid.)

Of course, the ideas that mark policies are socially embedded and rooted in a specific time and context. Sennett (2003) has made a remarkably clear analysis of the shame of dependency that has traditionally informed the social and institutional context of American welfare. It is a 'culturally specific' (ibid., p. 29) shame belonging to a liberal ideology in which the condition of those who depend on the help of others tends to be seen as degrading and the need for social assistance as a stigma. Thus the present state of welfare – which has been downsized to outsource services, rely on the willingness of the community to become mobile and make intervention more selective and temporary – has its roots in a political and cultural tradition that has exasperated the concept of independence.

We therefore have to understand the link between social policies and the social worlds that they themselves help to forge. There is no lack of tools for accomplishing this. Today the analysis of public policies can rely on a range of different approaches, as against a tradition of research that for a long time privileged individual interests and strategic rationality as the keys to explanation.

The work of Hall (1993) and of Sabatier and Jenkins-Smith (1993) certainly marked a turning point here. To Hall (1993) we owe the concept of the *paradigm* of policy, a framework of ideas that specifies the nature of the problems, the objectives and tools of a policy 'Like a Gestalt, this framework is embedded in the very terminology through which policymakers communicate about their work, and it is influential precisely because so much of it is taken for granted and unamenable to scrutiny as a whole' (ibid., p. 279). From this same perspective, Hall analyses the processes by which the theories of John Maynard Keynes became the foundation for macro-economic policies in the British welfare state.

> Once adapted to the organization of the British financial system, Keynesian ideas were institutionalized into the procedures of the British Treasury and formalized as the neoclassical synthesis in many standard texts. They specified what the economic world was like, how it was to be observed, which goals were attainable through policy, and what instruments should be used to attain them. They became the prism through which policymakers saw the economy as well as their own role within it.
>
> (ibid.)

The metaphor of the prism – which, by decomposing light, illuminates and transforms reality at one and the same time – is very effective in showing the power of ideas, which are all the more powerful, the more they are taken for granted. In harmony with this perspective, Sabatier and Jenkins-Smith (1993) have analysed policies as belief systems organized on three levels. The first is the basic nucleus, from which policy actors draw the identity and principles on which action is based. Fundamental values, world views and more general normative rules belong here. The second level regards strategies relating to a specific sector of policies. The third level concerns the choice of tools in line with the strategies in question. The result is that more radical change is the sort most unlikely to occur, precisely because it questions the basic fabric of values and norms.

Rein and Schön (1996) have instead concentrated on frames, the diagnostic/ prescriptive narrations that guide both analysis and action, highlighting the way they 'try to "hitch on to" norms that resonate broader cultural themes in society' (p. 89).

As can be seen, the categories of analysis differ but there is a common intention: to place the cognitive/interpretative dimension of policies in the lime-light, with the representations, categorizations and definitions they incorporate 'about what is to be done and how' (Capano, 2003, p. 783).

One approach that develops this line of research in an original way focuses on tools for governing. According to Lascoumes and Le Galès (2007), its two founders, we should avoid considering policy tools as purely techni-cal, 'natural' instruments, thus moving beyond the functional approach dominating the conceptualization and study of public administration, for which attention to instruments is justified merely by the need to identify the means best suited to the established objectives. The point is that the tools of public action incorporate, fix and give rise to values, interpretations and representations of what is at stake, as well as theories and rules on action. They are both technical and social instruments that establish regulations for social relations 'between governors and governed' (ibid., p. 3). Moreover, the tools that are adopted to reach specific aims contribute actively, and according to their own logic, towards structuring the action and tracing its direction, with outcomes that are sometimes unexpected or unprecedented (ibid.).

> Public policy instrumentation is therefore a means of orienting relations between political society (via the administrative executive) and civil society (via its administered subjects), through intermediaries in the form of devices that mix technical components (measuring, calculating, the rule of law, procedure) and social components (representation, symbol).
>
> (ibid., p. 7)

A highly interesting field of research opens up here as to how tools play their own role in policy and in transforming it dynamically. Focusing on tools can, in fact, help to understand the change in a public policy: 'change may come about through instruments or techniques, without agreement on the aims or principles of reform' (ibid., p. 16). Change does not necessarily demand that significances and objectives be agreed upon, nor does it always follow a direct and transparent trajectory. From this point of view 'stressing policy instruments is yet another way of criticizing the 'heroic' view of policy changes often put forward by the actors' (ibid.).

In general, policy change plays a key role in cultural approaches, generally dissatisfied with how this issue is addressed, either with reference to the individual actor or in terms of a functional perspective. Analyses centring on significances, norms and values have contributed to placing learning in the limelight and to suggesting interpretations of change equipped to stand up to the incoherence and ambiguity of policies and the pockets of resistance and innovative energy they are normally surrounded by. In a way, it has meant embracing a more disenchanted and less prohibitive vision, so that the transformative effects that the changes set off can be acknowledged, even when they do not affect the deeper policy levels.

One reason supporting the choice to concentrate on these aspects is precisely the need to take into account contradictory dynamics and the interweaving of their persistence or changes. We might consider the dynamics regarding the supranational level of Europe, which are so important and so controversial. For years there has been discussion on the role played by the Union in the process of harmonizing and creating convergence between the policies of the Member States. On the one hand the incomplete and fragile nature of these dynamics as regards the substance of policies is quite obvious. On the other hand, it can nonetheless be seen that a common language has emerged around certain key issues, for example social cohesion and activation. One complication that must not be forgotten is that a common framework does not mean that significances and perspectives are really shared.

## The institutions

Implicit in what has been said up to now is the fact that the cultural dimension of policies refers back to their institutional dimension. Indeed there are extremely close conceptual and empirical links between these two dimensions. Coming across ideas is almost inevitable if we are interested in studying policies by focusing on the constraints and rules, formal and informal, that affect and sustain social interactions and the way in which societies change through time; i.e. according to a basic definition that is widely agreed upon, the institutions.

The relationship between ideas and institutional analyses has gained a special place in the study of public policy, ever since Hall and Taylor (1996) in one of their seminal papers managed to create order in the constellation of concepts and theories leading back to neo-institutionalism, identifying three main approaches in it:

1  rational choice institutionalism, which conceives of institutions as tools of strategic calculation for the actors;
2  historical neo-institutionalism, which associates institutions with formal rules and conceives of the dynamics of social causation as 'path dependent', i.e. mediated 'by the contextual features of a given situation often inherited from the past' (ibid., p. 941);
3  sociological neo-institutionalism, according to which many institutional forms and procedures should be seen 'as culturally-specific practices', 'frames of meaning' (ibid., p. 947) guiding actions and decisions and, by means of the dynamics of isomorphism, diffused through organizational fields.

It is this last approach that disrupts the conceptual divide between 'institution' and 'culture'. As Hall and Taylor have emphasized, 'the two shade into each other' (ibid., p. 947). On the one hand, 'culture' itself is redefined as an institution' (ibid., p. 948).[2] On the other hand, the institution does not only influence the strategic calculations of actors but also shapes their preferences. This gives rise to the role played by the logic of what is appropriate, as a vehicle for the relationship between institutions and wider social/cultural environments: 'Institutions influence behaviour not simply by specifying what one should do but also by specifying what one can imagine oneself doing in a given context' (ibid.).[3]

Many complicated issues arise here. I shall limit myself to indicating some critical points:

●  In order to analyse policies processes, on the one hand the resources of action available in specific social contexts and their degree of aggregation and integration are significant, while on the other hand what also matters are the institutions with which these resources interact, since they create rules of influence, transmit organizational models and provide incentives, levers for action, power resources. In other words, the relationship between the political-administrative institutions and society presents itself as a relationship of co-determination.

• The issue of how processes of institution building develop and what confers 'legitimacy' or 'social appropriateness' on some institutional arrangements (March and Olsen, 1989) is central. There are various ways in which these processes can take root and flourish. In many cases what is decisive is the definition, by the public authority of a framework, of rules setting up ties and opportunities. In other cases, institution building makes use of social practices through which new cognitive and normative frameworks are created and shared by the actors involved in the definition and collective solution of a problem.

• Just as crucial is the issue of change. Inertia is a typical attribute of institutions, which, as such, are defined by their tendency to stabilize and lean towards continuity and persistence. Institutional changes are not, therefore, very frequent, particularly changes that are profound or radical. Nonetheless, even partial or incremental changes or adaptations should be taken into account; they are not so rare but just as significant in terms of the dynamics that are brought into play.

We shall go into these issues in more detail later in the book. For now we should add that a specific advantage of focusing on ideas and institutions in the study of public action regards the relationship between knowledge/ information and policies. This relationship is a central theme in public and scientific discourse, which are both directed towards emphasizing the need for policies to be based on information and data that satisfy objective conditions. The important point is that a different perspective should be adopted, in a way opposite to the prevailing one. I refer more precisely to the research programme on the informational basis of policies (Sen, 1990; de Leonardis, 2009; Salais, 2006, 2009), which investigates public knowledge as a social construction. It highlights the normative dimension of information and knowledge on which public decisions are based and how they are founded 'on processes of choice, selection and justification. In a word, their political nature' (de Leonardis, 2009, p. 75). As Sen maintains (1990, p. 111):

> The informational basis of judgment identifies the information on which the judgment is directly dependent – and no less important – asserts that the truth or falsehood of any other type of information cannot *directly* influence the correctness of the judgment. The informational basis of judgment of justice thus determines the factual territory over which considerations of justice would directly apply.

This perspective challenges the very claim to objectivity of knowledge and data. As Salais (2009, p. 2) argues:

Before becoming information, economic and social reality is shaped by cognitive frameworks (the categories and social processes involved in knowledge). These frameworks build and select, for the members of a community, information (and assessment) about what is and what is not important as a problem to be dealt with by the community (and the State).

Thus, the indicators that a decision-making process refers to condition the scenario, since: 'any indicator (or guideline) selects what is worthy to be known or not and, so doing, basically builds the reality that is relevant both for the deliberative process preceding the decision and for the action to be' (ibid., p. 11). Therefore, attention should be paid to what is taken for granted and is thus invisible, even in the case of statistical tables. In fact, a table is not just a collection of data but a procedure for putting together individual situations (Salais, 2006) which are considered equivalent (in terms of employment and position on the job market), taking it for granted that they all come into the same category. Instead, it cannot be assumed that this is so. In this perspective Salais analysed labour policies and the relative indicators. The social and legal definitions presupposed by these indicators change over time. What is defined as a 'job' in Europe is no longer what used to be associated with a model of full employment. Moreover, the definition changes from country to country. In the case of the United Kingdom, for example, the prevalent definitions lead people who work for only a few hours a week to be defined as 'employed', whereas the same is not true in other countries. In any case, the way the information on which decisions and policies are based is organized has very practical consequences. The choice of the European Union to refer to a definition according to which one hour of work a week is sufficient to qualify as employment affects national decisions, acting as an incentive for labour market deregulation.

In recognizing and investigating the 'political' nature of public knowledge, the research programme on the informational basis of policies sheds light on more general aspects. In the first place, the relationship between ideas and practice (actions, interaction and decisions) is not at all linear: it is circular and retro-active, affecting the very ideas it is informed by. As Béland and Cox (2011, p. 4) stress, 'ideas are constantly in flux' as they are reproduced and redefined by the actions and interactions they give shape to. The circularity implies self-reproduction mechanisms, in which premises and actions mutually confirm one another. If the mechanism does not allow these premises and actions to reflect back sufficiently, an authentic 'black box' results, which makes issues and choices opaque, concealing them behind technical or factual characteristics or reducing them to a matter of necessity. Nevertheless, these mechanisms are normally interwoven with elements of tension and contradiction. And there is always the possibility of slips, deviations, real changes.

In the second place, focusing on the cognitive and normative dimension of policies does help to open up the black box, i.e. to acknowledge and debate the perspectives that tend to pre-constitute decisions and implementation. What comes into play here is not only the need to problematize what presents itself as a given fact, but also the possibility of tracing new and different perspectives.

Perspectives of this nature, like the possibilities of developing them, direct us towards the complex relationship of interdependence between institutional constraints and agency – freedom and powers – of the subjects involved in policy making. We shall now go on to deal with agency.

## Agency and capabilities

Amartya Sen's capability approach is relevant to this framework because it allows us to clarify the agency of the recipients of policies, highlighting on the one hand the density of collective decisions in terms of norms and values in social matters, and on the other hand the interdependence between the individual and the social dimension of freedom.

Sen bases his considerations on a connection between the issues of equality and freedom. According to Sen, a correct approach to equality needs to acknowledge that individuals are radically different in terms of their personal characteristics, social aspects and environment. Thus, equality of resources does not imply actual equality in the possibility of realizing ones objectives, because what can or cannot be done also depends on the range of physical and social circumstances that influence people's lives (Sen, 1992). For this reason, failure to take into consideration the substantial differences between individuals can produce profoundly anti-egalitarian effects.

The capability approach takes into account the differences between individuals, linking them to their underlying freedom. In fact Sen supports a perspective that sees freedom not as the absence of constraints and external limits (negative freedom), but as the real possibility of doing or attaining something (positive freedom). This approach is the basis of the distinction between functionings and capabilities. Functionings are the states of well-being of a person, for example being well-nourished, in good health but also happy and self-respecting, or taking part in the life of the community. If functionings are well-being, capabilities are the individual freedom to attain well-being (Sen, 1992, p. 76). Thus capabilities are the freedom to choose the option an individual has reason to value. This is where we once again come across both the differences between individuals and the understanding of freedom in terms of real or substantial freedoms.

This sort of freedom involves the social context and the way it supports, increases or reduces individuals' options. The options are influenced by various factors: economic opportunities, political liberties, social powers and the enabling conditions of good health and basic education. But at the same time "the institutional arrangements for these opportunities are also influenced by the exercise of people's freedoms, through the liberty to participate in social choice and in the making of public decisions that impel the progress of these opportunities' (Sen, 1999, p. 5). Though individual, capabilities are linked decisively to the social and institutional opportunities that allow them to be developed and put into practice. From this point of view, choice is always a social process. Moreover, by taking part in public choices, individuals can influence these opportunities.

It is in this perspective that we should view conversion factors, i.e. those factors that intervene when resources and formal rights are converted into practical freedom of choice. According to Sen, both personal characteristics (such as age, gender and health) and factors of a social nature (such as norms and models of behaviour), as well as environmental and institutional differences, should be taken into account. It is thus in the conversion factors that we see the importance Sen attributes to the interaction between the social dimension and that of individual choice and action.

At an empirical level, conversion factors can operate in various ways and combinations, with implications that are not the same with respect to the freedoms and capabilities attained. Emphasis should be placed on the role of policies in this framework, in particular social policies, as contexts where, by means of conversion factors, different levers for developing capabilities can be used and encouraged. This is a role that calls into account the three main points in Sen's reasoning.

First, the capability approach shifts the barycentre of equality and well-being from the distribution of individual income to freedom of choice. This does not mean, however, that access to resources and the relative responsibilities of public institutions are of no importance. The shift is rather from resources as such to those resources that are always necessary make it possible to be and to do (de Leonardis, 1993). Policies thus carry dual importance: (i) for making resources accessible and (ii) for acting on the conversion factors that influence the use of resources in terms of capability (Sen, 1992). Sen recognizes the importance of public policies with particular regard to 'social opportunities' and 'protective security'. Social opportunities regard the action every society promotes in favour of education, health or social welfare and which directly influences the individual's substantial freedom to live a better life and take part in social life. Protective security involves measures such as unemployment benefits or income support (Sen, 1999, p. 40).

Second, as Salais (2008) emphasizes, there is a fundamental relationship between Sen's idea of freedom and power. Salais (2008) reports an example of Sen's that regards two different ways of being free in an environment free from the risk of an epidemic. The first consists of giving individuals the option of staying or leaving. The other consists of implementing health policies that do away with the risk of an epidemic, so that individuals have the possibility of living in a healthy environment. Policies of this nature allow access to real freedom – and powers – for everyone, precisely because they free people from having to make an individual choice when faced with the risk of the epidemic. 'A public policy that eliminates epidemics is enhancing our freedom to lead the life – unbattered by epidemics – that we would choose to lead' (Sen, 1992, p. 65).

Third, the capability approach underlines the close connection between freedom and values. This is where Sen places his reflections on the 'judgement of justice' and the information on which it is based, to stress that collective decisions of importance for capability, in which public priorities regarding well-being are compared and defined, always incorporate value judgements and choices regarding value, even when they 'conceal' them. From Sen's point of view, these very choices should be the subject of public debate. This means public debates should be attended, at which the value judgements that implicitly or explicitly guide decisions are made quite clear. Attendance at these debates is in fact a crucial component in the exercise of democracy and responsible social choices (Sen, 1999, p. 10). Sen insists on this point and consequently on the importance of public evaluation that allows the priorities and perspectives brought into play – many of which tend to conceal their choice of values in 'cultivated opaqueness' – to be placed under scrutiny (ibid., p. 110).

Fourth (and consequently), the freedom that Sen is concerned with includes the involvement of citizens in public debates at which options and priorities are discussed and established: 'The exercise of freedom is mediated through values, but values are subject in turn to the influence of public discussion and social interaction, which are themselves influenced by participatory freedom' (ibid., p. 9). When choice regards predetermined options there is no real freedom. According to Sen, the freedom that counts is, in fact, the liberty to act 'as citizens who matter and whose voices count rather than living as well-fed, well-clothed and well-entertained vassals' (Sen 1999, p. 288). The conditions for voice expression are complementary to the conditions necessary for good health, proper nourishment, etc. Sen emphasizes that voice is neither an alternative nor an accessory, but operates as an integral part of well-being.

From this point of view, Sen's perspective is fundamental for identifying the conditions for effective agency by the beneficiaries of social policies. As well as the exercise of substantial freedom, these conditions include the possibility of expressing and exerting the voice of the individual, i.e. debating, challenging and protesting.[4] It is precisely the relationship between capability, power and voice that confirms the difference between Sen's idea of freedom and the neoliberal idea of choice.

## Notes

1   For an in depth-analysis of these approaches see Muller (2000); Palier and Surel (2005).
2   Following Hall and Taylor (1996, p. 948), this reflects 'a "cognitive turn" within sociology itself away from formulations that associate culture exclusively with affective attitudes or values toward ones that see culture as a network of routines, symbols or scripts providing templates for behavior'.
3   Discursive neo-institutionalism should be placed here. This fourth approach, according to Schmidt (2011) accords particular attention to interactive processes and to actors engaged in a 'communicative discourse of deliberation, contestation, and legitimization of the policies' (p. 86).
4   According to Hirschman's (1970) well-known concept of voice.

# 2 What is social in Europe?

This chapter deals with the issue of the social dimension of Europe and its uncertain prospects in the present context of crisis. In the first part I look at Europe by focusing on the fabric of principles and norms that have fostered the various histories of the welfare states and the constellations of motives that have combined to animate them. It is certainly not my intention to give an exhaustive account of all the complex issues involved; even less do I intend to celebrate the past in a nostalgic vein. The fact is that remembering the ideas in which the welfare state has its roots helps us understand the scope of our present problems and what is at stake in the erosion of Europe's social dimension. In the second part and on this basis, I sketch the parabola of the European social model, pointing out the greater subordination of the social to the economic.

## A common heritage

### Universalism

There is no doubt that we should start out from universalism. This principle – a normative pillar of the so-called 'glorious thirty (years)' – which guaranteed growth and well-being to the populations of certain European countries from the period immediately after the Second World War to the mid 1970s, intends social protection to extend to all citizens, as members of the same national collectivity and therefore entitled to the same rights. Universalism has an equalizing quality which is opposed to two other sorts of logic: corporative-categorical logic associating protection with employment, discriminating between employment and non-employment (assuming paid work outside the family as a parameter for defining the positions of beneficiaries and the relevant protection) and dividing the beneficiaries into segments enjoying different types of protection; residual logic according to which social protection should be reserved for the poor and needy.

In the post-war Europe of the 1940s this principle benefited from a quite exceptional combination of social energy and political impulses. It is doubt-less true that in continental Europe the welfare state bore the categorical and employment-linked mark of so-called Bismarckian welfare. Nonetheless, universalism also attained some wide-ranging achievements. This certainly happened in northern Europe, which was its cradle, as documented, for example, by the *Folkpension*, the pension introduced in Sweden in the 1940s and financed by general taxation instead of contributions from workers. But it also happened elsewhere. In Italy the national health system, set up in 1978, although re-adjusted several times, today still recognizes health as a right of all citizens. The British welfare state which, thanks to policies adopted by the Labour government and to the Beveridge Report that inspired them, gave rise to a new social pact after the second world, was imbued with universalism. In his documentary *The Spirit of 45*, Ken Loach describes the social and political climate that made this pact possible, laying all the odds on the possibility of building a more just and cohesive society, radically different to the one that had condemned masses of people to poverty, ill health and unemployment before the war. This prospect was filled with 'a spirit' that upheld not only individual life projects but the very possibility of people organizing themselves as a collectivity, in a society. As Bauman (2009, p. 34) argues, the welfare state is organization for human cohabitation that tends to unite its members in the attempt to protect all people and each individual from the morally devastating effects of the war of all against all. In other words, it is a way of organizing society that institutionalizes solidarity by sharing and socializing risks (Ferrera, 1993).

The limits in some of the ways that universalism has been implemented are evident and well known. However, many of them highlight the need to make adjustments rather than reject the principle as such. A recurrent criticism regards the not always successful relationship between universalism (and its equalizing function) and individual differences, more precisely the discriminating effects of measures that, precisely because of their universalistic approach, do not take these differences into due account. The adoption of approaches and tools of positive discrimination normally aims to neutralize these effects, assuming as its target subjects and groups that are marked by differences. Rather than challenging universalism, this makes it possible to strengthen its equalizing potential. As regards gender, for example, it is now evident that the unequal load of caring responsibilities that burdens men and women due to the division of labour in the family requires specific and dedicated policies, as well as services and measures addressing citizens in general.

### *Equality*

Universalism does not necessarily mean equality.[1] Indeed the principle of equality has played an important but limited part in the histories of European welfare states. According to the normative theories of social citizenship, one for all Marshall's (1950) equality associated to the status of citizenship, where the members of the same collectivity are equal because they all have the same rights and are bound by the same obligations (equal citizenship, as Marshall defines it), is not opposed to the inequality that constitutes a market economy, far less does it imply the failure of the latter. It is true that in some European countries, between the 1960s and the 1970s, the most intense social claims and protests, whose main objectives were work and the protection linked to it, gathered under the flag of equality. Generally, however, there has been no side with an organically and programmatically egalitarian institutional agenda. From this point of view, the Scandinavian welfare state is a singular case and not the norm, because of the greater conviction with which egalitarian objectives were pursued right from the beginning through work, income support, care services, education and the greater impact of redistribution. To varying degrees, this impact is also to be seen even where an explicitly egalitarian normative horizon is lacking. In other words, social policies can actually create more equality between people even when equality is not number one on the agenda.

The link between welfare, universalism and equality is further complicated by changing approaches to the issue. Indeed, 'the substantive meaning of equality or inequality is powerfully bound by nation and epoch' (Esping-Andersen, 1999, p. 7). Moreover, behind these terms stands a huge mass of normative theories and several problems, some of which are still in search of a solution. In the latest debates, the idea that has long held sway of equality as equality of resources – derived from economics – is facing an agreed demand to recognize the differences and/or see individual freedom as something to be made the most of. It is in this light that we can view the growing interest in the potential of applying Sen's approach which, as we have seen, distinguishes equality of resources from real equality in the possibility of realizing personal objectives: one does not necessarily equate with the other. Indeed, people are profoundly different in their individual characteristics and social circumstances and, once these differences are ignored, an egalitarian project ends up by increasing the specific inequality involving capabilities.

### Rights

The alternating fortunes of universalism interweave with those that have marked the institutionalization of solidarity and recognition of the right to social protection. According to Heclo (1981), the invention of insurance schemes in Bismarck's times made it possible to move from the random and exceptional nature of charity to the certainty of standardized methods of calculation. Actuarial science has played a key role in this move. However, it was the certainty of possessing rights (so-called 'due rights') that subsequently gave this invention its true weight: social protection, recognized as a right, becomes 'due'. This was connected to the new pact between the State and citizens, which committed them reciprocally to a (variable) nucleus of rights and obligations. The pact held out until the mid 1970s, when the oil crisis caused a slowdown in its programmes and tools, which had even managed to make their way into countries with a conservative political tradition. From the 1980s onwards it has become patently obvious that it is in a critical state, since certain essential reasons and conditions are now lacking.

The historical matrix prevailing in social rights in Europe is the protection deriving from work, thus giving a lot of space to categorical criteria and derived rights – which individuals access through family membership. Nonetheless, Scandinavian welfare systems, universalistic and oriented towards equality, are marked by their tendency to recognize social rights in the form of individual rights and to protect citizens independently of their position with respect to the market, for example by developing child and elderly-care services as tools of equal opportunities (Saraceno, 2013a, p. 78).

In any case, the difference between measures based on rights and measures of a discretional nature is blatantly obvious in the case of economic assistance. The absence of any right to support in the case of poverty and the consequently random nature of intervention, for those who experience it as beneficiaries, often means being exposed to processes of stigmatization and social devaluation, as well as extreme difficulty in overcoming the condition of need.

### Social justice and democracy

The pact between the State and citizens at the basis of the welfare state has determined a very close connection between social justice and democracy. According to Marshall (1950, p. 72), social citizenship is a status which includes 'the right to share to the full in the social heritage and to live a life of a civilized being according to the standards prevailing in the society'. This, in a non-restrictive sense, also means participation in public life. More precisely, on the one hand social rights take shape as 'enabling' compared to civil and political rights (Nussbaum, 2000); on the other hand, only in a democratic regime do social rights acknowledge protection from risk and vulnerability coherent with the status of citizenship. Thus, on an ideal level, social justice and democracy are linked by a relationship of interdependency. In other words, the redistribution of resources and the redistribution of power go hand in hand. At the same time, access to an adequate range of resources means that there is a real possibility of taking part in social life and this is not just a formal prerogative or a privilege for a chosen few.

We know very well that the history of social policies is fraught with situations in which things did not go quite like this. The first social insurance schemes in Europe came into being under Bismarck's authoritarian government. In Italy, social welfare made a lot of progress under the fascist regime.[2] However, democracy is an essential element in the frame of reference in which we historically identify the distinctive nucleus of the welfare state. Indeed, what the latter has promised 'is not merely social policy and redistribute basic risks, but an effort to rewrite the social contract between government and the citizenry' (Esping-Andersen, 1999, p. 33). In other words 'democracy and the welfare state are sewn from the same fabric' (ibid., p. 8).

## Today

This is, so to say, the original legacy that the welfare states have brought to the organization of European societies, with all its limits and its merits. In this legacy some inter-connected fields of tension have been active for a long time.

First, the territorial borders of social citizenship have been called into question. In the last century in Europe, these borders were essentially national ones and citizenship in general took the form of belonging to a limited political community (Bauböck and Guiraudon, 2009), operating as a means for relationships and mutual recognition. Today, the borders are blurred and stratified. The European Union has become a laboratory for increasingly differentiated territorial realignments of citizenship (ibid.) and new ways of assembling citizenship (Clarke et al., 2014). As to social citizenship, dynamics of territorial differentiation have questioned the model (rather than the fact) of citizenship as belonging to a community defined by the space of the nation state. At the same time, the process of European integration has redefined its spatial architecture, interfering in national rules of inclusion/exclusion and partially creating a disjuncture between social rights and national territory (Ferrera, 2005).

Second is the transition towards active implies overcoming the concept, dating back to Marshall (1950), of citizenship as status (Evers and Guillemard, eds, 2013). This transition is as relevant as it is ambiguous. Indeed, it comprises both the tendency to reinforce the contractual aspects of social citizenship (Handler, 2003) and the central role attributed to empowerment and participation (Newman and Tonkens, 2011).[3] In the perspective where policies for activation coincide with inclusion in employment, prevalent in the EU, turns into a tendency to condition social entitlements to work has gained strength. Well-known cases are the *welfare to work* measures in the UK (like the *jobseeker's allowance*, a measure that foresees the obligation to actively look for work, reporting regularly to the job centre). In a way, the right has to be deserved. This calls into question the distinction between deserving subjects and non-deserving subjects, which is the original normative body from which aid for the poor stemmed in modern Europe: the former (widows, orphans, the elderly, the sick, etc.) *non-workers because unable to work*, thus considered deserving of assistance: the latter *non-workers though able*, thus considered undeserving of assistance.

The conditioning of rights is considered by many a pillar of the reorganization of European welfare systems. There is endless debate on this issue. However, empirical evidence fails to confirm the central role or need for the obligation to work with respect to the aim of making people independent. In their research on local interventions in the field of social assistance in Europe, Saraceno and his team (ed., 2002) demonstrate that the most effective protection systems – those that most successfully deal with the risk of producing dependency – are the Swedish ones, which are more generous and universalistic. Instead, a long period of dependence on social assistance is normally explained by the fact that the support is insufficient to allow individuals to start a new life: measures exclusively addressing those in serious conditions, together with limited economic benefits, result in a population of beneficiaries who find it hard to make themselves independent of social assistance.[4] It should be stressed that Scandinavian welfare systems envisage a firm connection between economic assistance and measures for professional training but not the obligation to work. We should remember, referring to Castel (2003), that strictly speaking rights are such because they are not negotiable: at most the way they are exercised may be negotiable.

An important group of transformations hinges on freedom of choice, a concept that tends to be sketched according to the template of the free market. The penetration of commercial elements into the decision-making ganglia of social protection is linked to a twist by citizenship towards the logic typical of commercial exchange. This is where the figure of the citizen makes way for that of the consumer, free to choose between different suppliers but hardly equipped to take part in the public space of collective decisions (Clarke, 2004; Barber, 2007). The measures that were introduced into several sectors in the United Kingdom (including education and health) from the 1980s onwards, thanks to radically pro-market positions, paved the way for the affirmation of freedom of choice as the principle for reorganizing regulation and provision (Crouch et al., eds, 2001).

As we shall see in Chapter 8, consumerism is not necessarily the same as empowering, particularly where the citizen/consumers are in fragile conditions. There are a great many open questions as to the repercussions that the consumerist twist taken by citizenship may have on the public dimension of welfare. In the case of the UK, the cradle of freedom of choice, it has been discovered that 'the extension of consumer identities produces a form of individualism and a rejection of the legitimacy of public authorities' (Newman and Tonkens, 2011, p. 193).

Freedom, in general, takes pride of place in the rhetoric and justification summoned up to support the changes in policy orientation over the course of the last few decades, promising to free individuals and collectivities from the tethers of public intervention, which are criticized at one and the same time as being inadequate, unsustainable and intrusive. However, what we have to understand is the sort of freedom we are talking about. Mainstream interpretations, following in the tracks of the metamorphoses that have taken place in the economy and the neo-liberal project, tend to accentuate aspects such as isolation and self-interest and ignore the fabric of relations that mediates the constitution of individual being.

As well as many problems, however, there are some interesting innovations. Apparent in locally-based social policies is a processual notion according to which citizenship, besides being defined by formal prerogatives, is constructed in practice. One effect is the blurring of boundaries between political and social citizenship. In some cases, in fact, local forms of citizenship strengthen or create social entitlements, thus providing an open space for citizens participation (García, 2006; Beaumont and Nicholls, 2008; Newman and Clarke,

2009). Consequently, reinforcing entitlements is bound up with the development of agency and voice on the public scene, and the interdependence between social justice and democracy is revealed. Besides locating itself, social citizenship tends to assume in this way a political value implying a right to take part in the exchange of ideas and the possibility to influence collective decisions. Although recent, this shift towards citizenship as a process is supported by robust theoretical bases and arguments. Not by chance, public debate gives increasing importance to Sen's theory of capabilities, which links entitlements, resources, freedom to be and to do, and tends to conceive citizenship as a construct of capabilities (Chapter 1).

The scenario is fraught with contradictions. In fact, as new opportunities develop for citizens in the context of local welfare, so there is a growing number of individuals, mainly migrant workers but also refugees and asylum seekers, who lack rights or are classifiable as 'denizens'.

Lastly, it should be noted that whilst the issue of freedom reigns unchallenged, that of equality has assumed a low profile. There are many reasons for the lack of popularity this issue encounters on the public agenda and in terms of its priorities (Evers and Guillemard, 2013). Its lack of political importance should, however, be related, according to Castel (1995), to the decline of the social model it referred to: a salary-earning society, defined by the central importance of salaried work and the forms of protection going with it and fuelled by economic growth and confidence in social progress and the dynamics of upward mobility. This social model was based on the hierarchical differentiation of positions and, at the same time, on their continuity. When it was abandoned, it made way for the theme of social exclusion to emerge, which is instead connected to a dualistic model based on the contrasting positions of in and out, those who are inside and those who are outside. In other words, once the mechanisms of the salaried society had started to clog, the problem became to reduce the risks of social disaggregation. However, this perspective conceals the intermediate situations between the two extremes of in and out, i.e. situations of vulnerability that come from profound transformations in the world of work and the precarious nature it has taken on.

## The European social model

The dynamics of transformation of the constellation of norms and values in whose wake the European welfare states developed are broadly superimposed onto the parabola of the European social model. This is a model of society whose distinctive nucleus is a combination of social protection, economic regulation and industrial relations based on social dialogue (Scharpf, 2002). According to Alber (2010, pp. 102–103), the European social model points to both a social situation and a combination of shared values.

> Europeans like to pride themselves on having a unique social model that combines economic efficiency with social solidarity. Even those who are

fully aware of the remarkable diversity of social models within the EU usually agree that European nations fundamentally differ from those in other regions of the world, particularly from the US, and particularly with respect to their social policies.

One aspect linked to this is the institution of a transnational level of social citizenship, taking concrete shape in, for example, the regulation of working conditions.

Despite this, the equal standing of social solidarity and the objective of economic growth is a promise that the model has found it difficult to maintain right from the beginning. When the European project for integration took its first steps forward in the 1950s it revolved almost exclusively around the economy. Issues linked to solidarity and social rights were left to the decision-making spheres of the national governments. This was partly because of the latters' determination to maintain their own specific regimes of social protection, and the fact that a highly asymmetric relationship was imposed between the economic and the social (Hyman, 2011). Indeed, the economy 'was supposed to provide the cement binding large European countries together, in order to avoid future wars: it was believed that social progress would naturally flow from economic integration' (Barbier and Colomb, 2014, p. 25). This original spirit, little inclined to give importance to objectives of redistribution and social solidarity of transnational scope, has left its mark on the model and most of its machinery. In the Union Treaties the emphasis is placed fully on the market and on competition (Ferrera, 2005). The predominance of negative integration mechanisms, leading towards the removal of obstacles to the development of a transnational market, over those of positive integration (implying the harmonization of regulations) has played a decisive role in sanctioning this lack of symmetry (Leibfried and Pierson, 1995, eds, 2000). As Hyman (2011, p. 15) argues, there is 'a self-reinforcing dynamic at the heart of European integration: intensified market liberalisation both follows from, and in turn reinforces, the subordination of social policy to the overriding priority of competitiveness'.

Under Delors' term of presidency (1985–1994), however, social matters did gain ground for some years. In this period a supranational level of rules and financing developed, which influenced the choices adopted by the Member States on social issues. The process of harmonization and the strategy of convergence regarding social policies were equipped with the necessary tools hinging on mechanisms of incentivization and evaluation. The main tool is the Open Method of Coordination which, by benchmarking and ad hoc measures (statistics and indicators), is supposed to bind national decision-makers to pursuing shared objectives.[5] It is thanks to the Open Method that multilevel governance officially becomes the regulatory infrastructure for the harmonization of policies. According to the White Paper of the Committees of the Regions, 'this mode of governance implies shared responsibility by the different levels of power involved and is based on all the sources of legitimate democracy and the representativity of the various players involved.'

The Open Method of Coordination was inaugurated in 1997 in the context of the European Employment Strategy. A little later, in the Lisbon Summit of 2000, the cohesion strategy was launched – a principle that inspired the founding treaties of the Union itself. As we read in the conclusions of the summit, the objective established then was 'a new strategic objective: to become the most competitive and dynamic knowledge-based economy in the world, capable of achieving sustainable economic growth with new and better jobs and greater social cohesion.' Strictly speaking, in the European sphere cohesion indicates mainly the need to reduce territorial disparity and reinforce social links. Cohesion also evokes the need to coordinate economic, labour, social and environmental policies so as to make their mutual interdependence evident, as well as to direct economic growth according to parameters of sustainability. In these terms, cohesion strategy is potentially a decisive element for realizing the European social model, thanks also to financing made available by several programmes. Nonetheless, convergence has been scarce and the coordination of national policies on social matters has generally produced modest results (de la Porte and Jacobsson, 2011). The Open Method has gradually revealed its lack of impact on national culture and political choices and has now become a marginal tool.

In the background a glimpse can be seen of the divergences and conflicts that the European social model reflects, in particular the conflict between political actors inspired by market-linked solutions and political actors tending towards social perspectives. It should also be remembered that, despite adopting legislation that has recognized certain social rights, the latter have been subordinated to economic rights (for example freedom of movement). According to Barbier and Colomb (2014, p. 25):

> social rights are considered solely in terms of how they might be affected by market functioning (or vice versa, how they might affect the market's functioning). But applying them 'for their own sake' is not, strictly speaking, an explicit political task of the EU.

2004 to 2007 is a significant period for understanding the ambiguities and weaknesses of social Europe. The redefinition of the Lisbon Agenda in 2005 resulted in the affirmation of an economic idea of cohesion embedded in competitiveness. The prime importance given to employment has been a constant item in EU priorities ever since and reflects the conviction that the reduction of poverty may be 'the natural consequence of more employment and a more competitive economy' (Saraceno, 2013b). These events, together with the enlargement of the Union to 27 countries and the defeat of the pro-Europe front at the referendums on the Constitutional Treaty organized in 2005 in the Netherlands and France, contributed definitively to weakening the Open Method of Coordination (Barbier and Colomb, 2014). What is important, according to Supiot (2010), is that the entry of the ex-Communist countries provided the opportunity for giving a new impetus to the European social model but and yet this opportunity was wasted. Indeed, the path to reunification was not pursued in a spirit of uniting peoples but in the spirit of aligning the east to the rules in force in the west. Enlargement thus resulted in undermining the political bases of a social model that was already frail (p. 26).

Lack of symmetry between the social and economic spheres, scarce integration with respect to social issues, weak coordination: these are the traits of social Europe facing the financial and economic crisis of 2007–2008. From this moment onwards, lack of balance and frailty become more evident. In line with the logic of austerity, the hierarchy of priorities is dominated by the issue of the economic stability of the Member States, first and foremost those in the Eurozone (Natali, 2012), in whose service a package of tools is created[6] based on the *ex-ante* and *ex-post* control of national budget policies. In addition, the perimeter of European coordination is extended and comes to affect policies never previously touched upon, such as salary policies and collective negotiation (ibid.).

For the social dimension there was a window of opportunity lasting some months, from 2008 to 2009: faced with the radical nature of the crisis, a fairly broad political front in the European Union and Member States assumed a position in favour of mechanisms for 're-regulating capitalism'. However, this did not last long. The prospect was promptly overturned and the systems of protection, regulation and industrial relations – the heart of the European social model – from then onwards were accused of being the decisive element contributing to the crisis (Degryse, 2012).

All that supporters of a social Europe can do at this stage is place their hopes in the Europe 2020 strategy, which approves the key objective of a mart, sustainable and inclusive growth and encourages the strengthening and coordination of policies considered decisive for reaching this objective, such as education and training. Moving in this direction, programmatic lines and measures have been adopted, such as the Youth Employment Initiative, in 2013, which aims in particular to support young 'NEETs' (i.e. those outside the circuits of education, training or employment) in regions with an unemployment rate of over 25 per cent; and the Youth Guarantee Initiative, again in 2013, aiming to ensure that all young people under 25 have the opportunity of a job, an apprenticeship, an internship or continuous training measure within four months of leaving school or losing a job. At the same time, in February 2013, the Social Investment Package was adopted and hailed by many as the new paradigm of social Europe (Chapter 4). Mainly connected to measures for childhood, education, training and employment (i.e. the fields of public intervention considered crucial for the development of human capital), the theme of social investment identifies a potential relationship between the economic and the social which is the opposite to the neo-liberal approach: instead of being considered a cost, social protection is considered a factor of production and thus necessary for economic growth (Palier, 2013).

The commitment of Europe to a social dimension thus seems to have regained some ground but many doubts remain as to its impact and practical implications. In fact, social issues weigh less than economic objectives when the latter are presented as a necessity. As Daly (2012) emphasizes, the very fact that growth comes onto the Europe 2020 agenda as its sole objective makes the slight importance of the social dimension quite clear. Even though inclusive growth is mentioned, reference is made exclusively to employment, training and the modernization of the job market (Daly, 2014) whilst the social dimension is basically reduced to fighting poverty (Saraceno, 2013b). One eloquent indicator is clearly spending: social investment is assumed as the model to refer to for social policies, yet suffers huge cuts in its main fields of intervention (Morel, Palier and Palme, eds, 2012).

## Facing the crisis

The social aftershocks of the crisis – now known as the Great Recession – have been drastic in all countries. In 2013, 22 countries had employment rates below the 2008 level.[7] The strongest losses were in Greece (−13.4 per cent), Spain (−9.9 per cent) and Cyprus (−9.3 per cent).[8]

The crisis has affected mainly the more vulnerable social groups, in particular young and low-skilled people (Bieling, 2012). However, in 2013 24.5 per cent of the EU population were at risk of poverty or social exclusion. Between 2008 and 2013 the number of vulnerable people increased by more than 20 per cent in some countries (Cyprus, Greece, Malta and Luxembourg).[9]

At the same time, most European countries have cut spending on welfare policies (including health, education and transfers to the poor) and have undertaken reforms, mainly in the sectors of unemployment benefits, labour market flexibility and pensions (van Kersbergena, Visb and Hemerijck, 2014).

In this shared context of growing constraints and problems, the countries of northern and central Europe have not only managed to preserve the nucleus of their own welfare systems (though with cuts in social spending) but have also reacted better to the crisis. Due to the combined effects of the crisis and austerity measures, in the welfare systems of southern and eastern Europe spending on social protection, which was already lower to begin with, is further and, indeed, severely reduced (Natali, 2012). Thus the differences and fault lines between countries are becoming more marked and dynamics of dualization are emerging 'between resilient and falling countries' (Saraceno, 2013c, p. 350).

The case of Greece clearly shows the impact that the crisis and austerity have had on citizens' living conditions (Dimoulas, 2014). In 2012 minimum salaries were reduced by 32 per cent for those under the age of 25 and 22 per cent for everyone else. As a consequence of the drastic reduction in resources and health services, between 2008 and 2010 a 43 per cent increase was recorded in the death rate of newborn babies and 20 per cent in those born dead. The death rate has increased amongst the elderly, too: between 2008 and 2012 the increase amounted to 12.5 per cent between the ages of 80–84 and 24.3 per cent after the age of 85. AIDS has increased due to cuts in the supply of single-dose syringes and condoms to drug addicts. Illnesses that had been eradicated have reappeared, for example TBC and malaria (Kentikelenis et al., 2014).

The gap is wide and deep and obviously not limited to Greece alone. In 2013 employment rates among EU Member States ranged from 52.9 per cent to 79.8 per cent. Northern and central Europe had the highest rates, in particular Sweden, Germany, the Netherlands, Denmark and Austria. Greece, Croatia, Spain and Italy were at the lower end of the scale, with employment rates below 60 per cent.[10]

The roots of dualization, however, are to be found in the period preceding the crisis and are linked to structural differences that have been exasperated by the policies put into practice in the Eurozone and by the fiscal austerity adopted as a strategy for economic recovery (Palier, Rovny and Rovny, 2015). As well as models of social protection, asymmetries between political economies are crucial variables (Hall, 2014): the export-led growth models of northern Europe have been able to take advantage of the monetary union far more than the demand-led growth models of countries in the south (ibid.).

Apart from the degree to which they were exposed to the crisis, European countries also differ in the responses they have come up with to its aftershocks. In some countries the crisis response has been retrenchment: for example, in the UK cuts in public services have been severe and local government lost 27 per cent of its central support over four years (Taylor-Gooby, 2012), whilst the role of the private, non-profit and for-profit sectors has increased in the provision of services (van Kersbergena, Visb and Hemerijck, 2014). The most radical cutting back of welfare is found in the weakest political economies (e.g. Greece). Instead, other countries have adopted strategies coherent with the social investment perspective, including childcare, care of the elderly and active labour market policies (ibid.).

The debate focuses on a number of factors in order to explain these differences. Several scholars place the emphasis on historical approaches and national beliefs (Greve, 2014), and on political and institutional variables. According to Shahidi (2015), the fiscal crisis – 'whether real or imagined'– is a powerful factor in shaping policy responses and in determining change in welfare states. Where the problem of fiscal instability of the State has dominated the public agenda, the legitimacy of welfare has been considerably eroded and various strategies of recommodification have been adopted. In this way, social policies have been subordinated to the objective of dealing with the fiscal crisis, a problem that 'has returned as a core political concern across the landscape of advanced capitalist countries' (ibid., p. 677).

However, the crisis has brought to light and sharpened four interrelated deficits that directly or indirectly weight on the social dimension of Europe:

- A deficit of social solidarity. The case of Greece is a clear demonstration that social solidarity, i.e. support for the victims of the crisis, has remained basically a national issue whilst mechanisms of support between states to prevent Greece's bailout have been activated all too obviously. At the same time, the moral discourse accompanying the circumstances of Greek public finances have devoted overwhelming attention to the Greek citizens and their presumed duty to settle the debts run up by previous governments (Streeck, 2013b).

- A deficit in economic integration. According to Habermas,[11] the sovereign debt crisis that emerged from the banking crisis had its roots in the absence of a truly common financial and economic policy and real convergence amongst Member States. As Pochet and Degryse (2012) argue, in this framework it has been wages, labour law and social security, i.e. the bases of the European social model, that are to be considered and used as the adjustment variables (in terms of competitiveness and productivity).[12]

- A deficit in democracy. As well as the supremacy of market-making mechanisms, social Europe's parabola calls into question the well-known problem of the Union's 'democratic deficit' and the enormous weight of decisions not open to public debate (Degryse, 2012).[13] Lack of transparency and accountability should be seen in connection with the techno-cratic register of the decisions taken by the Commission and the power that corporate lobbyists are able to exercise from the wings (Storey, 2008). According to Streeck (2013a), today the European Union operates as a catalyst for the liberalization of European capitalism, a liberalization machine which gives vital lymph to market forces. In relation to this, Streeck speaks of the consolidation State, i.e. centring on the objective of consolidating public finances, with reference to a supranational regime where it is the European Union and financial investors who coordinate to regulate the functioning of national states. In other words, democracy has been fully tamed by the markets (ibid., p. 138).

- A political deficit. The problem of the EU's institutional design with a currency union but lacking a political union stands at the centre of a wide-ranging debate (Delanty, 2014). The political difficulty exacerbates the difficulty of bringing to life a European society. According to Eder (2014), Europe is evolving towards a system of stakeholder groups competing amongst themselves. In these conditions, it becomes a container for a plurality of 'demoi', leaving intact the primacy of national bonds, so that the existing European society is 'a sum of peoples governed by supranational bureaucracies' (p. 235).

As things now stand, any conclusion about Europe risks being premature. Better, then, to continue by asking ourselves: what is social in Europe?

## Notes

1 The theme of equality is dealt with in an extremely wide-ranging debate that is impossible to go into here. For a basic summary of the issues at stake, see Carter (2012).

2  On the origins of the welfare state, see, amongst others, Alber (1982).
3  As for present re-elaborations, de Leonardis (2011) distinguishes four main versions of active citizenship: one focusing on the citizen as consumer; one seeing the citizen as entrepreneur – 'social' entrepreneur or 'entrepreneur of him/herself'; one conceiving of citizens as responsible individuals/families; lastly, citizenship as voice and participation.
4  Ibid. Three interdependent variables are considered by research in order to account for the different outcomes: the institutional and policy frame; the characteristics of the local society (job market, family structure, the models of relationships between public/third sector); individual characteristics.
5  There are three essential phases: the definition of guidelines and common objectives for specific sectors (jobs, social inclusion, etc.); the elaboration of national plans by each country; the evaluation of results confirmed by a comparison of best practices and reference to pre-established indicators. The mechanism foresees both an inter pares evaluation, and evaluation by the Commission and the Council (Sacchi, 2008).
6  The best known tool is the so-called Fiscal Compact, approved in 2012, which contains norms and constraints for reducing the public debt of Member States, including the inclusion of a balanced budget in 'binding provisions of a permanent nature – preferably constitutional'. For a critical analysis, see Degryse (2012).
7  http://ec.europa.eu/eurostat/statistics-explained/index.php/Europe_2020_indicators_-_employment
8  http://ec.europa.eu/eurostat/statistics-explained/index.php/Europe_2020_indicators_-_employment
9  http://ec.europa.eu/eurostat/statistics-explained/index.php/Europe_2020_indicators_-_poverty_and_social_exclusion
10  http://ec.europa.eu/eurostat/statistics-explained/index.php/Europe_2020_indicators_-_employment.
    As for social exclusion and poverty, in 2008 the distance between the countries with the lowest and the highest risk was about 30 per cent, and in 2013 this gap was about 33 per cent (ibid.).
11  http://www.theguardian.com/commentisfree/2015/jul/16/jurgen-habermas-eu-greece-debt-deal
12  '(…) what were known as 'competitive (currency) devaluations' in the days before monetary union must today be converted … into "competitive wage devaluations", "competitive labour law regulation" and "competitive retirement pension and health care devaluations"' (ibid. p. 212).
13  Since the 2014 European elections, for the first time citizens had greater influence on the designation of the President of the Commission. In fact, the choice must take into account the election results and has to be submitted to the European Parliament. In the past, the choice was reserved for the heads of government of the Member States.

# Part II

# Public action and social policies: Dynamics

# 3 The changing architecture

In the search to identify the factors that come into play in the transition towards a post-Keynesian or post-Fordist welfare state, for some time now the literature has highlighted the appearance of new social risks that put pressure on traditional systems of protection and are connected to two main fields of change (Taylor-Gooby, ed., 2004):

- the socio-demographic dynamics related to the ageing population, the greater family diversification and instability, and increasing migratory flows;
- the transformation of the economy and employment, in particular a rise in the number of women on the job market, the increase in unemployment and the spread of atypical forms of work.

The interplay of these dynamics has produced social risks relating to lack of self-sufficiency amongst the elderly; the difficulty of reconciling work outside the family with childcare or care of other frail or dependent family members; the risk of being trapped in work or careers that are precarious and/or disqualifying; and the marginal condition of migrants.

These, however, are only one face, and a complex one at that, of the transition in European welfare systems. The other face regards the institutional architecture and powers that risks and social demands, old and new, are confronted with. Here, a decisive role is played by the changes set in motion in the wake of the neoliberal project between the end of the 1970s and start of the 1980s, when a vast number of reformers in different national contexts shared the assumption that a more streamlined and less centralized State, whose ranks and spending had been pared down, was more efficient and provided more appropriate responses. Within this framework comes the growing prospect of reorganizing public powers with the aim of transforming the relationship both between public and private and between central and local authorities.

The debate on the impact and implications of changes taking place in this direction has not become any less heated over time. In any case, the forms and dynamics of power that once marked a whole social, economic and political world have changed. The (central) State no longer has the monopoly over public decisions or over services provided. In most European countries, according to processes that depend on their history, their political and administrative structures, the logics of reformers and the constraints and opportunities present in each specific context, the most deep-seated nerve-endings of welfare's institutional structures have been affected. At the same time, the process of territorial reorganization, marked by deterritorialization and reterritorialization, has advanced. The national scale of public action has come under pressure on the one hand from increasingly intense processes of internationalization and the advance of powers that are detached from traditional territorial delimitations (including those of Europe) and on the other hand from the re-emergence of dynamics of territorial differentiation (including the various forms of devolution).

In this chapter I shall go more deeply into these dynamics, with a view to shedding some light both on the logics underpinning them and on the consequences for public action. First of all, however, a scenario must be sketched.

## A scenario

All chronologies are arbitrary and fail to tell the whole story, especially when they can only be allowed limited space. However, there is no doubt that to grasp the present climate of welfare and public action, the starting point must be assumed as the rise of neoliberalism, a system of ideas that, as Crouch (2013) argues, is based on the belief that the free market is the best way to organize human affairs and that it is always preferable to states and politics, which not only are inefficient but also endanger freedom. This belief would not have produced such a profound effect in shaping the institutional and social structures of such diverse European countries without the political strategies and tools of the 'Thatcher revolution' (Faucher and Le Galès, 2010), which swept the UK from the end of the 1970s onwards and was then to spread all over Europe. Thanks to the British Conservative governments that followed, for over a decade deregulation dominated a political agenda that intended to get rid of the Keynesian institutions of welfare (the so-called *roll-back neoliberalism*), convinced that the spontaneous play of market forces alone was sufficient to ensure efficient economic regulation (Peck and Tickell, 2002). The models of classic microeconomics and the postulate of the rational, instrumental actor are the basic cognitive and normative reference points for the reforms undertaken in this sense (Faucher and Le Galès, 2010).

A second, decisive phase came in the course of the 1990s, and was dominated by the Third Way and Blair's New Labour. According to Peck and Tickell (2002), in this period neoliberalism changes its strategy and, faced with the failure of deregulation in key sectors such as transport and employment, starts to follow the path of state-building, making use of tools of governance and regulation that mitigate the mechanisms of commodification, whilst preserving the core of it. *Roll-out neoliberalism* – as the two scholars define it – thus reveals the limits of radically pro-market formulas and, at the same time, leads to a highly pervasive and influential form of neoliberalization.[1] In other words, it becomes evident that the core of the neoliberalist project is to mobilize State structures to build a market society (Faucher and Le Galès, 2010) and that this construction can make use of quite different tools and strategies.

In the lapse of time between these two phases, decisive events and problems for European welfare establish themselves in a gathering wave that breaks, with devastating impact on our own times, in the 2007–2008 crisis. Streeck's (2011) thesis is that this crisis is the manifestation of a basic lack of balance in 'democratic capitalism', the social, economic and political form characterized by the co-existence of two opposing regimes for allocating resources: the market on the one hand; democratic politics and the choices taken in this context in terms of needs and rights, on the other. Ever since the 1970s, capitalism has been attempting to delay the crisis – to play for time – facing the lack of balance with tools such as inflation, public and private debt. Thanks to these expedients, democratic politics have managed to give the impression of growth capitalism, capable of ensuring material progress and redistributing market and social opportunities (Streeck, 2013). The financialization, that has overwhelmed the economy and processes for accumulation through mechanisms of 'privatized Keynesianism' (Crouch, 2009; Streeck 2011), marks the most recent phase which starting from the 1990s lasts until the Great Recession of today. As Bieling (2012) rightly recalls, financialization has a very strong impact on the reproduction mechanisms of different areas of the economy and society, for example through the privatization of public infrastructures and pensions, or the reorganization of the systems of private enterprises. More precisely, it transforms 'the micro-, meso- and macro-dynamics of capitalist economies' (Jessop, 2013): it alters the behaviour of non-financial organizations 'through the rise of shareholder value as a coercive discourse, technology of governance, and vector of competition'; it increases the influence of the financial sector; it penetrates into everyday life, for example obliging the labour force to have recourse to credit to maintain its standard of living; it leaves the economy more exposed to the recession and 'more liable to the downward spiral of debt-deflation-default dynamics' (ibid.). In any case, all the solutions experimented in the endeavour to solve the conflict between market and democracy have failed one after the other and the most recent failure has led to the upheavals we are well aware of.

## Institutional changes: New public management and governance

In the light of what has been said, the latest crisis is a dramatic sign that democratic capitalism urgently needs to find new tools for dealing with the contradictions implicit in it (Streeck, 2011). It is extremely difficult to say what these tools might be. What is a little simpler is to sketch the web of changes that most closely regard social policies, public action and welfare in this context.

At the heart of these intertwining changes we find a central transformative line: the shift from a role of command and control, also implying the dominance of a public regime in the provision of services, to a role of enabling, enhancing the potential for social self-organization. This shift entails two corollaries of equal significance with respect to the issue of public action. The first corollary is that the definition of general interests no longer rests on the public decision-maker in a monolithic fashion. The hierarchical model whereby general interests are fixed and acknowledged on the basis of criteria of (legal-rational) legitimacy on the part of public authorities thus loses ground. There is now a demand to identify new frameworks of public action capable of supporting the confrontation between a variety of actors (Rhodes, 1996). The second corollary relates to the structures of provision, where the changes are linked not only to the respective presence of public and private organizations, but also to the regulative framework which the dynamics of coordination and the criteria for the allocation of resources form part of. This could be the case, for example, of the public administrations' convinced preference for the market model (Crouch et al., 2001). But it could also be the case where a public–private partnership of a cooperative nature is set up (Ascoli and Ranci, eds, 2002).

Two phenomena should be highlighted within this framework.

First is the affirmation of a strategy for reorganizing the public sector centring on regulatory mechanisms of marketization and on the model of New Public Management (NPM). In its simplest definition, marketization is an attempt to bring together the State and the market (Crouch et al., 2001), and it implies three guidelines: (1) separation between public guidance/financing/control and public/private provision; (2) competition between providers (public and public providers as well as public and private); (3) consumers' 'freedom of choice'. The organizational complement to marketization is NPM, which has penetrated into a fair number of European countries thanks to a considerable body of programmes adopted in the United Kingdom which acted as trailblazers.[2] The key concepts are accountability and the reduction of costs but also devolution and freedom of choice. NPM has met with increasing favour as a solution that can be extended to different contexts thanks to an interpretative framework built on three basic assumptions: modernization, innovation and efficiency (Hood, 1991, p. 4). In fact this model promotes 'managerial modernity' in services tailored to fit the market and economic rationality, and tends to present itself as radically different from previous approaches (ibid.). As Power (1997, p. 47) maintains, NPM could quite simply be classified as 'the desire to replace the presumed inefficiency of hierarchical bureaucracy with the presumed efficiency of the market'. The geography of change is vast. In keeping with a climate that places a lot of faith in the self-organizational abilities of social and economic actors, requiring less State, the organizational principles of hierarchy and reference to the law have lost ground almost everywhere. As well as this, the public sector really has become lighter and more stream-lined. Between 1976 and 1998, the space of the twelve years that coincide with the most intense period of administrative reorganization, the number of

British civil servants fell from 762,000 to 481,000 (Rhodes 2000; Suleiman, 2005).

The ways NPM has been put into practice are the subject of critical arguments of various natures, equally distributed between those who complain of the tendency not to keep the promises made and those who document their most undesirable consequences. According to the former, the introduction of managerial recipes has meant an increase in the burden of administrative procedures to be waded through, due to mechanisms of management that exasperate the fragmentation of work, imply more rules and conditions and make the monitoring and verification of results top-heavy. What happens in administrations reflects the affirmation of a logic of power and command that privileges economic/mathematical knowledge and mechanisms of quantification. From this point of view, it is just one aspect of a more general process of bureaucratization which is the direct product of the neoliberal model and affects the whole of society (Hibou, 2012). The second type of argument raises issues of values, in particular regarding the universalistic approach, the profile of equality and the public dimension of administrative action.

In any case, to Hood and Dixon (2015) we owe a sober, overall account of the thirty years of NPM in the public sector in the UK has undergone: their conclusion is that government spending has increased (though not to a very great extent) and results have deteriorated, especially in terms of fairness and consistency of public administration.

The second phenomenon to be investigated is normally summed up as the shift from government to governance. Rhodes (2007, p. 1246) defined governance as 'governing with and through networks', indicating the following characteristics: interdependence between organizations; constant interaction between the members of a network, caused by the need to exchange resources and negotiate mutual aims, rooted in trust and based on the rules of play agreed upon by the participants in the network; a significant degree of participant autonomy with respect to the State. The difference between these collaborative and networking interconnections, on the one hand, and the hierarchical structure and logics of authority characteristic of government, on the other, could not be clearer.

Actually, not all scholars believe that this marked distinction is a satisfactory expression of the empirical situation. There is no doubt that governance has reduced the space and legitimacy of government. Nonetheless, public powers do not disappear but come up against complex reorganization (Lascoumes and Le Galès, 2007). More precisely, public authority downsizes its traditional role of command and control (linked to the dominance of a public regime providing services) to assume enabling functions that aim to provide incentives to the social potential for self-organization. In this way, a way of governing takes shape that centres more on enabling than on doing, finding its legitimacy by using the logics of mobilization and activation (ibid.). Scholars who draw on Foucault and on the governmentality conceptualization of power have shown that in this way a transformation of public authority takes place, which continues to exercise power and control but does so 'at a distance'.

One basic problem is that the differences between government and governance are often set out in normative terms, particularly in public discourse and by highly influential international organizations such as the World Bank. Normative perspectives end up by taking for granted what is empirically a variable and frequently problematic phenomenon, such as, for example, the cooperative trend, the orientation towards collective interests and the effects of spreading democracy (Bagnasco and Le Galès, 1997; Geddes and Le Galès, 2001; Mayer, 2003; Bifulco and de Leonardis, 2003; Newman, 2005). Amongst the most convincing criticisms of governance are those directed at this normative tendency. The strength with which governance has entered into public discourse is equal to the distance that normally separates the rhetoric and the practice of it (d'Albergo and Segatori, 2012). According to Swyngedouw (2000), governance is a model endowed with a high capacity for legitimization but contradicted in practice by problems like the strengthening of old and new forms of authoritarianism.

The most controversial issue, from this point of view, is the relationship existing between governance, democracy and new forms of citizenship. Until the early 1990s, the concept of governance was mainly associated with the market-oriented perspective emerging in the wake of neoliberalism. In its empirical reality, the association between governance and the market has exhibited three main aspects: the prominent role played by business companies in policies (especially local) and in public–private partnerships for economic growth; the application of neo-managerial principles to public administration; the marginal role of citizens and communities in decision-making. At present, the discourse on, and approaches to, governance are mainly centred on themes like the involvement of the local community and the development of participative and deliberative decision-making processes. Some scholars use the term 'new governance' to emphasize characteristics such as interdependence between institutions and society, co-steering, shared goals and citizen participation. The UK case can be considered paradigmatic because of the policy practices that it has inspired, with an increase in programmes based on community regeneration through the adoption of participative methodologies. The same move towards participatory governance is to be found elsewhere, for example in France, Germany and Italy. Actually, the framework hinging on local governance and participation has become an authentic convention in local agendas (Taylor, 2007) emphasizing in particular the inclusion of interests that in theory are weak and only slightly concentrated in the local network.

Participatory governance, therefore, should in theory involve not only a transformation of power but also its transfer to individuals and communities through experimentation with new forms of citizenship, especially in local and urban contexts (Blakeley, 2010).

Nevertheless, the concrete forms assumed by governance raise numerous issues in this regard. First, it is not clear what legitimacy can be associated with decision-making processes not subject to the forms of control that usually regulate the relationship between representatives and represented (Papadopoulos, 2000). A related issue is the scant transparency of the structure of responsibility. In 'disorganized' governance networks, characterized by a redundancy of levels of action, the question 'Who is accountable?' sometimes goes unanswered (Newman, 2005). Such networks, moreover, are criticized for affording limited access to weaker and more dispersed stakeholders (Lafaye, 2000; Eizaguirre et al., 2013), as is very apparent when the agenda is controlled by economic actors. At any rate, the logic and tools of power can change without the latter necessarily being relinquished or redistributed.

Following the suggestion of Geddes (2010), one should consider a continuum of possibilities whose extremes are two very different forms of governance. One is the 'neoliberal' extreme, which pertains to a pro-market perspective dominated by competitiveness and economic growth, whilst other policy priorities, such as social inclusion and environmental sustainability, are regarded as being dependent upon, or subordinate to, competitiveness. The other extreme is contestatory governance, which, even when it concerns economic objectives, has the primary purpose of increasing local democracy, social inclusion and participation.

## Territorialization

Also coming within this framework of redefinition of public action is the process of territorialization, which mainly concerns two intertwined phenomena: the territorial reorganization of public powers and the tendency to take the territory as the reference point for policies and interventions.

In general the territorial dimension is an important element of difference between governance and government. The latter is based on a strict relationship with the territory and the correspondence between the State, national borders and society. In fact, the modern State took shape through the neutralization of localistic and territorial dynamics and the State/national dimension underpins modern citizenship and democracy (Ferrarese, 2011). One consequence of this is the affirmation of the concept of territory as an administrative space indifferent to the specific characteristics of the context, both standardized and standardizing (Estèbe, 2005). Today the relationship between the State and the territory is more complex, due to a dual shift, which on the one hand reterritorializes, through processes of devolution and forms of federalism, and on the other deterritorializes, attaching itself to decision-making processes at supranational levels and through supranational organizations. As Le Galès (2002) argues, polycentric governance indicates this new space of power and decision-making, which is the field of conflicts and dynamics of changing and redistributing power. Brenner (2004) has analysed how this resetting of political space, which radically transforms the state scalar organization, involves dismantling the 'regulatory formation of spatial Keynesianism' across the western European State system. Since governance is linked to the dynamics of the construction of new scales for state intervention, the latter should be examined:

not only as a site for political strategies but also as one of their key mechanisms and outcomes ... State scalar structures are now understood to be historically malleable; they may be ruptured and rewoven through the very political strategies they enable.

(Brenner, 2009, pp. 125–126)

According to Keating (1997), over the past few decades in Europe the territory as a whole has been in the throes of re-invention. Keating refers in particular to the dynamics of regionalization[3] which began when the Europe of the Regions promoted by Jacques Delors was launched between the 1980s and the 1990s. Since then the Regions have played a leading role not only in national politics but also in Europe, experimenting with new forms of collective action and territorial regulation. This entails the end of the naturalized idea of the territory once and for all. It is, indeed, evident that a Region is not a natural entity but a social construction, with a territory, political space, and system of governing institutions (ibid.).

Multilevel governance is the tool created to coordinate this geometry of power and processes, which is at the same time stratified and dynamic. It is entrusted with the task of facilitating 'the coordinated action by the European Union, the Member States and local and regional authorities, based on partnership and aimed at drawing up and implementing EU policies' (The Committee of the Regions' White Paper). Multilevel governance should allow for common choices and action, at the same time drawing on the autonomy of decentralized tiers. It thus points to a relationship based on multiscalarity and the interdependence between actors 'involved in a continuing process of negotiation across a range of policy fields' (Allen and Cochrane, 2010, p. 1166).

Regionalization is, of course, only one aspect of reorganization. In the new territorial order, cities, too, are leading actors, nourishing new forms of politics, economy and culture (Sassen, 2006). The Europe of the Regions has been swiftly flanked by a Europe of the Cities. By exploiting opportunities like structural funds offered by the EU, cities have become political actors in the European space and they search for legitimization and representative roles (Le Galès, 2002). Thanks to urban and regional policies developed over the past thirty years, the EU has changed the institutional and economic context in which cities are placed, favouring the formation of a political space in which various levels of governing interact, vertically or horizontally (ibid.).

The importance and significance of localization should be placed in this perspective, which highlights the interdependence between local and global. Globalization has marked not the decline but the rise of local.[4] In other words, 'The local is not transcended by globalization, but rather ... the local is to be understood by global relationships' (Savage, Bagnall and Longhurst, 2005, p. 3). First, the dual focus local/global is crucial for understanding the dynamics of reorganization of society that have come into play on an urban scale in response to the changes induced by globalization: the 'recentrings' (*recentrages*) as Bagnasco (2003) defines them, or the new forms of integration between economy, politics and culture that are particularly to be found in cities. Second, in the mobile and stratified geometries of rescaling, localization indicates the political-institutional process through which 'the State 'shrinks', downsizing back to local to become more effective and more agile' (Castel, 2005). This implies that greater proximity between governors and governed should in theory promote the recruitment of communities' to processes of governing (Clarke, 2008).

We thus come to territorialization in policy approaches, which, put simply, consists of the tendency to adopt an integrated approach to a combination of problems (social, physical and economic) concerning the specific needs and resources of delimited areas and communities. Quite common are actions based on a principle of positive discrimination targeting disadvantaged areas and intended to redistribute and equalize opportunities. The idea that interventions and competences should be territorialized has been gaining ground ever since sector-based approaches to local development proved inadequate and, at the same time, the spatial aspects of problems such as social exclusion became significant issues in the public debate (Madanipour, 1998).

Understood as a set of arrangements interacting with specific local conditions, local welfare lies at the intersection between the two pathways of territorialization: the rescaling of welfare powers and the design of policies targeted on contexts. In fact, local welfare is associated with the role assumed by local governments and public-private networks in decisions on a very wide range of issues. Besides, local welfare is also linked to the redefinition of the approaches and tools of public action in which reference to the territory is the key to recalibrating policies with a view to satisfying a range of demands that have become of prime importance, such as shaping services and intervention to fit the specific needs and resources of a collectivity, recognizing the active role of the recipients and citizens in these policies, and making use of potential local cooperatives. In this light local welfare occupies a decisive role in the arrangements through which public agendas have attempted to deal with some of the more evident limits of the welfare state (fortunately not all welfare states to the same extent): the tendency towards standardization and uniformity of intervention, the hierarchical and authoritative mark of relations between state and citizens, and the relegation of beneficiaries to a passive role.

Implicit and explicit forms of localization of welfare and rescaling of social policies have taken place in almost all European countries over the last thirty years, although the timing and ways vary according to the country and context in question, as do the implications (Kazepov, 2008). In particular, since the 1990s the rhetoric of subsidiarity and the demand to boost active labour market policies have encouraged a redistribution of regulatory powers towards subnational levels, in which the latter have gained a certain financial independence (ibid.).

In any case, talking about local welfare does not just mean talking about the scale that delimits the actors, powers, needs and responses of welfare, but also (i) the networks existing between actors – public and non-public – which emerge locally where the vertical and horizontal axes of governance intersect; (ii) the responses that are identified and negotiated amongst these actors; (iii) the specific demands and social problems to be met; and (iv) the basis of the available resources that can be activated in the context.[5] The innovative drive in the localization of the design and implementation of policies is in fact normally associated with the possibility of new actors emerging, as well as new ways of conceiving problems and solutions and new resources, as summed up by the notion of social innovation (Chapter 9).

Overall, reterritorialization can be summed up in two intersecting perspectives, the first perceiving the territory as the stake in a game of political reorganization, and the second perceiving it as an action system. Both entail conceptual reorientation and the 'discovery' of the territory as a dynamic entity that is active and 'under construction' (Governa and Salone, 2004, p. 797). This notion of territory values the local level but extends its horizons, connections and confines, since it places the interdependence between local actors and other scales and networks of varying dimensions at its centre (Moulaert and Vicari Haddock, 2009). This new approach is consonant with the 'spatial turn' that took place in the social sciences during the 1980s. It was discovered, as Mayer (2008, p. 414) puts it, that 'social interactions and social relations under capitalism could be better understood as societally produced in historically specific social spaces'. The focus is on space, which is no longer considered inert, or a container, but the fruit of active production.

## Problems and opportunities in changing public action

The roots of the processual dimension of public action are greatly entangled. The three models shown in Table 3.1 sum up the debate on marketization, governance and territorial reorganization. As previously mentioned, the classic model of government is founded on the correspondence of national territory, society and citizenship. The participatory shift in governance and the territorialized and localized profile of public action in welfare mutually strengthen one another. The mobilization of networks and resources for action involved in local governance is in fact potentially associated with a redistribution of power that tends to favour citizens.

Nonetheless, as previously mentioned, this cannot be taken for granted. In fact many local governance structures operate mainly with a view to allowing market logics and economic and financial interests to penetrate the public domain, in an attempt to correspond to objectives of growth and competi-

*Table 3.1* Governance and territory

| Government | Marketized governance | Participatory governance |
|---|---|---|
| National territory as the medium (standardized and standardizing) of citizenship | Territory as resources to be exploited | Territory as a system of action and resources to be set in motion |

tiveness. As a consequence, the territory can become a mere reservoir of resources to be exploited in the name of competitiveness. A highly eloquent example is that of housing, which is generally witnessing the growing weight of financialization mechanisms frequently induced by public–private networks. The marginalization of objectives of inclusion and democratic participation is not such a rare event in governance. Moreover, a large body of research shows that even when watchwords like 'participation' and 'empowerment' prevail, citizens are not necessarily endowed with greater power as a result.

One crucial point is the availability of resources. Thanks to welfare re-organizations that have been inspired by the principle of vertical subsidiarity, local governments have acquired greater responsibilities but in some cases this happens in the absence of a sufficient allocation of resources due to the logic of the 'devolution of penury' (Mény and Wright, 1985). In this way, greater freedom of action is thwarted by the scarcity of resources. In any case, localized policies may increase territorial inequalities or simply redistribute them (Hadjimichalis and Hudson, 2007), challenging democratic responsibility (Keating, 1997). These problems are becoming all the more acute due to cuts in public spending following the crisis and to the strategy of austerity. Moreover, the check on spending is a typical domain of central State power. With the crisis, this type of power has strengthened, giving rise to mechanisms of recentralization that are particularly restrictive in the case of social policies.

Paradoxically, it may happen that the local becomes 'a trap', because it is taken for granted that local is inherently good (Purcell, 2006), for example by assuming that devolution of authority will produce greater democracy. The problem is that local democracy is fragile. Experiments with this in different countries and environments can help to bring new life to traditional mechanisms of consensus and to contrast the political apathy that has been affecting all Western democracies for some time now. But it is impossible for them to be sufficient. In his passionate analysis of American democracy as 'inverted totalitarianism', Wolin (2008) maintains that the participation of citizens in local political life is an essential resource for overcoming problems such as growing disinterest and the manipulation of consensus. But it is not enough.

> Democratic experience begins at the local level, but a democratic citizenry should not accept city limits as its political horizon. A principal reason is that the modern citizenry has needs which exceed local resources … and can be addressed only by means of state power.
>
> (ibid., p. 291)

What is more, local practices of participation seem quite fragile in the light of post-democracy, as Crouch (2004) has called it, pointing to the system of exercising power in which ' … policy is decided in private by the integration between elected governments and élites that are almost exclusively economic interests' (ibid., p. 6).

Therefore we need to gain a better understanding of the effects arising from the combination of problems and opportunities in changing public action, with particular regard to the possibility of social organization and innovation which germinate in the folds of governance.

The following chapters are devoted to this. At this stage we may already conclude that too much hope has been placed in territorialized governance as a means to generate innovations for citizenship; but while we need to moderate that hope, we should not abandon it.

## Notes

1   In this light, Peck and Tickell (2002) refer to the importance assumed by programmes centring on the community, to discourse on social capital, to local partnerships and the various forms of mobilization of associations.
2   In Great Britain the programmes adopted by the Conservative governments and those by Labour bore the mark of the same blueprint and were virtually seamless. Amongst the best known are these regarding healthcare and those linked to the tools of Value for Money, hinging on the three Es: economic efficiency, efficiency and effectiveness. The programme Next Steps, launched in 1988, provided for devolution of many public services, placing them in the hands of a system of agencies directed by managerial figures. With the programme Citizens' Charter (later renamed Service First), the objectives of reform shifted towards access, transparency, the promotion of choice and improvement of the standards according to which the service was implemented. Amongst the tools that gain greater importance are those associated with the stages of checking and control. The creation of the National Audit Office in the 1980s, for example, had profound repercussions on the autonomy of local authorities, setting up a quite rigid system of definition and measurement of standards (Le Galès and Scott, 2008).
3   As Ferrera (2005) notices, the initial phase of regionalization, which began in the 1970s and 1980s, took place within national borders and was animated by the need to make the administrative burden sustained by the central State somewhat lighter, the search for more efficient policies and services that were also closer to the citizen, and the social demand for decentralization of decision-making. The last few years of the past century saw the advance of 'a new wave' of regionalism which, in Keating's (1997) by now classic analysis, differs from the past in that it takes place not within states but within the wider sphere of the European Union and the global market. Three factors contribute to its development: functional change (driven by globalization), institutional reorganization (devolution and European integration), and political mobilization within the Regions.
4   One implication is that globalizing social relations accentuates the social need for the local, which can be seen as a defensive reaction, induced and reinforced by globalization (Castells, 1996).
5   Andreotti et al., (2012); Bifulco (2014). The concept of a local welfare system does, in fact, indicate the specific configuration of needs, resources, formal and informal arrangements involved in the design and implementation of policies emerging from the interplay of the economic, political, social and cultural aspects of a local context (Andreotti et al., 2012, p. 1926).

# 4 The social investment

Arising on the terrain of the crisis of the welfare state, the Social Investment (SI) perspective indicates a strong and explicit link between social protection and economic growth. One cornerstone consists of active labour market programmes that give priority to the objective of social inclusion through participation in work, unlike traditional passive policies, which provide compensation for non-participation in work (Borghi and van Berkel, 2007). Equally important are the interventions held to be crucial for the development of human capital: measures for childhood, education, training and lifelong learning.

In SI the same logic of incentivization and mobilization of individuals resounds as permeates the practices and rhetoric of governance. As already mentioned, the processual declination is a basic aspect of public action, and just as ambiguous.

The chapter begins by focusing on the ambiguity of the SI perspective and of activation, reporting the critical debate that has developed on these themes. I shall then tackle this ambiguity by developing a question: what sort of agency comes into play in activation and social investment? Therefore, I will concentrate on models of agency guiding public actions, linking them with current dynamics of individualization. The comparison between freedom of choice/punitive responsibilization and interdependence/capabilities is the line of investigation in the final part.

## Common but not shared perspectives

Unlike the neoliberal creed, according to which social spending is simply a cost, SI is based on the thesis that social policies are productive factors and, consequently, necessary to economic growth (Morel, Palier and Palme, 2012, pp. 353–376). According to Jenson (2012), there are three main lines along which the thesis is developed: the decisive role of knowledge and learning for the future of our societies (linked to the emphasis placed on policies regarding human capital); the tendency towards building the future rather than improving present conditions (the starting point for the attention to childhood and policies for contrasting the intergenerational transmission); and the idea that the success of the individual is a benefit for everyone.

There is widespread and bipartisan consensus on SI. Many stress that its strongest point is the way in which it reconciles social and economic aspects, distinguishing itself both from neoliberalism and from the Keynesian model.[1] As Cantillon (2011) comments, its supporters tend to present it as a new model capable of complementing the 'old' welfare state with enabling strategies. What is more, many take the view of 'social expenditures as most justifiable when they lead to the accumulation of a range of individual and communal capital' (Daly, 2011, p. 4).

In fact, the normative significances and implications of this perspective are not at all free from ambiguity. It is no coincidence that increasing efforts are being made to pinpoint specific aspects of it and, in particular, its differences compared to the neoliberal model (Hemerijck, 2012; Hemerijck, 2013). Morel et al. (2012), who have given us a broad summary of the issues at stake, maintain that social investment disassociates itself from the idea that 'any job' is a good thing, idea that is the pillar of active neoliberal-style policies and is associated with the risk of providing an incentive for precarious and under-paid employment. In their opinion, SI re-launches the issue of activation in a perspective that recognizes the strategic importance of the quality of work and, unlike neoliberal programmes of deregulation and dismantling of the public sector, acknowledges the value of the State's role as financer and provider of the services necessary for developing human capital, especially concerning edu-cation and training. Partial continuity with the Keynesian vision should thus be acknowledged, in particular with regard to the conviction that the State must reconcile efficiency with equality and that social policy can operate as a premise for growth (ibid.). Unlike the Keynesian model, however, SI looks to the future rather than to the present. At the same time, the profile of social justice tends towards prevention rather than reparative logic, since priority is given to providing equal opportunities of access to work and reducing as far as possible the transmission of inequality between generations. One important break with neoliberalism would be this public commitment to the objective of equal opportunities, to be pursued by means of investment in individual skills.

The most critical commentators have many strings to their bow, starting with the issue of work. On the one hand, recognizing that opportunities are not equally distributed means that in order to effectively promote access to employment various types of services and support must be provided (Jenson, 2012). On the other hand, the idea that work is the main path to integration and social inclusion remains the initial assumption. This leads to devaluing unpaid work and activities carried on outside the marketplace (Cantillon and Van Lancker, 2013) and, in particular, 'risks concealing both the need and the value of the work of caring, paid or unpaid as it may be' (Saraceno, 2009, p. 61). One implication of this is that issues of work/family reconciliation policy at EU level may be depicted as employment rather than family policy issues (O'Connor, 2005; Lewis, 2006). The fact is that employment not only tends to be considered the solution (according to the 'work first' principle) but the way in which it is conceived encourages an instrumental declination of social policies. The objective of raising the employment rate amongst women is, in fact, normally motivated economically by the need to increase the contributional basis of social security and not by the need to promote women's aspirations.[2] Policies on childhood also suffer instrumental distortion, when children are considered as 'working citizens' of the future rather than 'child citizens' of the present with social rights, despite the fact they are not productive (Lister, 2003). In this way childcare and education policies centre on employment priorities rather than on children's well-being.[3]

Moreover, the space reserved for those that cannot access employment – because they cannot 'be activated' – still has to be understood. According to Cantillon (2011), the notion of social investment is not significant for those most deprived of resources, such as frail, elderly or disabled persons.

The relationship between protection and promotion is another thorny issue. The decidedly preventive/promotional orientation means that the importance of protective measures as premises for social investment action tends to be neglected. As to social justice, the break with neoliberalism goes hand in hand with its distance from the classic welfare state: unlike the latter, which envisaged repairing social damage caused by the market, the objective is to equip citizens with the skills that allow them to access and adapt to the market (Laruffa, forthcoming). This implies a shift regarding priorities and core values, from equality to inclusion (Evers and Guillemard, 2013, p. 366). The aim of compensating for social damage is thus only marginal (Vandenbroucke et al., 2011) and redistributive mechanisms weigh in favour of young people, those who are active or can be activated. All this makes the limits of this perspective evident, particularly if it is taken as the sole and overall point of reference for policies. Cantillon and Van Lancker (2013) are quite convincing when they argue that 'social investment perspective cannot and will not ensure social progress for all if it is not complemented by a firm commitment to traditional forms of social protection' (p. 561).

The critical comments are convincing but at the same time it should be stressed that they concern composite and unclear normative frameworks.

As Barbier (2005, p. 286) has been arguing for some time about active labour market programmes: 'The adoption of a common language does not mean that the concepts have blended smoothly or that ideas on activation all agree'. Rhetorical uses and 'ritual conformity' are rife. In fact the perspective of activation has established itself on the various national agendas in terms of a common language that starts out from the European Employment Strategy, the tool for coordinating national policies on employment, introduced in 1997 and foreseeing the elaboration of EU guidelines to be taken into account in the national plans. Nonetheless, neither the roots not the operational formulas of activation are unequivocal. Although a minority, wider perspectives are also present (for example in some northern European programmes) that do not hinge on employment but are associated with themes such as participation and community development (Hvinden, 1999).

SI, in which activation is one of the central axes, has all the characteristics of a *quasi*-concept, highly flexible and open to a multitude of interpretations (Jenson, 2010).[4] This is a resource for public action and policies, which are able to appeal to different significances (ibid.). European initiatives and discourse make use of this potential, reinforcing some significances and ignoring others or combining them (ibid.). This means that even under the same SI umbrella a range of different approaches and implementations are to be seen (Esping-Andersen et al., 2002). The northern European countries tend to combine measures for the development of human capital with solid social protection (Morel et al., 2012). They can boast simultaneously of good economic growth, high levels of education, a high employment rate for women, less transmission of poverty between generations and a more satisfactory network of assistance for the elderly (Palier, 2013). The measures adopted in the United Kingdom reveal clear continuity with neoliberal programmes for reducing public commitment and restricting entitlements and benefits in welfare. In the rest of Europe only modest attempts have been made to move towards social investment (ibid.).

## Individualization

Because the main aspect here is ambiguity, analytical keys have to be found to help sieve through real experiences, identifying their logic and implications.

The individualization of the policies and models of agency underpinning them are a precious line of investigation to follow. The starting point is the tendency to take the individual as a point of reference and metric for models of intervention. This tendency takes shape in a range of formulas and declinations. One fairly widespread tendency is to provide tailor-made services and intervention, shaped to individual characteristics and circumstances (Borghi and van Berkel, 2007; van Berkel and Valkenburg, 2007). At the same time individualization gives importance to the personal ability to adapt, thus diminishing the importance of social and institutional contexts, i.e. the reasons for recognizing and exercising collective responsibility (Daly, 2011; Lewis, 2001).

One of the most significant and at the same time slippery areas in the affirmation of an individualized policy model is, indeed, that of responsibility. The shifting relationships between individual and collective responsibility are quite evident in the concept of employability, which implies a definition of unemployment as the result of individual deficiencies (Borghi, 2011). The responsibility for ensuring adequate conditions for the individual's access to employment is placed on the individual herself or himself (Bonvin and Farvaque, 2003), who has to demonstrate satisfactory engagement in job seeking and skills development. This means that measures mobilizing collective and institutional resources and affecting the demand for labour become irrelevant. One aspect of activation policies common to different countries has been, as is known, their one-sided focus on the supply side of the labour market (van der Aa and van Berkel, 2014).[5] Where more general social conditions and contexts vanish from the scene, this emphasis on the responsibility of the individual tends to end up placing the blame on her or him, according to the typical mechanisms of blaming the victim, which imply the prevalence of a moral and moralizing register in interventions and their underlying categories (de Leonardis 2000).

Similar dynamics can be recognized in those provisions of economic assistance which, whilst stating that their aim is to make beneficiaries autonomous and responsible, oblige them to agree upon 'contracts' that establish restrictive conditions for access to benefits.

Thus the idea of 'a more proactive individual responsibility for results' (Taylor-Gooby, 2011, p. 454) is certainly prominent in the social climate forming the background to the institutional agenda of activation and SI. As mentioned in the first chapter, this is part and parcel of the neoliberal normative and cognitive stamp according to which problems and solutions in public action take shape. Individualization is therefore the fruit and engine of a model of social organization that encourages all individuals 'to consider themselves part of, and to help constitute, a responsible society' (Newman and Tonkens, 2011, p. 181). Also coming into the group of responsibilities are (ibid., pp. 180–181):

- economic responsibilities, which require citizens to contribute to the cost of services or assume the financial responsibility for their conditions of well-being;
- democratic responsibilities, which see individuals involved in public life in view of their status as citizens;
- care responsibilities, which reinforce individual obligations towards vulnerable members of both the community and the family;
- consumer responsibilities, referring to the freedom to choose suppliers and services (ibid.).

As regards models of agency, the basic image of an independent, responsible and autonomous individual, the 'self-possessed and self-directing subject' (Clarke, 2008; Rose, 1996) is the focal point. This, then, is the cognitive and normative matrix that has forged public action in its recent, tortuous evolutions (not only in social policy) (Borghi, 2011; Daly, 2011). What needs to be underscored is that this matrix, nourished by the various liberalisms that permeate European social and institutional life, is not monolithic, but includes numerous elements of tension and contradiction. Indeed it furnishes the background to policies inspired by 'active welfare' in different ways, whether dealing with recognizing the citizen-consumer's freedom of choice, or triggering processes of social inclusion via work, or promoting public participation. In addition, the interventions set in motion may either increase agency or else rob it of its potential, for example by stressing the dynamics of responsibilization to the detriment of a substantial increase in freedom or focusing on the activation of individuals who do not, however, have sufficient resources for this.

As we shall be seeing shortly, all this leads to analytical paths that reach to the core of the dynamics of individualization and their directions of change in the contemporary social world.

## What sort of agency? Problems

The models of agency traced above are therefore linked to the social dynamics through which today's typologies of individuality, their tensions and contradictions are developed, affecting the notion of the individual that has gained force in Western modernity: free from ascribed ties, free from status and traditions, the individual is sovereign because she or he is autonomous and free (Pitch, 2007).

In essential terms, the concepts of autonomy and freedom respectively indicate: (a) the ability to 'give laws to one-self' planning one's own development, and (b) the possibility of choosing and acting without constraints. Yet they still remain quite vague and controversial.

Actually, as Sennett (2003) clearly points out, the theme of autonomy has interested theoretical reflection, public debate and the social life in Western countries driven by two different positions.

One perspective – which counts a founding father of sociology, Durkheim, among its inspirers – conceives of autonomy as always being socially mediated by relations of interdependence. Another perspective has its main source in the tradition of liberalism and stresses the capacity for self-government, separation from others and the irrelevance of connections. The path along which these two perspectives have developed is also interwoven with the theme of freedom. Here, we come to the classic distinction between negative freedom and positive freedom (Berlin, 1969). The former is defined by the absence of external constraints and limitations. The latter, instead, involves the possibility of actually doing and attaining something: it is the substantive freedom discussed by Sen (1999), which is the liberty to live the life you place value upon. In the light of this distinction, the principle of autonomy marking social and institutional practices reveals paradoxical consequences. Honneth (2004) discussed these aspects focusing on the effects of two processes. On the one hand, individual self-fulfilment has become an institutionalized social expectation, which people must conform to. On the other hand, this has been turned into an 'ideology of de-institutionalization' which, by pursuing the project of individuality free from social and institutional constraints, has led to the manifestation in individuals 'of a number of symptoms of inner emptiness, of feeling oneself to be superfluous, and of absence of purpose' (ibid. p. 467).

The ideas of liberty and autonomy have assumed an unprecedented importance as principles for the organization and re-organization of contemporary society. According to Boltanski and Chiappello (1999) these ideas have been assimilated into the new economic order and into arguments legitimizing the capitalism of today, thus softening its impact. On one hand, referring to individuality gifted with autonomy, creativity and capacity for initiative assumes unprecedented normative importance. Ehrenberg (1998, p. 4) argues this 'new normativity' is pervading late-industrial society, urging each person to become himself or herself. On the other hand, some changes now under way question the real possibilities individuals have to take charge of their own projects. Since collective agreements on social and work protection have weakened, security has given way to autonomy almost everywhere (Boltanski and Chiappello, 1999; Castells, 1996). But the shift can have very unequal implications. Some subjects may draw advantages from it while others are forced to agree for the lack of an alternative. Thus autonomy becomes a particularly cogent principle precisely when what Castel (1995, 2003, 2009) defines as the social supports of individuality tend to weaken – collective rights, resources and regulations that have historically nourished it in Western modernity.

In other words, the problem is the increasing gap 'between individuality as a decreed condition and individuality as the practical and realistic ability of auto-affirmation' that Bauman (2000, p. 26) focuses on in analysing 'liquid modernity.' Under these conditions, freedom may imply a negative sense of lack of relationships and isolation. A tendency of that sort may lead to the development of isolated individualities, devoid of the social and institutional resources that mediate the power to determine or change one's life. A related tendency is the proliferation of typologies of individuality whose freedom is defined mainly by their being active and gifted with initiative. The two possibilities are not antithetical. Even in this case, the construction of social bonds seems to be unfavourable, and the power to influence the conditions that determine quality of life is limited (Bauman 1999; Sennett, 2003). Furthermore, there is the risk of a hypertrophic development of individual responsibility. As Beck (1992) argues, today we are induced to look for biographical solutions to social contradictions. This means that individuals are held to be solely responsible for problems that have social origins.

Thus, the perspective of individuality privileged by today's 'spirit of capitalism' risks amplifying the problems that the negative sense of the term 'individualism' has been underscoring in the European context – the primacy of self-interest, the devaluation of society and of the collective aspects of social life.

Nevertheless, not even the most pessimistic analyses hold that the situation of agency emerging in this picture is unambiguous. There are new and old forms of inequality, concentrations of power and heteronomy, just as there are possibilities of emancipation (Paci, 2005). They are often fairly contingent and variable combinations, so that hypotheses about them have undergone close empirical analyses. As well as this, it would be as well to take into account the variety of existing individualisms (Dumont, 1984). As Lukes (1973) highlights, the concept of individualism has complex cultural roots and has taken on different meanings in time and space.[6] Regarding the political cultures in which it is articulated, individualism is a pseudo-unit composed of a variety of ideological and ideal elements (Urbinati, 2009).[7] Rather than hindering it, some forms of individualisms favour the particular relationship between individual and collectivity which leads to associated action, reinforcing specific features of our times, such as the freely chosen, composite and reversible nature of aggregation (Dekker and Van den Broek, 1998; Ambrosini, 2005). What should be remembered, however, is that in the wake of individualization a social demand for autonomy has developed that nurtures individual aspirations regarding lifestyle, work and family cohabitation capable of satisfying the demand for self-determination and self-realization (Paci, 2005).

## What sort of agency? Opportunities

The ambivalences that individuality encounters today help to explain why agency is a tangle of opportunities and constraints. In order to deal with opportunities, I shall seek support in two concepts: interdependence and capabilities.

First, interdependence is a precious aid in attempting to reformulate the theme of autonomy in a register free from blame or moralizing. It has been dealt with by Sennett and by Castel, amongst others – two authors whom I have already referred to on several occasions here, whose very similar positions should nonetheless be kept distinct from one another.

Sennett (2003) upturns the thesis of welfare as being equivalent to dependency, a central point in those (public and scientific) arguments that have pushed for an end to the welfare state. In his opinion, the welfare state has had the merit of considering dependency linked to the need for help as an inevitable factor in modern society and a problem that has to be faced (ibid., p. 173). Its limit has been to transform beneficiaries into passive spectators of their own needs. The problem is thus not dependency in itself, but the specific institutional architecture that has denied users of public bureaucracy the opportunity for coming to grips with their own dependency (ibid., p. 177). The welfare state, which wished to make dependency respectable, has ended up confirming that particular lack of respect that consists in being invisible and without a voice. On the other hand, the reformed structures of welfare, whose public provisions have been reduced in order to outsource services, rely on the voluntary mobilization of the community and make intervention more selective and temporary, pursuing an idea of autonomy as a lasting condition of self-sufficiency. It is a relatively easy task for Sennett to show the liberal tradition as the main source for feeding the shame of dependency and it is the concept of independence that has prospered in this tradition and attracted his attention. In particular, he criticizes the idea that independence, as the ability to self-govern oneself, is equivalent to separation from others, from the same human interaction that produces it. Finding support in Donal Winnicott, Sennett argues that autonomy is strength of character based on the perception of others, i.e. it institutes a relationship between people instead of sanctioning differences that isolate them (ibid., p. 124). Conceived in this way, autonomy allows Sennett to proceed with a reformulation of the issue of dependency in terms of interdependence. And it is here that he appeals to sociology, in particular to Durkheim, who was convinced that 'social cohesion occurs because one person is always dependent upon another in order to achieve a sense of completeness'. Dependency supposes incompleteness in itself; completeness requires the resources of another which one may not well understand' (ibid., p. 124). On these solid bases he grounds his conviction that the autonomy-dependency opposition is a false one and should thus be overcome, placing interdependence at the centre of the discourse. In this perspective, interdependence implies both differentiation and connection and the reciprocal acknowledgement that a person needs others to be autonomous. In other words, to speak of interdependence means placing in the forefront what Dubet (2005) defines 'a dialogical model' of the individual, in which 'the activity of the individual is autonomous but the conditions for this activity do not belong to him.'

Castel's reflection assumes a different register, the diachronic register of social history. The theme of interdependence only apparently occupies second place here. Backed by a considerable study on the development of salaried society, Castel (2003) maintains that the model the welfare state has referred to is not a society of equals but a society of similars 'in which all its members can take part in interdependent relations because they have available a reserve of shared resources and shared rights' (ibid., p. 33). To speak of interdependence thus means focusing on the relationship between the individual and society and the way in which, through history, this relationship has been mediated by social property,[8] i.e. the institutionalized social protection of the welfare state, thanks to which the necessary rights and resources are ensured 'for controlling one's own destiny' (Castel and Haroche, 2001, p. 106). The support for individuation, Castel calls them, which make it possible to access the 'self-ownership',[9] to exist positively as an individual developing personal strategies (ibid., p. 48). From Castel's perspective and in contrast with liberal individualism, the individual is such because he lives in society and 'in society a person takes part in essential relations with the collective' (ibid., p. 103). The collective he refers to consists in arrangements such as rights, regulations and representative organizations. As Castel investigates the past to understand the present, his main problem is the erosion of these arrangements due to the crisis of the welfare state. It is this erosion that explains the emergence of a figure with the specific individuality of modern times: the individual by default ('individu par défaut'), defined by the lack of resources and support that prevent her or him from affirming herself or himself positively and participating in society. It is the other face of the individual by excess ('individu par excès') who seems to have filled the world 'with the demands of his egotism, in a subjectivism with no point of arrival' (ibid., pp. 143–144).

Compared to the model of autonomy prevalent today, the idea of interdependence reveals rather limited performative power. In the eyes of many, it seems inclined to adhere to a perspective based on separation, self-sufficiency and the irrelevance of connections. At the same time, there is the tendency to make freedom coincide with freedom from institutional ties, which a long period of the Nineteen Hundreds established as the condition for gaining a certain amount of social security. A freedom that risks being understood primarily as negative freedom: the freedom from (Berlin, 1969). Instead, if the focus is placed on interdependence, both the social mark of individuality and the contextual and therefore limited nature of autonomy and individual freedoms come to light.[10]

This perspective sheds light both on the, on the contextual – and thus limited – nature of autonomy and on the social dimension of freedom.

Second, from here it is only a brief step to capabilities. The dual link between interdependence and capabilities is one of the most original contributions from Martha Nussbaum, according to whom individual agency implies a social fabric of interdependencies, in which the capability of giving and receiving care by creating connections is practised (Nussbaum, 2000). Nussbaum has also given a clear account of the social dimension of capabilities in her concept of combined capabilities, which places the emphasis on the link between the individual and social dimensions of capabilities. In this perspective, there are combinations of capabilities (and the promotion of them) when internal capabilities, those possessed by the individual, manage to combine appropriately with external capabilities, those that derive from organizations, institutions and contexts.

Though following a different route, the idea of freedom Sen refers to with regard to choice and agency gives the same importance to the connection between social and individual. As said in Chapter 1, individual capabilities are decisively linked to social contexts and institutional opportunities which allow them to grow and be practised (infrastructures, economic possibilities, institutional, legal, political powers and so on)[5]. At the same time, collective action increases the possibility of individual choices, setting up new ends and means for getting there (de Munck, 2008).

Precisely because the social and individual dimensions of capabilities are complementary, the substantial freedom implies different powers to those normally attributed to the consumer over the market. The freedoms that are dear to Sen include citizen involvement in the public debate in which options and priorities are discussed and fixed. The point is that this debate involves the attribution of values in which the substantive freedoms are rooted. It is in this light that voice assumes relevance as the 'political' expression of capabilities. More precisely the *capability for voice* is 'the capacity to express one's opinions and thoughts and to make them count in the course of public discussion' (Bonvin and Thelen, 2003). It is equivalent to powers of choice, and at the same time a premise to, and result of, public democratic debating. Based on these terms on the value of freedom, the capability approach sheds light on voice as an attribute of agency.

From this point of view, the development of agency needs voice to be amplified, instead of punitive dynamics by stressing the individual responsibility. In other words, agency implies powers and not blame. One point to remember is that to give substance to the figure of the individual equipped with this power, resources remain relevant, just like the policies that make them accessible and redistribute them. This is why the promotion of capabilities is not an alternative to protection but presupposes it. At the same time agency is not a given fact or a premise but develops through processes that increase powers and freedom. As Zimmermann (2006, pp. 477–478) comments:

> freedom should not be considered as a state, but as a process of interactions and power relations. Rather than manifesting itself as a given and stabilized condition, it occurs through permanent doing. As a consequence, the capability issue is not only a matter of enjoying freedom of choice and being able to convert it into effective achievements, it also raises the question of the production of capabilities and their changing set over time.

Policies thus have a decisive role to play in triggering and sustaining these processes.

## Conclusions

What has been said up to now about agency, activation and social investment helps to start opening up the black box of policies and highlight how social policies are embedded in the social fabric they themselves contribute to producing.

The triangle of interdependence/substantive freedom/voice and the triangle consisting of self-sufficiency/market freedom/moralization seem useful analytical tools for bringing to light the different models of agency incorporated in policies, in particular for distinguishing between figures of individuality embedded in – and consisting of – social bonds, and desocialized figures.

Truth to tell, the spirit of the times does not seem particularly inclined to appreciate types of agency that are not desocialized and commodified. Nonetheless the opportunities exist, as will soon be seen when discussing participation.

## Notes

1 Hemerijck (2012), who is amongst the founders of the theory regarding this perspective, considers the Social Investment State as the third phase of welfare state reconfiguration.
2 Saraceno (2009) places another connected issue in the limelight: when the theme is the reconciliation of paid labour and care, in the context of the EU equal opportunities are considered as options to be offered to women to access the man's world of paid employment, rather than options to be offered to men so that they can share the responsibilities of caring.
3 Lister (2006). In connection with this, Lister (ibid.) recalls the distinction between two different ways of considering children, as 'beings' or as 'becomings'. Unlike the latter, the former values children in the present and not just as potential adults.
4 Following Jenson (ibid.), quasi-concepts have been generated by academic research but they also entail a common-sense meaning open to multiple interpretations.
5 Nonetheless, lately activation policies seem to focus more on the role and responsibility of employers and there is an increase in 'demand-led' labour market

policies that offer public recruitment and training services for employers (van der Aa and Rik van Berkel, 2014).

6  In the original French meaning, individualism stresses the threat to social and political order, while in the US it refers to the idea of a cohesive society based on equal individual rights, and in Germany to the organic unity of individuals and society (Lukes, 1973).

7  According to Urbinati (ibid.), besides rationalistic individualism and utilitarian or possessive individualism, there is also democratic individualism, which affirms that the political system must protect individual rights. This typology of individualism is said to be rooted in American political cultures.

8  Social property is 'a counterpart of private property, a property for obtaining security now made available to those who were excluded from the protection afforded by private property' (Castel, 2003, p. 31).

9  Thus, which make it possible 'to be your own boss, the owner of your own person and your own actions' (Castel and Haroche, 2001, p. 14).

10  This perspective has for some time affected different areas of scientific debate. Some years ago, Gilligan (1982), an American psychologist, studied moral choices, distinguishing two different modes for forming a judgement. The ethic of responsibility, which is normally referred to by women, places the interdependence between oneself and others in the limelight. The ethic of individual freedom, instead, more frequently informs the morals adopted by men and is based on the concept of equality, giving expression to the acknowledgement of equal respect due to each individual. This articulation reflects the simultaneous presence of two perspectives for perceiving and interpreting social reality. Two visions which, by giving different definitions of the relationship between separation and connection, in any case 'reflect the paradoxical truth of human experience: the fact that we know ourselves as separate only insofar as we live in connection with others, and that we experience relationship only insofar we differentiate other from self' (ibid, p. 63).

# 5    Participation

Citizen participation has become one of the most important topics on the institutional agenda in many European countries and in a number of different public action areas, particularly at a local level. The interest that the theme arouses is on a par with its vagueness. Whilst there is a certain consensus over understanding participation as the citizen's involvement in public decision-making, the concept is polysemic and it tends to result in a variegated spectrum of procedures. Moreover, it is affected by a large body of normative theory, in which two distinct perspectives emerge: the theories of participatory democracy, which stress the direct involvement of citizens in public affairs, and the theories of deliberative democracy, which emphasize mainly the virtue of dialogical and reflective processes (Papadopoulos and Warin, 2007).

On local welfare agendas, participation is normally associated with strategies for promoting the active role of the beneficiaries and/or social inclusion. In this sense it is an integral part of the reorganizations of social policies that have taken place over the last few decades, and a vital key to gaining an understanding of the agency theories they incorporate and convey. As a result, participation brings together a very diverse range of modes for focusing on the role of recipients: as users who contribute to providing a service, either individually and/or as family members; as inhabitants mobilized for the regeneration of a decaying neighbourhood; as stakeholders; as members of third-sector organizations or communities involved in local solidarity networks; and as citizens with rights who belong to a political community (Newman and Tonkens, 2011).

The present chapter brings into focus some issues regarding the relationship between voice and participation. The starting point, as I have mentioned elsewhere (Bifulco, 2013), is Woody Allen's *Melinda and Melinda* (2004). The gist of the plot is as follows: before going to a funeral, four friends gather around a restaurant table and show off their storytelling skills by narrating the tale of a woman – the same woman seen from two different angles, two Melindas in fact. But while one version is tragic, the other is comic. In the first, Melinda encounters grief and despair, while in the second she ends up moderately happy. Thus, the outcome of Melinda and Melinda can indeed be an effective way to indicate the complications arising when analysing certain social phenomena that clearly display both negative and positive features.

Participation is deeply affected by such complications. In scholarly and public debates, supporters and sceptics confront one other with the same vigour. Seen from a comic point of view, the vicissitudes of participation are complex and not always edifying, though they may count on a happy ending. While recognizing the difficulties involved, supporters tend to underline positive aspects, such as more efficient mechanisms of consensus and an improvement in the democratic process. On the side of tragedy the fact that the practices of participation rarely keep their most ambitious promises weighs particularly heavily.

What this chapter holds is that we should not consider differing stories of participation as being in conflict with one another, but understand how they meet and blend in an empirical social reality. There, in fact, the practices of participation tell not just two stories, but many more. In the following paragraphs I shall describe the dimensions, factors and questions that can help us gain a fuller comprehension of these discontinuous stories. I shall then focus on the relationship between participation and voice, posing the questions: (i) 'What powers are involved in participation?'; and (ii) 'How are they constructed?'

First, however, the context requires some clarification.

## The context

Following in Moini's (2012) footsteps, two different cycles of participation can be distinguished in Europe. In the first, which comprises the 1970s and the 1980s, participatory practices are associated with widespread and intense social mobilization. Their main characteristics are the central importance of collective identity: conflictual connotations, very slight structuring, and the reference to egalitarian ideologies. The second cycle, from the 1990s up to today, is distinguished by 'top-down' dynamics and the essential role of public administrations as promoters of opportunities for participation. Widely present in many sectors (in the fight against social exclusion, in local development and the regeneration of decaying neighbourhoods, in environmental policies), these forms of participation have only slight ideological connotations, a low level of conflictuality and they tend to concentrate on issues of very limited importance (ibid.).

The present phase is thus characterized by an institutionalized profile of participation. According to Lascoumes and Le Galès (2007), participation procedures belong to a growing typology of policy instruments that omit reference to authority and privilege the activation of individuals tending to involve them as key elements in policy practices.

An important point is that in the passage from the first to the second phase, the political, collective and conflictual side of participation grows weaker. What is more, today participation is marked prevalently by the aggregation of individuals and individual instances and no longer by mobilization in a broader political sense (de Leonardis, 2011b; Neveu, 2011). This is the context in which the theme of participation acquires such importance that it becomes, as Blondiaux and Sintomer (2002) maintain, a real imperative. In their words, it is the manifestation of 'a new spirit' of public action that is solidifying in a wide repertory of instruments and technologies (juries, plans, committees, etc.). Various factors combine to establish it. As already mentioned, the European Union is a very effective vehicle for a collection of styles and models of action hinging on the mobilization of citizens and civil society. Specific EU initiatives have encouraged this, for example the Urban programmes which, from 1994 to 2005, financed interventions for regenerating neighbourhoods in numerous European cities, rewarding participatory approaches in particular.

As well as this, various national programmes for urban development and regeneration assume participation as a methodological premise, if not as a true objective. The French *politique de la ville* is a very well-known case of an integrated and inclusive approach to the problems of urban peripheries. In the more disorganic Italian context, the (initially national and then regional) programmes known as *Contratti di Quartiere* (Neighbourhood Contracts) stand out thanks to their inclusive potential. Their main targets are urban areas with a prevalence of public housing (Bifulco, 2014). There are also experiences located where the local and the global intersect, such as Agenda 21, the action plans on environmental issues and sustainable development launched by the United Nations and normally promoted by cities and transnational networks of cities, which have strengthened the bond between territory, sustainability and involvement in local communities. In addition, it should not be forgotten that the localization of welfare – which then tends to imply greater proximity between government and citizens and the valorization of territorial resources for action – have encouraged various forms of social aggregation and mobilization (García, 2006). The provision of opportunities for participation increases both in response to a social demand to open up decision-making processes, and to the need of policies and politicians to activate new sources of consensus and legitimation. As a consequence, prominent on the (local) governance agenda of social policies is an array of devices which are inclusive in a twofold sense: first, they are measures for the social inclusion of individuals and disadvantaged groups; second, they are instruments for involving these individuals and groups, as well as citizens in general, in public decisions and public life. In any case, it is mostly on an urban scale that different types of actors find opportunities for action, where the local, national and global intersect (Silver, Scott and Kazepov, 2010) and may well spark off innovation which, following the logic of democratic experimentation (Sabel and Dorf, 2006), strengthens the social bases for participation in public life. The range of intervention in question is vast and embraces the social services, security, socio-cultural integration, employment, the environment and the development of local businesses.

In this context there has been growing appreciation of the potential benefits of participation. These are held to include better understanding of the problems addressed and therefore more efficacious solutions, the enhancing of cooperative capacities and social capital, and revitalization of the democratic process. Moreover, policy-makers have become increasingly convinced that, by their very nature, many issues cannot be resolved without the involvement of the people who are affected by or jointly interested in them.

But there are also several problems. As already mentioned, practices do not always correspond to their potential or live up to expectations. Participation is not an automatic solution to the deficit of democracy that governance frequently suffers from. The number of participants tends to be low more or less everywhere. Moreover, the problems that appear on the agenda of participation are normally of modest scope and marginal. It should be added that participatory policies frequently assume individual and collective agency to be a pre-requisite. Indeed, inequality risks increasing in cases where the capacity to participate is considered a pre-condition for the allocation of resources.

As to the real inclusion of weaker interests and disadvantaged subjects, one issue that is strongly debated is whether the importance assumed by participation comes at the expense of the redistributive aims of social justice (Fainstein, 2010). It is nonetheless true that where citizens do have a real say in decisions that are relevant to their well-being there are tangible redistributive effects (Silver, Scott and Kazepov, 2010).

The basic problem is the scenario that provides the background to participation. According to Moini (2012), participation has favoured the consolidation of neoliberalism by helping to contain its costs and political contradictions. There is no need to embrace these positions totally to agree on the fact that the hopes raised by participation are excessive in these times of post-democracy, in which the considerable erosion of democratic powers goes hand in hand with the spectacularization of politics and the reinforcement of the transnational political-financial oligarchies (Crouch, 2004).

This does not mean that these hopes should be completely abandoned. The social stuff that practices are made of is a mixture, a composite that is not always well amalgamated. This is why participation 'should not be liquidated as the smiling face of neoliberism' (Newman and Clarke, 2009, p. 67): it takes shape in a widely diversified range of possible developments. The problem is to understand how these should be analysed.

## A few distinctions

Participation should always be distinguished from connected issues and phenomena, on which it is often superimposed. It should, for example, be distinguished from deliberation, which in its true sense is identified by the dialogical-rational model, based on dynamics of communication and argumentation. Unlike participation, which does not exclude conflict, this model assumes that dialogue allows the actors to transform their positions reciprocally and have them converge in a common perspective.

As said in Chapter 3, participation and governance is certainly a combination to be carefully explored.

Another concept that intersects with participation is empowerment. The two themes gathered strength together as guidelines for action, just as those pertaining to community involvement were gradually gaining space. Actually, concepts of empowerment may be very different but they can be schematically ranged in two opposing positions.

The first tends to decline empowerment in terms of a mechanism for responsibilization, precisely as outlined in Chapter 4 on activation and SI, in relation to the idea that each individual is solely responsible for his/her successes and failures. From this point of view empowerment is the equivalent of a sort of 'punitive' responsibilization centring on the moral obligation to make an effort. Failure or inaction can consequently be classed as misdeeds. What is valid for individuals in their relationship with institutions and organizations is also valid for greater or smaller collectivities. Empowerment can thus be very burdensome. In fact, the more limited the resources available, the more difficult it is to honour the obligation to tackle problems.

A different viewpoint links empowerment to the power of citizens to trace their own project for development, taking part in the relevant decisions. It is, so to speak, a positive approach, which connects responsibility to the real possibility to choose the actions one accounts for. In this case empowerment has a political rather than moral connotation because it involves a comparison between interests and powers in which many actors are legitimized to debate on important collective issues. Furthermore, it appeals specifically to the responsibility of institutions to create conditions in which this exchange can take place.

Presented in these terms, the two perspectives of empowerment are obviously ideal types. Yet, the empirical dynamics are normally mixed and the distance between ideas and practices, approaches and realizations is a known aspect of public action.

In both versions, however, empowerment affects the relationship between the collective and the individual dimensions. However, the directions and significance of this relationship are different. In the punitive perspective, the link between individuality and the more general social context is blurred and the collective dimension involved is mainly the narrow one of the community (Amin, 2005). The positive perspective implies the availability of a rich basket of social and collective resources (social mobilization and organization but also institutional rules, norms and rights) both as a premise and as a product of individual empowerment.

Resources are of great importance. The restrictive formulas of empowerment are coherent with cuts – even drastic ones – in social protection. Strategies marked by the dictates of 'making an effort' complement cuts in public funds – sometimes considerable ones. Instead, perspectives hinging on the redistribution of power imply both the redistribution of resources and their reconversion, which does not exclude saving and rationalization.

## Dimensions, questions, factors

Besides nourishing debate between supporters and critics, the research has attempted to construct certain maps for finding the way in the investigation of practices. Arnstein's (1969) classic categorization paved the way for analyses centring on different typologies of participation. His famous ladder is broken down into eight steps which are, from the bottom up: manipulation and therapy, equivalent to non-participation; consultation and placation, which correspond to tokenism; partnership, delegated power and citizen control, all three associated with citizen control. As Bishop and Davis (2002) observe, the analytical scheme proposed by Arnstein and the classifications that have been formulated in its wake tend to consider participation as a continuum, thus incorporating a value judgement. The assumption is, in fact, that 'not all forms of participation are "real". This risks making direct democracy the only test for a participative mechanism' (ibid., p. 18). Besides this, the notions of participation as a continuum presume that there exists a shared idea and a methodology of 'real participation'. But participation is a discontinuous form of interaction (ibid., 2002).

To understand and analyse this discontinuity, we must recognize that practices vary according to different dimensions that correspond to specific questions (Table 5.1). More precisely:

- Inclusivity: who participates? The problems implied here are those of openness and access (Papadopoulos and Warin, 2007; Paci, ed., 2008). The ability to participate is not smoothly distributed and there is the risk that those subjects with a higher level of agency and voice, better access to information and greater expert knowledge will be at an advantage (Fraser, 1997; Geddes 2000; Bifulco and de Leonardis, 2003; Vicari Haddock, 2005; Bifulco and Centemeri, 2008; Silver, Scott and Kazepov, 2010). Problems of acknowledgement and legitimacy must then be taken into account. In fact, not all subjects enjoy sufficient credibility for their interests to be considered as legitimate by the policy-makers (Papadopulos and Warin, 2007, p. 30).
- The quality of interaction: how do people participate? In participation, interaction may leave room for cooperation or conflict, as well as opportunism; it

*Table 5.1* Dimensions and questions of participation

| | |
|---|---|
| Inclusivity | Who? |
| Quality of interaction | How? |
| Effectiveness | For what? |
| Institutionalization | Where? |

Source: based on my elaboration of Smith and Wales (2000); Papadopoulos and Warin (2007); Bifulco and Centemeri (2008); della Porta (2008).

may be integrative or aggregative. Della Porta (2008) speaks of the 'quality of discourse' to underline the importance of discussion with respect to the changing of preferences and the construction of shared interests. Several scholars highlight the quality of deliberation and the expectations linked to it: competent policy-making, consensual decisions, learning processes, increasing mutual respect and recognition, and a stronger sense of community (Smith and Wales, 2000).

• Institutionalization of participation: where does participation take place? This dimension concerns the spaces of participation, and what level of formalization and acknowledgement they are given. It is connected to variables such as the visibility and stability of participation procedures, as well as the possibility that these procedures may evolve into learning processes (Bifulco and Centemeri, 2008).

• Effectiveness: what is one taking part in, or for what? As well as questioning the processes, the consequences of participation must also be taken into account (Silver et al., 2010). This means focusing first and foremost on what is at stake in participation and how wide-ranging its effects are (d'Albergo, 2012). Second, if and how participation really affects institutional powers and mechanisms, i.e. the 'political' effectiveness of participation (Fung, 2006; Paci, 2008).

It should be pointed out that the theoretical option these questions refer to – and on which a fair number of research studies converge – places the relationship between the individual actor and the social and institutional dimension at centre stage. The debate on the factors that favour social participation has traditionally been dominated by approaches centring on the individual actor (Almond and Verba, 1963). Naturally, there are different positions in relation to this and such a wide range of arguments to support these positions that they cannot be dealt with here. What can be done, however, is to recall that one of the most evident limits to perspectives focusing on the individual is 'the impossibility of proposing to pinpoint collective phenomena simply by putting together data on the characteristics of individual actors' (Diani, 2008, p. 59).

Thus specific windows of opportunity help to understand how and why participation develops in particular contexts. More precisely, the following factors have to be taken into account, referring to three main dimensions: the temporal dimension, the political-institutional dimension, the social/cooperative dimension.

*Time.* Giving importance to time means paying attention to mechanisms of path dependency, and so to the weight of history, traditional practices and consolidated institutional balances, without allowing this to lead to deterministic options. Historical events allow us to understand what sort of past the practices carry with them, so to speak, the past they have been influenced by but which they can also distance themselves from to some extent. For example, the comparison between France and the United States made by Donzelot et al. (2003) demonstrates quite clearly the influence exerted by political and institutional traditions of policy-making on the practices of participation but also the entanglement of persistence and change that takes shape in the long term.

*Political-institutional architecture.* Focusing on the political-institutional architecture sheds light on factors such as systems of local government, political coalitions and cycles of political change. In Italy the season of participation begins about halfway through the 1990s, thanks to the combination of three processes: devolution, the reform of the local electoral system, and the reorganization undertaken in some public sectors (particularly local development). In the UK and France participation comes, at least partly, in response to a demand for change which affects the centralized structure of the State (Bacqué, Rey and Sintomer, eds, 2005; Imrie and Raco, eds, 2003; Raco, Parker and Doak, 2006).

*Social organization.* Participation is sensitive to potential for cooperation and levels of organization and aggregation in local societies. However, we should not assume that there is a simple cause-effect relationship at work. The most famous participatory experience in the world, the Porto Alegre Budget, could only count on very few resources at the outset in terms of the cooperative fabric existing in the local community (Abers, 1998). The strengthening of this fabric is a result of implementing the Budget, which operated as a learning arena for cooperation. The Italian context is very interesting from this point of view. A number of research studies carried out in different parts of the country demonstrate that the opportunities offered by participatory policies increase social capital that was originally compromised or very slight. At the same time availability of resources is no guarantee of positive results. In a study on participation in local social policies in Italy, Bifulco and Centemeri (2008) show that participation is only partially connected to a mobilized and organized local society.

*The rules of participation.* The rules governing participation are resources as important as the social capital or potential for cooperation. Lowndes et al. (2006) refer to Ostrom's concept (1999, p. 38) on the rules in use, i.e. 'the specific combination of formal and informal institutions that influence participation in a place' and which shape the behaviour of politicians, public managers, leaders of the community and citizens (p. 542). Thanks to the rules in use, public authorities provide incentives for mobilization and establish a normative context in which participation is seen as an appropriate sort of behaviour (by citizens and decision-makers). This confirms 'the creative ability of individuals to evolve and develop rules that facilitate cooperation and collective action' (ibid., p. 560).

*Problem-setting and categorization mechanisms.* The importance assumed by participation in policy agendas not only reflects the influence of the European framework but also the mechanisms by which problems are categorized and paired with specific solutions in national and local contexts. In some cases the institutional agendas tend to consider participation as a solution in itself. In fact there is a great difference between participation being understood as a strategy for attaining specific objectives – for example for increasing consensus – or as an objective in its own right.

*Political leadership.* In many European countries the decline of mass parties has directed the search for consensus into less traditional channels, especially at a local level. The drive towards participation by local politicians arises from their need to put down roots for their personal influence and consolidate it, gaining understanding of a local situation and building alliances with leaders of the communities and private partners (Bäck et al., eds, 2006).

*The social bases of participation.* The controversy regarding 'bottom-up' and 'top-down' practices is longer and as bitter as it once was. In fact many agree that for participation to develop, interests and motives for participating must be fuelled (Borghi, 2006; Bonetti and Villa, 2014) which in turn reinforce social competences and intelligence. According to Fung and Wright (2003, p. 18), participatory experiments establish new channels for exercising and developing knowledge, intelligence and interest in formulating solutions in the people who are directly interested in an issue.

## Voice and capacity to aspire

When we tackle the issues described above, it becomes evident that, unlike Melinda's, there are many stories that can be told about participation, all more or less pleasant or disappointing. But to gain a better understanding of these differences, we should now focus on the dynamics and conditions of agency in participation.

As already said in Chapter 4 exploring the connection between activation, voice and capabilities, participation represents the most 'political' face of the individuality dominant in the framework of activation and the models of agency that inform it.

It is by following on from these lines of thought that I will arrive at the questions posed at the beginning of the chapter: What are the powers of participation? In what way are these powers expressed and developed?

To answer these questions, I will now take into consideration the link between voice and participation from the viewpoint put forward by Appadurai (2004, 2013) who, in his dialogue with Sen, develops his concept of 'capacity to aspire'. This capacity concerns 'how human beings engage their own futures' (Appadurai, 2004, p. 63) and the normative frameworks from which desire and imaginations of the future take form. It is tied to the possibility:

> to have a more complex experience of the relation between a wide range of ends and means … to explore and harvest diverse experiences of exploration and trial, because of their many opportunities to link

material goods and immediate opportunities to more general and generic
possibilities and options.

(ibid., p. 61)

Using a telling metaphor, Appadurai speaks of a 'navigational capacity',
which feeds on the possibility of using the maps of norms to explore the
future and formulating 'real-world conjectures and refutations' (ibid., p. 62).

Like Sen, Appadurai details this concept by focusing on the topics of development and poverty in India, in situations where opportunities for imagining a
future are few and far between. He is interested in revealing how such opportunities can be developed in order to overcome one of the major obstacles to the
realization of projects of well-being for the poor, i.e. 'a binary relationship to
core cultural values, negative and skeptical at one pole, over-attached at the
other' (ibid., p. 75).

This outlook illustrates the original way in which Appadurai understands
culture, emphasizing on the one hand an orientation to the future,[1] and on
the other a pragmatic dimension. The capacity to aspire, in fact, 'thrives and
survives on practices, repetition, exploration, conjecture and refutation' (ibid.,
p. 66). Put differently, by means of voice, which is precisely 'the capacity to
debate, contest, inquire, and participate critically' (ibid., p. 79). Appadurai is
very clear on the relationship between capacity to aspire and voice. He feels
that one of the most serious forms of poverty is not being able to have voice:
'how can we strengthen the capability of the poor to have and to cultivate
voice?' (ibid., p. 63). All his thinking is directed towards showing in what
sense voice and capacity act together and reinforce each other. 'It is through
the exercise of voice that the sinews of aspiration as cultural capacity are built
and strengthened, and conversely, it is through exercising the capacity to
aspire that the exercise of voice by the poor will be extended' (ibid., p. 83).

The experiences he refers to show very clearly how voice enters into play in
the construction of the capacity to aspire. His analysis of home exhibitions
and toilet festivals[1] demonstrates that the crucial point is to create spaces for
public sociality and official recognition which are accessible to poor families.
Thanks to the exchange of ideas they activate, these events become public and
political, besides being occasions for socialization and enjoyment. They stage
a visibility politics which reverses the conditions of invisibility the poor are
normally subjected to. In this sense the capacity to have aspirations is to be
considered not only a cultural capacity but also a public and political one.

This means that the capacity to aspire cannot be considered a condition for
interaction. On the contrary: the practices thanks to which this capacity is
produced must be brought to the fore. Appadurai refers particularly to 'public
dramas' and 'ritualized social performances', i.e. to practices that generate
'new states of feeling and connection' which change the terms of reciprocal
recognition. In these situations the capacity to aspire can activate by bringing
about a change involving the collective and normative context in which action
and imagination take shape.

One episode reported by Appadurai himself may help to clarify this point. About ten years ago, in an important meeting of the United Nations devoted to the problem of housing, in the UN's New York headquarters, a group of fifteen or so members of the Alliance (a grassroots Indian movement) obtained permission to build a model for a house and various models of sanitary services in the middle of the hall in the main building, thus initiating an extraordinary political event. Kofi Annan himself, then head of the UN, was a surprised and interested spectator, finding himself surrounded by the songs and dances that the Indian and South African women involved by the Alliance improvised for the occasion. The festive spirit left an indelible mark on the UN officials present. Therefore:

> for a few brief moments the political power and magic of the UN had been drawn into the space of the urban poor and the highest representatives of the United Nations were surrounded by the voices, the songs, the dances and the physical exhibits of the poorest of the poor – their true constituency.
>
> (Appadurai, 2013, p. 287)

The production of agency therefore has an exquisitely collective dimension. Appadurai points out that capacities are never isolated and always belong to local groups of values, ends and means. The imagination itself is 'a collective social fact', the property of the collectivity and not only an individual faculty. It is indeed at this point that the dialogue with Sen becomes more intense.

> Freedom, the anchoring good in Sen's approach to capabilities and development, has no lasting meaning apart from a collective, dense, and supple horizon of hopes and wants. Absent such a horizon, freedom descends to choice, rational or otherwise, informed or not.
>
> (Appadurai, 2004, p. 82)

The capacity to aspire, therefore, connects Sen's freedoms with 'norms that frame social lives' (ibid., p. 66), recognizing in the poor the power to articulate them or draw fuel for desiring and realizing other possible lives.

Though this perspective prioritizes situations of dire poverty, it can be applied to a far wider range of circumstances. The imagination, as Appadurai (1996) emphasizes in another very well-known text, is an essential driving force of collective mobilization. What is valid in 'normal' situations is even more valid in extreme conditions, where mobilization is all the more necessary and complicated. In fact, from his point of view the way out of poverty comes from a context of interactions in which visions of the future, agency and voice are simultaneously constructed:

> Since the work of development and poverty reduction has everything to do with the future, it is self-evident that a deeper capacity to aspire can only strengthen the poor as partners in the battle against poverty. This is

the only way that words like participation, empowerment, and grass roots can be rescued from the tyranny of cliché'.

(Appadurai, 2004, p. 82)

The capacity to aspire is therefore necessary not only for having desires and projecting the future but also for reinforcing democratic participation in the forms that Appadurai (2002, p. 46) terms 'deep democracy', characterized by 'internal criticism and debate, horizontal exchange and learning, and vertical collaborations and partnerships'. As de Leonardis and Deriu (2012, p. xiv) observe:

> the capacity to aspire is an encouragement to investigate the space of what is possible ... The capacity to aspire has to do with the possibility of imagining and exploring the margins for opening up possibilities and thus experimenting with them and trying them out.

One last consideration should be made as to the spatial dimension. Generally speaking, the space for possibility that Appadurai refers to is not exclusively local. Or rather, it is not a local space understood and experienced as a space that is self-sufficient. The capacity to aspire tends to feed on connections between different levels, as shown by the story of the sanitary services at the UN, where we find (i) an Indian association with local roots in the community and in contexts of extreme poverty (ii) whose range of action extends way beyond the local perimeter (iii) involving people coming from different parts of the world. Cosmopolitanism from below, Appadurai defines it. A cosmopolitanism where the desire:

> to connect with a wider world ... begins close to home and builds on the practices of the local, the everyday and the familiar ... A cosmopolitanism that builds towards global affinities and solidarities through an irregular assortment of near and distant experiences.

(2013, p. 270)

The processes through which the capacity to aspire is produced are thus spatially qualified by the drive to extend the confines of what is local, i.e. the place they start from. This drive, it is worth repeating, is the basis for a different geography of the local, which does not intend to deny the local but 'to combat its indignities and exclusions' (ibid., p. 271). A point of view that is open to promising generalizations as regards social policies and the relations existing in this field between community, institutions and local contexts (Bifulco, 2013).

## Conclusions

Appadurai's perspectives help us to advance along the path already traced with regard to activation, making it possible to understand how voice calls into question the collective horizon that both circumscribes and fuels action and imagination. In this way we are led to the recognition that the differences between stories of participation depend on the conditions for exercising voice and the possibilities of mobilizing in order to think out and realize one's future.

From an analytical point of view, it is thus necessary to observe if and how policies that insist more or less directly on participation fuel agency and voice. From a normative point of view, steps should be taken to make the destinees 'active partners', who develop freedom and desires and manage to formulate projects for their future that do not merely repeat scripts already written on the basis of social conventions and the cultural norms of the context.

In actual practice voice is not so common. There is action taken under the banner of participation that merely justifies inequality and people's lack of power. But there are also cases in which people really do decide and bring about a change in their future. And since the ideas incorporated in the policies have performative power, agency is nonetheless a field for change.

As Blondiaux and Sintomer (2002) suggest, participation should be taken seriously. This does not mean to be optimistic but, on the contrary, that a disenchanted analysis of practices has to be made without thinking that the latter are all mere repetitions of the same old script.

## Note

1 The Toilet Festivals Appadurai refers to are public initiatives organized by associations of activists in some Indian cities in which toilets designed by the inhabitants of slums, i.e. people normally obliged to defecate in public and lacking the bare minimum of hygiene or dignity, are exhibited in public. These initiatives add up to a strategy of social acknowledgement, as well as a way of promoting technological innovation.

# 6    Public–private

Discussing welfare today means talking about the readjustment taking place in the boundaries between public and private non-profit and for-profit. The combinations vary from country to country, sometimes from sector to sector. Whatever they are, what counts is the spread of logics that are different to those typical of the public authorities, both in terms of decisions and in the provision of services.

The theme of the relationship between public and private is laden with normative implications, imbued with political reasons and options that are not always explicit. This chapter concentrates from a very selective point of view on two empirical fields: the contractualization of social policies, and EU orientations and regulations on social entrepreneurship. The aim is to shed light on the ambivalent transformations of the public and the questions they raise about both the social and the institutional spheres.

## Contractualization

As well as on a particular vision of the relationship between market and society and determined political actors, neoliberalization has hinged on the adoption of a wide collection of new instruments for public action (Lascoumes and Le Galès, 2007). Within this framework, social policies in European countries increasingly have recourse to contractual devices in regulating relationships between public administrations and both for-profit and non-profit private parties. In its simplest form, the phenomenon of social policy contracting recalls the transformational processes related to marketization, that affect not only *who* is involved (the public or private nature of the parties engaged), but also *how* they interact (the logics of regulation and public action). Nonetheless, marketization does not constitute an exclusive or unequivocal reference with regard to emerging contractual devices in social policies. In practice, the dynamics of marketization in European countries entail a variable degree of alternation and combination among various modes of regulation. In fact, we are faced with different forms of contractualization and a variety of contractual devices.

This variety can be traced back to the following main types (Bifulco and Vitale, 2006):

- contracts as buy-sell transactions (market-type);
- contracts as policy-making agreements (hybrid form between state and market);
- contracts as responsibilization.

The first of these coincides with the market-type contract, more directly related to marketization and particularly regarding health and social care policies. Health is a privileged developmental area for managed competition and quasi-markets in Europe (Le Grand and Bartlett, eds, 1993). Since the 1990s, marketization has reorganized the system of home-based care for the weak or frail (elderly people, people with disabilities, children) in many countries. This may result in two distinct regulatory models, depending on whether the role of purchaser is assigned to the public organization or to the citizen-consumer (Ascoli and Ranci, eds, 2002). Parallel to this, contractual regulation can avail itself of two dissimilar devices: (a) contracting out: that is, competitive tender or agreements between administrative bodies and providers (both public and private) related to a specific type of competition, competition *for* access to the market (in order to stipulate contracts with the public administration); (b) contracts based on the competitive offer among authorized providers, in this case there is competition *within* the market to attract consumers.

Not only the production of goods and services but also policy-making, primarily at the local level, tend to give increasing space to contractual devices as the decision-making arena opens up to diverse parties and institutions, both public and private. Under the name of pacts, conventions or, more precisely, of contracts, these devices redefine the form and content of relationships between public administrations themselves, with varying degrees of competence or involvement. Here we have a second type of contracting, based on agreements concerning complex problems and collective interests. Therefore, this kind of contract is, by its very nature, 'between state and market' (Bobbio, 2000). Public–private partnerships are the organizational pillars of policy fields involving these kinds of agreements, such as interventions for social inclusion or for neighbourhoods in crisis. At a local level in particular, they are made responsible for a range of tasks: catalysing and composing according to a unified intention the many different stakeholders; coordinating the various levels of government that interact along the European/national/subnational axis; setting up and stabilizing relations of trust and cooperation; transferring locally produced effects onto a broader scale. Thus, under certain conditions, partnerships can put into practice processes of 'institution building', i.e. the creation of rules, procedures, normative and cognitive frameworks for cooperation and coordination between issues and actors (Geddes and Le Galès, 2001; Donolo, 2005). It has to be said that partnerships (local ones) have found good supporters amongst politicians because they are generally considered adaptable and flexible modes of organization, and also because they are coherent with the more general tendency to redefine and broaden the involvement of the local community in public intervention (Geddes and Benington, eds, 2001; Corcoran, 2006). Indeed, in their most inclusive versions, with the widest openings to citizens, partnerships can result in participatory governance (Chapter 3).

We find the third type of contract, which we define as 'responsibilization' (Saraceno, 2002), in interventions for social inclusion. This is specifically to be found in policies for income support and placement (whether social or occupational) that are conditional and based on the assumption of reciprocal commitments by recipients and agencies. Two main typologies can be distinguished. The first, more deeply rooted in continental Europe, is based on the acceptance of reciprocal responsibilities by recipients and agencies, and on the mutual recognition of relational capacities (Borghi and van Berkel, 2007). The second typology, which is strongly influenced by the US perspective of workfare, centres upon the recipient's unilateral obligation to conform to a pre-established conduct, thus subordinating the right to receive benefits to the fulfilment of this obligation.

On this scenario, we can identify at least a few common elements, which correspond to different transformative transitions of public action. First, there is the transition from the logics of government to those of negotiation between actors and interests, typical of governance. A second transition refers to the increasing autonomy of local levels of government. Lastly, we have the transition from the logic of uniform and predefined services based on universal or categorical entitlement (citizenship as status), to the logic of personalized services (in the direction of citizenship as contract: Handler, 2003).

As the presence of hybrid forms indicates, the spread of contractual forms and devices calls for the frontiers between state, market, family and so-called civil society to be changed; thus, what is at stake is a redefinition of the role of the public subject on the one hand, and of the relationships between services (both public and private) and citizens on the other. However, the main attraction of the contractual model is a basic precondition of its 'market' type: managed competition. The idea is that making the most of the virtues of competition – i.e. efficiency, the diversification of goods and services and respect for the 'freedom of choice' of the citizen-consumer – requires the public regulation of market transactions. As a consequence, a public institution should intervene to perform a regulative function, i.e. to render competition effective, to counter any barriers to market access and any trust positions, as well as to avoid the risk of situations of partiality or collusion, to remedy the imbalances in information that typically plague the trade relationship between provider and buyer, and to define and test performance standards.

From this point of view, the market is conceived as a solution to the failures of the state (inefficiency and rigidity of offer). Yet its virtues only unfold on condition that a change takes place in public administration, involving both its regulatory role and the logics of management and organizational dynamics. More precisely, managed competition requires both the introduction of the structure of market incentives – for example, prices and tariffs – in the production of public services, as well as the introduction into public administrations of criteria and techniques of New Public Management (NPM). In this perspective, the infusion of 'market' action criteria in the public sector is a central aspect.

The reform of the UK health system during the 1990s is without doubt an exemplary case of policy change oriented in this direction. But once translated into practice, the reforms and policies were rife with hybridizations. Already under Thatcher, the development of competition between providers in the health quasi-markets was only partial. Research on the subject highlights a mix between formal and informal competition and collaboration between the parties, a mix that is not without situations of oligopoly or monopoly (Neri, 2009).

In general, regulatory forms and instruments with different political roots meet, alternate and often mix along the bumpy routes of contractualization. To a certain extent, this is linked to effects of institutional learning with regard to the problems and possibilities of the regulatory modes once they have been applied in practice. The problems of authority are all too familiar but the market itself does not appear entirely desirable once the results are visible, both in terms of inclusion/exclusion and in terms of public visibility and control. Quite apart from questions of principle, the documented effects often fail to conform to the objectives declared. According to Crouch (2013) the externalization and outsourcing practised in the name of market advantages in several public sectors have not reduced the costs to citizens, have not improved quality and have not produced greater freedom of choice.

Similarly, the development and institutionalization of cooperative relations and bonds of trust between institutions and organized actors in local society constitute important factors for social cohesion and the democratization of collective decisions. Yet cooperation presents its own problems, susceptible as it is to the risk of partial, closed and exclusive situations (Ostrom, 2005) which privilege certain selected actors. The border separating cooperation oriented toward collective use from cooperation of a particularistic nature is subtle, mobile and circumstantial. In the shadow of trust relations between public and private, discretional practices and ties of dependency, even personal ones, may develop according to types of logic that are coherent with the process of re-feudalization which, according to Supiot (2005), is more generally tied in with contractualization.

Mix and variety do not therefore imply that the effective range of contracting social policies should be reappraised. The main point to be made is that the changes involved are often ambiguous and can develop in several directions as well as in heterogeneous forms. However, the processes implied in them are not at all neutral. Even if they do not follow the linear paths pursued by the reference models, and often by the public philosophies that support them, they have been on the road for a long time, so to speak, have prompted changes and will continue to do so. There are a few hints in this direction even in Sweden, home of the universalistic ethos of welfare state (Chapter 6).

## Social market

The European Union plays a decisive role in spreading devices of a contractual nature which in turn act as engines for models of intervention and regulatory logics. The instruments of negotiation foreseen by European programmes such as Urban or Equal have given rise to a wide range of different modes of cooperation and partnership between the state and the market. Norms, too, have carried no small weight. The Bolkestein directive on public services approved in 2006 exalted the pro-market side of contractualization and the repertory of regulations typical of neo-liberalism, summed up by the triad consisting of efficiency, competition, freedom of choice.

The mix of diverse elements seems to be the privileged path in EU regulations and policy framing, too. The Prodi Commission is responsible both for the 2006 Bolkstein directive and for the launch in 2001 of the *White Book on Governance*, which opens the European season of collaborative governance.

Choices in favour of the private sphere entering the area of welfare are normally justified by discourse that emphasizes the need to connect the social and the economic. This argument is clearly emphasized in the European agenda on social economy, whose importance and scope of action grew in correspondence with the Social Investment perspective. The fact that its main mark is ambiguity is nothing new but should nonetheless be stressed. Social business is the keyword for European politicians and is widely approved in the bureaucracy and epistemic communities they refer to. The hierarchy defining the relationship between business/market and the social is not so clear, however.

The figures in the EU are considerable. At present social economy employs more than 11 million people, accounting for 6 per cent of total employment and 10 per cent of the European economy.[1] According to one of the sources that enjoys most credit with the European authorities, the list of sectors of intervention affected is getting longer:

> social security, social and health services, insurance services, banking services, local services, education, training and research, social tourism, energy, consumer services, industrial and agricultural production, handicraft, building, residential environment and cooperative housing, associated work, domains of culture, sport and leisure activities.[2]

One well-known piece of data in the scientific literature is the heterogeneous nature of the organizational and operational formulas labelled social enterprise (Teasdale, 2012): associations, cooperatives, foundations and real businesses. They all disrupt the boundaries between the public and the private, between the state and the market, since they do, in theory, have social aims and collective interests, despite being private subjects (non-profit but also for-profit). Apart from this, it is difficult to understand what else they have in common. What is more, at a national and/or subnational level the models of relations with public administration, the criteria for formal acknowledgement and the set of constraints and opportunities are clearly different.

Truth to tell, on several occasions the Commission has attempted to reduce this indetermination, particularly with regard to the term 'social enterprise'. A recent definition,[3] is the following:

A social business is an undertaking:
- whose primary objective is to achieve social impact rather than generate profit for owners and shareholders;
- which uses its surpluses mainly to achieve these social goals;
- which is managed by social entrepreneurs in an accountable, transparent and innovative way, in particular by involving workers, customers and stakeholders affected by its business activity.

At the same time, the Commission is doing a lot to promote social economy on different fronts and with all the tools it has available, including lines of financing that directly or indirectly document its value.

In tune with this orientation, social enterprises have been assigned a crucial role in the Europe 2020 strategy, in particular with respect to the objective 'to bring innovative solutions for social cohesion and inclusion, job creation, growth and the promotion of active citizenship'.[4] The range of motives adopted remains relatively unchanged:

Social enterprises contribute to smart growth by responding with social innovation to needs that have not yet been met ... They also create sustainable growth by taking into account their environmental impact and by their long-term vision. For example, social enterprises often develop efficient ways to reduce emissions and waste or use natural resources. In addition, social enterprises are at the heart of inclusive growth due to their emphasis on people and social cohesion: they create sustainable jobs for women, young people and the elderly. In other words, their key aim is to effect social and economic transformation which contributes to the objectives of the Europe 2020 Strategy.[5]

The prominence of social entrepreneurship rests upon solid bases in this context. Since 2000, social enterprises have had a structure representing them at a European level, called Social Economy Europe, aiming at promoting the values and reinforcing the recognition of social economy actors in Europe. With the launch of the Social Business Initiative (SBI) in 2011, a strategic plan was set in motion for facilitating access to funds by social enterprises and simplifying the normative framework. Moreover, social business is an integral part of the new 2014–2020 programming for community funds.

Although a lot depends on national and local contexts, the crisis does not seem to have slowed down this impulse. On the contrary, in public discourse the crisis is cited as an argument in favour of strategies for developing the social market. It is nonetheless probable that smaller organizations and in general those less equipped to deal with the logic of the market suffer more from the restrictions on the public budget. Instead, larger enterprises can more easily take advantage of the market areas that free up due to a State that is suffering under financial pressure, with its spending radically downsized.

Several questions are opened up by this scenario. We have to understand how the economic rationale of a business can be reconciled with solidarity, responsibility, the common interest, particularly now that the logic of profit and that of social usefulness are affecting one another in such a significant way. The shift in Europe's vocabulary is a far-from secondary aspect of the issue. The prevalent use of the term 'social business', rather than 'social enterprise' may in fact be assumed as an indication of a more accentuated market-based perspective.

The role of the third sector organizations involved in social enterprises also raises some questions. One thesis that has long been present in the literature and in public debate is that, thanks to their characteristics (pro-social inclination, proximity to social needs, organizational flexibility, internal democracy), these organizations may be an effective alternative to state and market failure, able to ensure satisfactory answers to old and new social problems and, at the same time, bring new life to social ties. In addition, the central importance assigned to the role of the third sector is in harmony with the orientations prevalent today, which emphasize the capacity for activation of individuals and the collectivity. However, this is a significant potential but should be subjected to careful observation. Many organizations are constitutionally of a dual nature, since they pursue both the interests of the beneficiaries and – as producers and providers of services – their own economic interests, in which a glimpse of some kind of conflicting interest can be seen (Polizzi, 2008). We should also be asking ourselves what foundation there is for the role of community spokesperson being attributed to the third sector, a role that on the one hand can be justified by the capacity to take up and report social demands but on the other hand is not subject to any institutional mechanism of representation or control (Bifulco and de Leonardis, 2003; Polizzi, 2008). The more general issue is that the cooperative inclination of civil society and its organized forms cannot be taken for granted. As Fraser (2013) notices, civil society – not only in its traditional form – is certainly not an irenic space for social relations. On the contrary, diverse sorts of domination have their roots there, together with hierarchies, exclusive mechanisms, unequal social status and political voice or unequal access to resources. This means that the civil virtues of society cannot be considered as a premise but are, if anything, a result (de Leonardis, 1998; Borghi, 2014). Instead, celebrations of civil society as the natural place for solidarity tend to absorb the latter into a moral register, reducing it to ethical codes of behaviour and personal virtue, to openness towards ones neighbour (de Leonardis, 1998, p. 65). Perspectives of this nature make differences of power, otherness or conflict invisible and thus irrelevant. The mediated and mediating dimension of institutions is consequently rendered irrelevant. The organizing principle is, in fact, that of immediacy, by definition hostile towards mechanisms of mediation, i.e. towards institutions, that 'mediate communication and exchange between strangers, the acknowledgement of the generalized other', fix a normative framework for the expression and regulation of conflict, look after and fuel social ties (ibid., p. 57).

A more general issue is that the concept of social has gradually become frayed and 'stretched'. If we look at the most recent initiatives taken at a European level, even outside the auspices of the EU, a shift towards the market becomes obvious. In fact social entrepreneurship, whose role is legitimized first and foremost by an inclination towards solidarity (with the consequent obligation for any surplus to be used for social purposes), is not the only alternative to the public sphere appealed to by the reorganizations now taking place. A strategy to which attention should be devoted, even though it is only at its very beginnings, is that focusing on investments with social impact: its aim is to attract capital and private (for-profit) companies with a potential interest in combining economic activity with social usefulness. During the 2013 G8, a task force was set up and an agenda drawn up on this issue, which has as its priority the identification of new market areas with social impact that are attractive to large financial investors.[6]

Seen from this point of view, the contractualization of social policies seems to have set off along a new path, on which it is not hard to see the intervention of financialization dynamics. Once again the UK acts as pathfinder. An instrument that has already been tried out, promoted by Prime Minister Cameron to support his Big Society programme, is that of the Social Benefit Bonds, through which private investors finance a public programme and receive earnings proportionate to the end result (Bryan and Rafferty, 2014). In this way, e.g. an intervention on prisoner rehabilitation and several projects on behalf of children have been financed. Should the intervention, which is in any case managed by the public authorities, prove unsuccessful, no profit is forthcoming. The fact that the main purchasers are not philanthropic organizations but investment banks and hedge funds (including Goldman Sachs) is proof of how deeply the logic of financialization has penetrated the social markets. The aspect that counts most is that 'financial ways of calculating are becoming more pervasive socially' (ibid., p. 891): the calculative logic of derivatives is also gaining a foothold on the social markets, implying formulas of specific contracting between public and private and special risk management based on shifting financial and other risks to people.[7] The change effected by instruments such as Social Bonds affects the State directly, as it implies the institutionalization of mechanisms of contracting out of risk based on 'deconstructing the State into a vast range of activities and means of determining which should be provided in-house and which could be acquired by contract' (ibid., p. 896).

It should be added that logics of this nature and instruments for measuring performance are spreading at the same rate. The question of the social value of the investments tends to be chained to that of the measurement of this value, *ex ante* and *ex post*. It is in fact assumed that the potential investors will only be attracted if their gain is measurable. This increases the pressure, already intrinsic in NPM, to develop impact-measurement procedures and result-oriented policies.[8] Again in the UK, the Public Services (Social Value) Act passed in March 2012 ratified the need for a metric to quantify to what extent the interventions led 'to a better functioning, socially cohesive and environmentally sustainable society' (Dowling and Harvie, 2014, p. 879). One effect is that what cannot be measured tends to lose value socially.

## Public

What is happening in the mix between public and private, through the spread of models of contractual relations, the growing contamination between the logic of non-profit and the logic of for-profit, the appearance of financial actors and financial logic on the social market (with emerging forms of pricing and trading of state risks), raises a question: what is public?

It is evident that the public dimension does not only involve the role covered by the State and its administrative structure. The dynamics causing the public–private mix to grow intertwine with those that make the uncertainty of what is public quite evident. It is uncertain how the decisional and regulative frameworks of welfare, the actors and organizations taking part therein, and the issues and interests which develop and are dealt with, are to be qualified 'public'. This uncertainty has several different implications. The nature of the actors involved is not a suitable criterion for revealing to what degree public action is public. And the public and the private are not two clearly distinguished spheres of action (Fraser, 1997).

I now come to the threshold of the issues regarding the concept of the public. I will take just two steps forward.

The first step consists in assuming a process-based perspective. The uncertainty as to what is public suggests shifting the attention from given realities – the public understood as characteristics of actors and organizations, or as a precondition for action – to the processes through which arenas, actors and issues may (or may not) become public (Bifulco and de Leonardis, 2005). The second step consists in outlining the criteria that define what is public from the perspective of processes. More precisely, the articulation of these criteria rests on certain conceptual points taken from theories on the public, notably four of them (ibid.). The first is visibility: the public, to begin with, is 'in public'. Interpreted from the point of view of processes, this condition focuses attention on the processes of 'visibilization', thanks to which problems and viewpoints on problems leave the private, or hidden sphere, leading to arenas of discussion which subject them to the filter of critical examination (Habermas, 1989). In this way, we witness the development of multiple positions (Arendt, 1958) and the range of different vocabularies through which problems, and the publics that face them and engage with them, simultaneously take shape (Dewey, 1927). Visibilization is made significant by another point: the processes of 'generalization', through which particular viewpoints and claims conflicting in these arenas activate a framework of references making them accessible to the judgement of others and acceptable as legitimate (Boltanski and Thénevot, 1991; Cefaï, 2002). The passage from the particular to the general refers us in turn to the third point: the setting up of common assets. In this case, the processes of publicization are related to bringing to the surface, through the dynamics of generalization, well-defined assets recognized as being common to a collectivity, linked to shared interests, and dealt with, cared for and utilized in common (Ostrom, 1990). Finally, the fourth point brings institution building and its corresponding processes to the fore: the acknowledgement of 'third parties', thanks to which interaction is regulated and plurality is mediated; the emergence, thereby, of a relatively shared normative fabric for the definition and treatment of general interests and common assets recognized as such; the creation and re-elaboration of the terms that translate the particular into the general; and attention to the necessary conditions for maintaining these processes open and active through time (Donolo, 1997).

This way of understanding the public has several implications.

First, it poses the question of privatism in a specific sense that points to the disappearance of those conditions and motives that allow social questions to be recognized as questions of collective importance (de Leonardis, 1997, 1998): a 'privatization of the social', a reduction of social issues to questions of private choice, action, relations interests and/or virtue. Interpreted in this way, privatism is affecting the whole scenario of welfare profoundly and regards both the public and the private – the commercial in the same way as the supportive. Sources of privatism are those organizations and public institutions that reduce the range of different positions rather than increase them, causing problems and solutions to crystallize and to take shape as irrefutable matters, cultivating the art of creating black boxes instead of sustaining the voice of citizens. In the same way, dynamics of interaction between public and private which perpetuate or reinforce the burden of particular interests, not subject to the constraints of (public) institutional mediation implied by the system of democratic representation, also produce effects of privatism. The third sector and social entrepreneurship, too, can fuel this kind of dynamics, with many variations. According to de Leonardis (ibid.), the privatism of the public–private mix has its roots in the tendency to emphasize the social capacities of self-organization, whether because a market model is adopted in which the self-regulatory mechanisms promise to compose the range of different interests at stake through private exchange, or because an ideal of supportive community is pursued founded on voluntary commitment and moral obligation, as such pertinent to the private sphere (Bifulco and de Leonardis, 2005, p. 221; de Leonardis, 1998).

Financialization aggravates the risk of privatism through dynamics where the following aspects converge:

- the expansion of private powers (Pizzorno, 2001; Mény, 2015), with relative lack of clarity in the decision-making spheres, problems of accountability and deficit of democracy;
- the growing penetration of the market into the areas of collective goods previously decommodified (Crouch, 2013);
- the spread of market-driven narrative and the connected desocialization of issues that welfare brings into play or, in Fraser's (2011) words, disenablement of the ethical substance of social protection.

Second, situations are not univocal. The differences between marketization/NPM and participatory governance do not constitute a watershed in terms of what is public in welfare. The dimension of visibilization should be considered in particular. As a form of 'governing by numbers' (Shore and Wright, 2015; Supiot, 2015), NPM has exasperated the naturalizing and reifying effects of technologies of measurement, auditing and ranking, which have spread through several sectors. Procedures developed in the name of transparency, and conceived 'as unmediated or unfiltered human access to reality' (Hansen, 2015, p. 204), paradoxically have effects of opacity as they make what they measure seem like an irrefutable fact, rendering both previous choices and possible alternatives invisible. Policies, decisions and their implementation are thus spared any confrontation with the horizon of what is politically possible (Hansen, 2015; de Leonardis and Giorgi 2013) and are placed 'beyond the realm of the contestable' (Garsten and Jacobson, 2013, p. 428).

Practices of participatory governance can prove to lack clarity to the same extent. Indeed, they can conceal unequal conditions of access to decisions or different power positions of actors, and may neutralize conflicting viewpoints with regard to what may be acknowledged as a collective problem (Fraser, 1997). These effects are aggravated by the affirmation of models of governance that emphasize consensus-oriented logic. Garsten and Jacobsson (2013) define these models 'post-political': they are characterized by dynamics of soft power, by 'subtle forms of steering and control, constraining and limiting the options available for political choice' (ibid., p. 422). The ideas they appeal to – dialogue, agreement, collaboration, etc. – reflect 'a 'harmony ideology' that relies on the good will of the subjects involved (ibid., p. 429). Here too, the result is the removal of the political nature of the issues and decisions at stake. In relation to this, Garsten and Jacobsson (ibid.) notice the compatibility between the moral register and the economic: what is really a matter of options and choices is transformed into ethics or economics, two forms that:

tend to go very well together. Ethical codes of conduct tend to work by way of voluntary engagement of partners, built on a general appreciation of market forces and on trust in the ability of involved organizational actors to find jointly beneficial solutions.

(ibid., p. 424)

Third, in order for there to be a public dimension, favourable conditions must exist for what Fraser (2011, pp. 147–148) defines 'the public sphere of civil society', an arena of public challenge and debate in which 'the tacitly diffused commonsense of "society"' is transformed into explicitly avowed propositional positions, subject to critique, on the one hand, and to explicit defence, on the other. Fraser sees the vitality of this public sphere as depending on the dynamics of emancipation that are capable of contrasting and submitting to public scrutiny the forms of dominion that the state, the market but also society itself bring into play. Incorporating these dynamics in Polyani's framework of double movement – marketization and social protection, disembedding and re-embedding – Fraser calls into question the idealized and over-simplified image of society, as well as unconditional criticism of disembedding processes. The public sphere of civil society implies bringing into focus the 'normative deficits of society, as well as those of economy' and 'struggles against domination *wherever* it roots' (ibid., p. 144). This means both contrasting the grip of the market as the master narrative of public policies, and avoiding irenic and naturalized visions of social life.

## Public administration

The end of the equation between public and state seems to multiply the difficulties in defining the role of the public administration.

A starting point for tackling this issue is to recall the changes that have generally affected administrative responsibility. The direct responsibility typical of bureaucracy (expression of the functions of command/control by public authorities and tasks of management/implementation directed by its administrative structures) has made way for the intermediary role of administrative responsibility, the pivot for post-bureaucratic administrative change. However, this intermediary role may have a very different premise and meaning. In collaborative models of governance it is not the attribute of a position but is linked to intermediary action between various and divergent strategies, interests and justifications. In managerial models it is defined by the position of the public administration in relation to the citizen in a triangular scheme: the public administration's responsibility is indirect, because it is mediated by private providers (Freedland, 2001). Financialization further stretches this chain of indirect responsibilities, which also includes in its meshes financial intermediaries and social investors.

These shifts in responsibility can best be understood in connection with two phenomena. One that has already been mentioned is the growing impact of

procedures of measurement and evaluation that have accompanied manage-
rialism from its very beginning (Clarke and Newman, 1997). Consequently,
administrative responsibility in marketized governance is mediated not only
by third parties (suppliers, financers, etc.) but also by a range of technical devices
that tend to transform what is really the sphere of public decision-making and
responsibilities into the form of objective facts. The parameters of measurement are themselves actually the fruit of choices. The notion of efficiency,
which is supposed to be the priority of the measurements 'expresses a value
judgement, not a scientific truth' (Poggi 2013, p. 136). In other words, it is
political in nature. More precisely:

> the neoliberal absolutization of efficiency is a legitimate *political* stance that
> seeks to give an acceptable or contestable orientation to public opinion, not
> a scientific theorem … There is no scientific reason why the general
> public, and political choices, cannot instead privilege, systematically or
> occasionally, criteria other than efficiency.
>
> (ibid., p. 137)

But efficiency has now been imposed as a technical-scientific fact, thereby
disenabling the political value of the choices that have taken firm shape in it
and the many different alternatives. Moreover, the growing recourse to ranking
and benchmarking techniques in several administrative sectors points to an
intensification of datafication (Hansen, 2015), with the implications previously mentioned: transparency devices adopted as key mechanisms for good
administration, which actually lead to less clarity; measures that have a retro-
active effect on what they measure, despite claims to objectivity; procedures that
overwhelm the substance of the matter. To sum up, bureaucracy through different means: no longer laws and regulations but measurements and data.
The Weberian and the neoliberal bureaucracy of NPM have far more in
common than it might seem. In addition, as Hibou (2012) has rightly pointed
out, both contribute, in different ways, to the process of bureaucratization
that has transformed and continues to transform modern societies. The cage
is made of glass, not iron, but a cage it remains (Bifulco, 2011a): control has
become softer but this does not mean that it has loosened its grip; transparency
is not necessarily equivalent to greater opportunities for knowledge and
choice but, on the contrary, can end up by reducing the field of options.

The other phenomenon is the growing importance attributed to the role of
coordination by public administrations in partnerships and governance.
Deprived of bureaucratic authority, public administration is encouraged to
anchor its legitimacy in processes and relations and thus assume the direction
of the networks of governance. But it is one matter for the director to limit
intervention to monitoring respect for procedures or, at most, rules, in a predefined framework that is assumed to be irrefutable. Instead, it is quite a different
matter for the director to bring the substance of issues into the limelight for
public acknowledgement and debate, i.e. options and priorities and the very

rules that constitute them. The former case reveals a functional and instrumental inflection in the role of coordination, identical to the traditional concept of bureaucratic administration as an instrument of politics, with the difference that in networks the relationship between administration and politics can be more mediated and less visible than in bureaucracy. In the latter case, the boundary between administration and politics is more blurred, the two spheres are closer and their connections more visible. In other words, the choices and options implicit in administrative action can be more easily recognized, even when they have assumed a firm shape as procedures and techniques. Between these two extremes there is an ample range of empirical situations and varying degrees of the relationship between administration and politics which, ever since Weber, has become recognizable as a field of strong tension central to statehood and the modern state. But to stick to the typical ideal, it should be remembered that in Weberian administration rational knowledge is a decisive instrument of legitimacy, as is the strategic balance between functions and powers. Nonetheless, this never completely removes the tension between administration and politics. In post-bureaucratic models we find both situations in which this tension is disenabled through devices that produce effects of privatization and depoliticization of issues, and situations in which, vice versa, the tension is amplified by administrative actions that actively promote public debate on the issues at stake in connection with inclusive decision-making processes.

## Conclusions

The questions touched upon in this chapter lead us to highly complex issues relating to the enabling role of the State. There are those who, like Mazzucato (2011), argue convincingly the need for an entrepreneurial State, capable of elaborating a strategic vision of development and willing to invest the resources necessary for achieving it.

Quite pragmatically, we can venture the conclusion that, as even many supporters of the mix acknowledge, what is still needed today is public responsibility for welfare. The alternative is to fuel the residual logics which turn social issues into the private problems of the needy, or consolidate private decision-making powers, exonerated from the constraints and obligations intrinsic in democratic powers. At the end of the day, public institutions are all we have for the moment to obtain a third party, indispensable for getting old and new social issues debated, acknowledged and treated as issues of collective importance (Bifulco and de Leonardis, 2005).

## Notes

1 http://ec.europa.eu/growth/smes/promoting-entrepreneurship/we-work-for/social-econo my/index_en.htm
2 http://www.socialeconomy.eu.org/spip.php?rubrique541

3   http://docz.io/doc/2983125/the-social-business-initiative-brochure
4   http://www.eesc.europa.eu/?i=portal.en.events-and-activities-social-enterprises-europe-2020
5   http://ec.europa.eu/internal_market/publications/docs/sbi-brochure/sbi-brochure-print_en.pdf
6   Social impact investments are conceived for generating a measurable social and environmental impact, whilst at the same time guaranteeing a financial return for investors.
7   A very clear example, outside the field of social policies in the strict sense, is the spread of work contracts that shift risks from employers to workers. One device which has become prevalent in Britain is the 'zero hours' employment contract, in which employer has no obligation to provide work and employee works only when requested (Bryan and Rafferty, 2014, p. 895).
8   As Chiappello points out (2013): 'The enthusiasm for impact measurement is therefore a sign of the times. It seems attractive, not because of its presumed efficiency, but because it offers an opportunity to organize the social services sector differently, by allowing for remote management by non-professionals, project-based contractualization for public and private financiers and the production of easily digestible information for potential investors.'

# Part III

# Public action and social policies: A changing social domain

# 7   Young school-to-work transitions

What measures and approaches are offered in Europe today to support young school-to-work transitions? What criteria of social justice come into play in the perspective of employability? What processes support the skills and capacities in young people's school-to-work transitions? What added value can the application of the capabilities approach (CA) bring to these processes? These are the main issues dealt with in this chapter, which focuses on findings from a European research study carried out in nine European countries (Italy, France, Poland, Switzerland, Austria, Germany, United Kingdom, Denmark, and Sweden) (Otto et al., eds, 2015,). The analysis looks at programmes and interventions that deal with problems, risks, or failures in one or more of the following transitions: from compulsory school to further education, from education/vocational training to the labour market, and from unemployment/being out of the labour market to employment. In identifying certain factors that sustain agency in young people's transitions, the chapter confirms the importance of the institutional dimension, which the CA calls into question in two ways: on the one hand by highlighting the close and complex relationship between individual agency and the normative fabric of society; on the other hand by assigning to institutions an important role in the processes of converting formal entitlements into real, effective and demandable rights and resources (Bifulco and Mozzana, 2011).

## Problems and solutions

Unemployment is certainly not a residual condition amongst young people in the EU. At the end of 2014, 21.4 per cent of young people between the ages of 15 and 24 in the EU-28 proved unemployed, with an overall unemployment rate of 9.9 per cent. The lowest rates were to be found in Germany (7.2 per cent) and Austria (9 per cent); the highest in Spain (51.4 per cent) and Greece (50.6 per cent).[1]

In times of crisis young people's difficulties are greater than those of adults. As well as unemployment there is also an increase in precarious working conditions, since young people are those most affected by the dynamics involved in rendering the job market more flexible (Eurofound, 2014). Sharing the same difficulties does not attenuate inequality, if anything it is increased. In fact, whilst young people are the most affected by the crisis, some young people are more affected than others (Schröer, 2015).

The intensification of global competition and the shift towards the knowledge society have nonetheless made education more important on the labour market (ibid.). The tendency for employed people in highly qualified and well paid jobs to grow is, however, accompanied by an increase in those employed in less qualified and poorly paid work, according to the dynamics of asymmetric polarization (Reyneri, 2011).

Policies supporting the school-to-work transition are thus required to deal with an accumulation of problems, old and new. In 2014 in the EU the percentage of early leavers from education and training was 11.1 per cent, with the highest proportion in Spain (21.9 per cent).[2] In the same year, 15.3 per cent of the population between the ages of 15 and 29 were not studying, working or involved in some sort of training (the so-called NEETs – Not in Education, Employment or Training).[3]

The times and ways of the school-to-work transition obviously influence young people's paths to independence, with differences between countries that reflect the more general characteristics of the welfare and education systems. In the Mediterranean countries and ex-Eastern Europe the transitions are longer and there is more delay in their paths to independence.[4]

As the problems gradually grew and became more serious, the issue of the transition of young people to work started to weigh more heavily on the public agenda in many countries. The solutions attempted include various types of measures to improve labour market entry, such as apprenticeship, vocational training, on-the-job training, job-search services, measures for reducing the numbers of early school leavers, and incentives to employers (Eurofound, 2014). At the same time a mix of regulation and deregulation of the labour market has contributed to increasing the flexibility of young workers entering and exiting it.

In general, the measures drawn up in the framework of employability, and shared by many countries, gave priority to the need for integrating education/ training and work experiences, for example by supporting young people with low qualifications (Germany), boosting the system of technical and vocational training (UK), boosting apprenticeships (UK, Italy) and creating programmes and packages of measures combining regulation, tax incentives, legal measures to this purpose (ibid.).

The choices nonetheless take place in contexts that vary in terms of their institutional balances, resources and approaches to intervention. These differences can normally be traced back to three distinct educational regimes (Atzmüller, 2012):

- The dual system integrates on-the-job training with public vocational education. In Germany it has been considered the 'silver bullet' for the transition from school to work for some time now (Düker and Ley,

2012). Other countries such as Austria and the Netherlands are characterized by policies and training systems organized along these lines. The system highlights the concept of 'professional vocation' (*Beruf*) as a source of identity and social integration (Atzmüller, 2012). Despite the good performances generally acknowledged as regards young people's access to employment, this system has to deal with problems regarding the quality of training and the availability of apprenticeships in companies. Moreover, because of the irreversible nature of the choices made between general education or technical-professional institutes, the strong mechanisms by which inequality is reproduced are quite evident.

- In the Scandinavian area a public universalistic system provides both general competences and professional competences, thus guaranteeing that choices are reversible and transitions can be made through educational paths (ibid., 2012). This system ensures the inclusion of young people in stable paths of employment better than the others but not all of them benefit from it in the same way (ibid.).
- The regime based on general skills is typical of countries like France, Italy and – with different characteristics – the UK. Transition from school to work is weakly institutionalized and young people who fail to complete a standard school education do not have much opportunity to access the professional training that is normally managed by the market.

The last regime is the one that most exposes young people to problems deriving from an insufficiently supported school-to-work transition and, more in general, to the risk of social exclusion. Nonetheless, today all European countries face difficulties in providing access to employment for their young people, in particular young people with low educational qualifications and migrant backgrounds, and some countries have made large investments in attempts to find a solution. In Germany, for example, local support structures and individual counselling for young people without an apprenticeship or employment have been set up (Düker and Ley, 2012). In France the national strategy as a whole has been reorganized, in an attempt to reinforce the coordination between different levels of government (Berthet and Simon, 2012). The central government has launched and financed local experimental programmes, such as those promoted as part of the *Fond d'Expérimentation pour la Jeunesse* (Experimental Fund in favour of Youth) which finances innovative programmes for students and young people under 25 years of age.

Coherently with the perspective of social investment, these issues are central to the European social agenda (Chapter 2). As has been repeatedly declared by the European Commission, strategical importance has been attributed to actions for reducing early school leaving and reintegrating into the education system those who have dropped out of school with low qualifications, giving them a chance of entering the job market (European Commission, 2011).[5] In 2012 the European Commission proposed the so-called Youth Employment Package. In 2013 the Youth Guarantee Initiative was launched, aiming to reduce the school-to-work transition time. In fact some observers have stressed that a distinction should be made between *guarantee of opportunity* and *guarantee of outcome* (OECD, 2014a). As the local case studies reveal, the Initiative increases opportunities for training, apprenticeships and internships but 'cannot ensure that unemployed young people are placed in a stable and lasting job, training or educational path' (ibid., p.10).

The key reference for policies of inclusion in employment is obviously that of active labour market policies. Whilst embracing quite a wide range of orientations and formulas of activation, these generally hinge on the concept of employability (Chapter 4). In its most restrictive sense employability is equivalent to the availability to do any sort of job at any conditions: 'Work first', the guiding concept for activation strategies, has often meant an increase in badly paid, precarious and poor quality work (van Berkel and Hornemann Møller, 2002; McQuaid and Lindsay, 2005). Young people are the main targets of the stricter and more demanding formulas (ILO, 2013), a strategy that has proved to produce more problems than benefits so far.

As argued in Chapter 4, employability is conceived of as a pool of individual characteristics and skills founded on adaptability and this is the basic theme of policies focusing on the supply side of the labour market. Yet the optimism regarding this approach is fading (Ellison and van Berkel, 2014). This is due to several factors, including their failure to reintroduce the more vulnerable unemployed, which were evident even before the crisis. Moreover, with budgets reduced due to policies of austerity, investing in the unemployed without any guarantee that a job may actually be found has become less attractive to the political decision-makers (ibid.). Attention is therefore (timidly) starting to be paid to forms of responsibility shared between public administrations and business enterprises, to matching between supply and demand-side policies and to employability conceived not only in terms of individual adaptability (ibid.).

As to measures specifically aiming to support transition, a high level of personalization in intervention is normally considered an essential criterion. Acknowledgement of young people's heterogeneity, their characteristics and demands are the basis for counselling projects and personalized support. In itself, under a single umbrella, the letters NEET include heterogeneous subjects and different reasons and conditions for not being at work or in education: young people experiencing deprivation or considerable social disadvantages, for example poor resources, a background of migration, disability problems or low attainment at school; but also young people who are termed NEETs for short periods, for example between two jobs (Schröer, 2015).

The strategies that are recommended in the context of the EU give particular importance not only to the need for personalized support but also to a sound coordination between institutional actors and levels, to the integration between measures in different sectors (education, employment, social services for children and young people) and to the possibility of intervening with a combination of general education, vocational training and practical working experience (Council of the European Union, 2011; Schröer, 2015).

A crucial problem area is, instead, identified in the quality of training. As highlighted by the Eurofound's (2014) report, there is the risk of traineeships being used as a source of cheap or free labour by employers. In many cases, instead of facilitating access to a decent job, traineeships risk trapping young people in insecure conditions that they find difficult to get out of.

## The informational bases of justice: Merit

The frames guiding policies are a mixture of cognitive categories, interpretative models and norms for action (Chapter 1). The criteria regarding justice that are incorporated in them and underpin the identification and evaluation of the options at play in decision-making are a basic ingredient, although often rather murky, in these mixtures. In other words, they are the 'informational bases of justice', that specify 'the variables that are directly involved in assessing the justice of alternative systems of arrangements' (Sen, 1992, p. 73).

As we have seen, the cognitive and normative bases of employability exalt the specific concept of a responsible individual who is adaptable and at the same time capable of initiative and achievement. Briefly, an individual who deserves his success or lack of success. In fact, merit is a fairly explicit normative reference point for employability and, more in general, the concept of equality that guides the prospect of social investment, designed to increase the opportunities for young people and consequently reduce the intergenerational transmission of inequality. In any case, merit stands out in the universalistic implications of its being founded on impartiality, whilst, by definition, involving mechanisms of selection. It promises not only to avoid creating situations of dependence and passivity but also to restore an equal balance (being selective) in the redistribution of resources and opportunities, neutralizing the worst consequences of inequality in social and family backgrounds, provision of resources, social and cultural capital.

These are the basic arguments that occur in discourse regarding merit. They tend to crystalize a complex universe of options, judgements and criteria for judgement and normalize them as common sense. Merit is really a category with a long and pregnant history. According to Sennett (2003), merit has its roots in Enlightenment, when a sort of social alchemy came about, thanks to which merit and talent became synonyms. Thus it is linked to the ambition typical of modern society: to open up a career for the talented and overcome the hereditary transmission of privilege and positions that count. Thus the idea that privilege must be deserved and individual capacity is the measure of this judgement establishes itself (ibid.). This prospect took shape in practice thanks to the development of a widespread bureaucracy of talent (ibid.). As usual Sennett surprises us: in fact normally we tend to consider bureaucracy and merit as two incompatible social and institutional universes. The essence of the argument is as follows: placing merit at the centre of attention is a criterion for organizing society that tends to honour inequality of talent and capacity. Meritocracy has thus corroborated and institutionalized an exquisitely modern type of inequality, which values individuals and the differences between individuals.

What became of merit after this? As Sennett (ibid.) again reminds us, it was the sociologist Michael Young who coined the term meritocracy. In his book *The Rise of Meritocracy 1870–2033* (1958) Young stresses in a critical tone the way the value attributed to merit has led to the success of methods for measuring individual gifts, particularly in schools, which confirm and legitimize the hierarchies and inequality in industrial society. However, the negative sense Young attributes to meritocracy has been upturned in a bipartisan approval. Towards the end of his life, Young even wrote a letter to Tony Blair, asking him to stop abusing the term meritocracy, but without success (Boarelli, 2010). Thus, the reference to merit raises several problems. One is to understand what we are talking about when we talk about merit. It should be remembered that it has a profoundly social dimension, starting from the mechanisms and criteria for its definition, acknowledgement and evaluation. Normative theories of justice can give precious indications here. One may stand for them all: effect should not be mistaken for cause. To speak of merit without touching on the social, historical and natural causes that condition individual performances actually means speaking about effects and avoiding tackling the causes (Urbinati, 2008). 'In the condition our society is in at present the acknowledgement of merit is rarely a factor of impartiality or justice' (ibid.). Seriously honouring merit – and the matrix of Enlightenment that makes it a pillar of the fight against the transmission of privileges and unjustified inequality – implies that individual ability and capacities should not be assumed or taken for granted or naturalized, but should be conceived of as the outcome of an interweaving of individual, social and institutional factors. In this weft individual choices certainly weigh heavily, just like public action and the resources that can support or discourage these choices. Second, the evaluation of merit 'is neither a neutral nor a simple procedure' but is a question 'of who is evaluated and by whom, by the systems of evaluation used and, first and foremost, who conceives of them and implements them' (ibid.). Third, there can be agreement on the fact that, if the objective is to act on the causes of inequality and not on the effects of it, intervening means both providing more opportunities and redistributing resources.

## Beyond employability: The Workable research

The limits to be seen in the more restrictive activation strategies have for some time been demanding a search for perspectives for inclusion in work capable of corresponding to the demands of a constantly changing economy and individualized society by increasing, and not reducing, the real opportunities for people's independence (Paci, 2005, 2011; Dean et al., 2005; Paci and Pugliese, eds, 2011; de Leonardis, Negrelli and Salais, eds, 2012).

Besides, as a consequence of the crisis, active labour market policies are undergoing tensions and evolutions. In fact, it has become evident that the national welfare systems that best correspond to the objective of sustainable and inclusive growth (established as part of Europe 2020) are those in which measures for employment and training are accompanied by protection and the promotion of equality (Morel, Palier and Palme, 2012). At the same time public and specialized debate is paying more and more attention to the capacities approach as a frame for reformulating the theme of activation and relationship between the knowledge society and economy.

Based on this approach, the European *Workable* research (Otto et al., eds, 2015,) examined programmes and interventions for young people with difficulty in the school/training/work transition in nine countries: Italy, France, Poland, Switzerland, Austria, Germany, Great Britain, Denmark and Sweden:

In three cases – France, Switzerland and Italy – the target was early school leavers; two cases – Denmark and the UK – dealt with the young unemployed; the subject in Germany and Austria was young people with no upper secondary school qualifications; the Polish case study concerned young people at upper secondary vocational schools with low skills; and the Swedish case studied graduates from higher education who were experiencing difficulties in securing the jobs they wanted.

The basic points of the theoretical framework are those already presented in Chapter 1:

- the focus is not only on individuals but also on social and institutional contexts, in line with the individual and at the same time social nature of capabilities;
- the rights and measures for social protection are not accessories but elements that determine the exercise of individual freedoms;
- the capability for voice of the recipients is crucial (de Leonardis and Negrelli, 2012).

'*Workable*' thus investigated the opportunities and constraints encountered by young people's choices and substantive freedom in the field of education and work, both seen as spheres for exercising and developing capabilities. This means that, as well as being inflected as a specific capability, education has been identified as a conversion factor that develops young peoples' capabilities in general terms. As Walker stresses (2005, p. 108) 'the sort of education that best expresses Sen's CA is the sort that develops ... the ability to take informed and reflective decisions'.

Starting from here, research has highlighted the difference between the traditional employability approach and CA. It can be summed up as follows:

- The CA perspective recognizes the differences between individuals, their life conditions and their capabilities. For this reason it stresses the role of social, institutional and environmental conversion factors that support individual biographies (Bussi, 2014; Bonvin and Moachon, 2014). Instead, the individualistic interpretation of employability ignores these dimensions. This implies a paradox, i.e. that in the end too little but at the same time too much is demanded of individuals. In fact, on the one hand employability requires mere adaptation to the demands of the market, independently of the aspirations, attributions of value and motives for choosing a life path people have reason to value; on the other hand, it burdens individuals with too much responsibility.

- As already mentioned, CA incorporates a model in which the responsibility is shared between the individual, public institutions and society. From this point of view it attributes to institutions a sort of 'enabling employability' function. This means that 'the public institutions involved in the delivery of employability policies will provide both resources and factors of conversion (thus create the social, personal – to the extent of possible – and environmental arrangements) that make the set of opportunities available to individuals valuable and possible' (Bussi, 2014, p. 21).

- Whilst employability emphasizes individual adaptation, CA brings to light agency qualified by reflexivity and voice (Borghi, 2005). Following Sen's approach, the possibility of making your own voice heard and count is an integral part of the process of developing skills and competences (Bonvin and Farvaque, 2003). What is more, as regards education, studies have shown for some time now that, whilst being equal in terms of performance, young people from well-off families obtain better qualifications than those from poor families, since they are able to express their preferences and mobilize their social networks (Berthet and Simon, 2012). At the same time, education influences voice, as well as work and more generally the quality of a plurality of dimensions fundamental for an individual's life.

- Unlike the employability approaches centring on the valorization of human capital as a tool for the economy, CA considers that skills are of value not only because they increase job opportunities but also in themselves, stressing once again the intrinsic value of education (Bussi, 2014). In fact, CA provides an evaluative metric according to which 'the economy must be assessed against its capacity to support the development of valuable opportunities for individuals (Kjeldsen and Bonvin, 2015, p. 231). Sen himself has emphasized this as an important distinguishing element between CA and the human capital perspective, which 'concentrates on the agency of human beings – through skill and knowledge as well as their effort – in augmenting production possibilities' (Sen 1997, quoted in Unterhalter, 2009 p. 212).

In this framework, the research posed the following questions: What opportunities and options are available to young people in the fields of employment, independence, participation in society? How can policies increase them? What factors facilitate the school/training-work transition?

To answer these questions, the nine case studies took the young person's own perspectives and his or her own choice into account, attempting to understand how these perspectives were influenced, constrained or enabled by economic and cultural environments and by institutional factors which translate central policy into local practices (Hollywood et al., 2012). Therefore, one aim of the case studies was to take a bottom-up perspective on the development of capabilities at different levels (ibid.):

- micro level: the subjective, professional and interactive level;
- meso level: the interactive, institutional and conceptual level;
- macro level: the political and societal level.

The research questions were addressed primarily through interviews (group and individual) with young people and other stakeholders (e.g. managers and staff), over a period of time lasting around 24 months (from 2010 to 2012). The observation techniques used consisted of participatory observation and focus groups, as well as an analysis of statistical data and documentation.

On the whole the results of the research confirm:

- the importance of interventions characterized by multidimensional and coordinated approaches, which integrate training and employment policies with those regarding housing, health and assistance;
- the importance of timely action for preventing early school leaving;
- the need to take simultaneous action regarding individual aspects and contexts (in terms of protection and the resources available) in order to increase opportunities and capabilities;
- the importance of voice and of the recipient's possibility of discussing programmes and intervention;
- the role of the capacity to aspire (Appadurai, 2004), i.e. the capacity to desire and imagine a future, mobilizing and reorganizing the social norms structuring the individual's life context;
- the role of the institutions.

The following summary, regarding a Polish programme, an Austrian one, a French one and an Italian one, does not do justice to the complexity of experiences and to the analysis carried out on them but it will at least give an idea of it.

### Case studies

**Poland: The Energet programme** (Sztandar-Sztanderska and Zieleńska, 2012) Under communism, professional training in Poland was provided directly by companies (ibid.). The period of crisis and restructuring that began after 1989 put an end to this role. Since then the system of professional training has been supported by State financing which is, however, insufficient even for ensuring adequate infrastructures. Since public financing depends on the number of enrolments, institutes necessarily have to find a way of attracting students. The offer of new specializations has been increased with this aim in mind but the lack of support for teacher training is a serious problem in terms of the quality of the teaching. This explains why it is almost exclusively students from disadvantaged family and social backgrounds who undertake this type of training. The Energet programme was created by a multinational energy enterprise and by the Professional School of Warsaw with the objective of providing students with some basic abilities and introducing the specialization as 'technician in energy engineering' in the professional curricula. The programme has allowed the institute to gain considerable financial, material and educational support. The company has financed scholarships, provided laboratory materials and enriched the school's offer of training. Moreover, it has been possible to organize extra lessons outside the compulsory school timetable, which is a quite exceptional occurrence in Poland. A psychologist, employed thanks to funding for the project, has organized extra activities for the students, and the teachers have made themselves available for some extra hours for individual consultations. The students have generally shown interest in the initiatives and style of teaching adopted, which is highly pragmatic, with the tendency to place value on experience. The increase in resources has not, however, solved the problem of inequality in terms of the students' knowledge and competences. The classes organized as part of Energet have resulted in a division into two separate groups: the brilliant students and all the others. As emerges from some interviews, in many cases this gap confirmed a self-image of 'unsuited for'. This is linked to the logic of evaluation adopted by the programme, which has only provided scholarships for those students with the most brilliant results and not for those who achieved improvement. All this is accompanied by limited voice. The teacher-student relations are regulated according to a model centring on hierarchy and asymmetry of positions. The implicit assumptions about who can speak up and how, typical of these environments, are linked to two recurring oppositions: the 'young' against the 'adults' and 'having competences' against 'not having competences'. The parents are in fact defined 'incompetent' both by the teachers and by the Energet technical experts. The students are considered 'immature' and 'lacking real-world competences'. In its implementation all this translates into an extremely modest 'capacitating' power, with the result that, despite the boost in resources, inequality and the positions at departure are confirmed.

**Austria: The SCAT programme** (Haidinger and Kasper, 2012)
The Austrian education system, like the German, traditionally centres on the 'dual system'. As a consequence, professional education is based on the integration of theoretical classroom education and practice, taught directly in the company, and apprenticeships are of enormous importance. In 2009, due to

the growing lack of places for apprenticeships in companies, the 'Vocational Placement Guarantee' was launched, contemplating supra-company training with the objective of providing a wider range of apprenticeships. 'SCAT' (Supra-Company Apprenticeship Training) is the denomination of this supra-company type of training which is conceived as a 'safety network' for young people who fail to access apprenticeships in the normal way. In the two-year period 2009–2010 16,314 openings for apprenticeships were financed in the SCAT programme as a whole with an expenditure of around 225 million euros (in 2008–2009 there were 10,213). The participants are mostly males from immigrant families, many of whom with a problematic or frail social background. In any case, the SCAT training programme is a high-threshold intervention and thus young people with learning difficulties or particularly serious social problems are excluded from it. The training is organized in the classroom rather than in companies, with groups of a maximum of 15 pupils: internships are nonetheless foreseen in companies as an integral part of training. The programme also provides tutoring and socio-pedagogic support for apprentices who experience learning difficulties in professional schools. The innovative aspects in the way this training is set up are its supportive nature and the workshop-style organization, even though some pupils complain of the lack of breaks and time for more creative activities. Right from the start, the young people are assigned tasks involving responsibility but this occurs in an organizational environment characterized by a fairly high level of surveillance which does not facilitate acknowledgement and valorization of the young people's individual abilities. In fact the SCAT programme offers very little room for young people's voice and choices. The system is deeply structured with few margins for developing the capacity of self-determination.

**Italy: The Trespassing project** (Bifulco, Monteleone and Mozzana, 2012)
The most significant piece of data regarding the situation in Italy is an institutional framework of residual and poorly integrated public policies which are not equipped to support the transition of young people, particularly if the latter are in a condition of vulnerability. Up to the present, neither the reform of upper secondary schools (centred on a stronger link between vocational schools and the world of economy and production, and on the regionalization of vocational training), nor the measures recently adopted for apprenticeships seem to have had any effect on the problem of the poor connection between education and work. Moreover the family environment and territorial context have a decisive influence on opportunities for education or the educational achievements (Fondazione Giovanni Agnelli, 2010). Choices of education reproduce social hierarchies: young people from wealthier and better-educated families choose high schools whilst the others enrol in technical or professional institutes. The Trespassing project started in 2009 in Naples (a city in the south well known for its problems of social and economic integration) thanks to the initiative of an association with a long history of mobilization on issues of exclusion. The area of intervention is a neighbourhood in the city

centre where different conditions of social disease have been accumulating for some time. The project, financed by the Region, offers internships in small businesses to young people between 16 and 18 years of age who have left school early. The intention is to offer paths of familiarization with work which make it possible to catch up on and valorize basic competences, not only of a professional nature but also social and inter-personal (Bifulco, Monteleone and Mozzana, 2012).

The methodology of the intervention is based on experience and on-the-job learning, as well as on the dual tutoring service that sees a company tutor working side by side with a teacher. At the end of the internship the participants receive a reference letter with an evaluation of their basic competences.

In all its phases the project makes room for the beneficiaries' point of view. Right from the selection interviews there is discussion and the young people's aspirations and expectations are discussed with them. In fact, in most cases the candidates express the general need for a job and it takes some time for them to say what sort of work and future they imagine for themselves. Those who are selected stipulate an educational contract with the association, which binds them reciprocally but which can nonetheless be reformulated as it proceeds. In practice the first week involves a collective work experience – for example the renovation of a public building – which has the objective of encouraging cooperative dynamics and provides the opportunity for young people and teachers to get to know one another whilst working side by side.

The association's profound roots in the social fabric of the neighbourhood enables stable collaboration with businesses and craftspeople, as well as the development of trusting relationships with the young people and their families. In fact the organizational model has all the characteristics of openness and resilience typical of a low-threshold service. This model favours considerable investment in the voice of the beneficiaries. Nonetheless, the whole project reveals evident weaknesses and is unable to make an impact on some decisive conditions existing in the context. The critical structural state of the Neapolitan labour market, the lack of resources for welfare and low integration between education policies and labour policies are historical and deeply rooted features of the city, which are only minimally affected.

This combines with the weak role played by the Region, which is, however, the administrative body that provides financing. The objective is to support the beneficiaries' faculty of choice, especially as regards the work environment but the end result is that individual competences in a given context are the centre of attention. This means that, once the internship is over, there is little opportunity for the young people's competences to be put into practice. Moreover, the limited resources provided influence the recipients' access mechanisms, leading to the selection of the most promising young people and excluding the weaker ones, who risk not succeeding. Institutional failings thus end by ratifying and aggravating a consolidated situation of scarce public resources and opportunities for work.

**France: The regional plan for Rhône-Alpes** (Berthet and Simon, 2012)
In France, too, the students' educational fate is highly correlated to their social origins. As to institutional design, it combines an intricate hierarchical and organizational structure of relationships with an important tradition of centralism. Education and training are primarily the responsibility of state schools, including professional training.

In the last few years some experimental programmes have made it their priority to fight school dropout. One of these is the regional plan for Rhône-Alpes, launched in 2008 thanks to an agreement between the regional Council, the Ministry of Education, the Regional Direction for Food, Agriculture and Forestry and the regional network of 'missions locales' (the local, inter-departmental structures for young people at risk of exclusion). The programme financed projects in professional upper secondary schools, both public and private, aiming to avoid early school leaving. Schools were asked to present proposals that foresaw in particular tutoring and consultancy services on choices of training, individualized follow-up for pupils, socialization workshops and improvement of competences. The plan was operational for three years (2008–2011) with an overall budget of 1.5 million euros financing 91 projects (out of the 125 proposed). The main axes of the project were teacher training, the organization of workshops, and individual consultation for pupils considered at risk. One tangible result is that the teachers were alerted and mobilized to deal with a situation where the problem of early school leaving tends to be externalized and entrusted to operators who do not belong to the teaching staff (psychomotor therapists, consultants, logopaedicians, etc.). The main limit from the perspective of capabilities is that the projects started after the choices of educational orientation had already been made. In fact, the projects were not conceived to reduce the constraints that condition choices of education but to avoid early school leaving. The only freedom allowed the young people is not to be obliged to leave school. In addition, the pupils can rarely withdraw from the interventions proposed and any resistance does not normally have the opportunity to be expressed.

It should be added that in many cases the projects devote attention to a limited number of aspects, prevalently of an individual nature – such as tutoring – neglecting any integrated work on the plurality of factors that lead to early leaving, such as those relating to health, housing, etc.

## Young people's transitions and capacitations

The case summaries show the traps normally encountered even by well-intentioned projects and, above all, highlight what it means to adopt a CA in order to analyse an intervention supporting the school-to-work transition. Briefly, what becomes uppermost is a specific way of understanding work and training, which encourages us to look not at the coherence between demand and offer or at the gaps to be filled in terms of employability, but at the opportunities young people have for formulating and realizing an autonomous life project through education and at the way skills, voice, agency are increased – or diminished.

These cases give proof of the processual dimension of capabilities: these are neither a given fact nor a precondition but develop if there are opportunities and contexts in which they can be exercised (de Leonardis, 1993). The added value that CA contributes to reflections and research on policies supporting young people's transitions derives primarily from this processual dimension. This perspective sheds light on issues that are frequently omitted in analyses that concentrate exclusively on data such educational results, indicators of performance, the figures on dropouts, expenditure and access to work (Sztandar-Sztanderska and Zieleńska, 2012). Instead of focusing on this data, CA does, in fact, focus on the importance of the educational process. From this point of view, what are fundamental are not only goods and services provided by schools or programmes (courses, infrastructures, training, etc.), but also mechanisms for increasing the chances that actually make it possible to exploit what is given. In other words, competences deriving from education as well as capabilities are not simply a state but raise the question of the processes by which they are produced and reproduced.

As a consequence, CA calls into question the issue of the desirable effects of education and the way in which the transition between education/training and the labour market takes shape. Instead of results such as the number of qualified or employed people, it highlights the range of possible choices for young people and the ways in which policies and measures influence their development. Consequently, attention shifts from the results (number/percentage of employed or unemployed) to the quality of employment (ibid.).

In addition, the need for young people to feel they are part of the educational process becomes quite clear. If this possibility is limited, then the range of options considered accessible also becomes limited – an effect that can be traced back to mechanisms regarding the adaptation of preferences. In other words, the capacity to aspire (Appadurai, 2004) is impoverished or becomes sterile. On the other hand, if policies focus on the individual only, and on his or her individual will to enter the field, without actions that aim to change the context, the responsibility for the situation ends up weighing on the shoulders of young people only.

In the cases we have just examined, institutional investment in the creation of opportunities for discussion on the educational options available is very slight and ineffective, if not lacking totally. This points to the difficulty of ensuring the conditions for a capacitating process of choice. It also confirms the importance of the institutions, not only in terms of resources, but also in terms of the possibilities that young people and families have of disputing the context of the choice, i.e. the possibility of their becoming active subjects of capacitating processes. The institutions play a crucial role as actors able to mobilize basic conversion factors: they can, in fact, give priority to individual conversion factors but, in the same way, they can strengthen and promote conversion factors of a social and environmental nature, influencing the constraints and opportunities provided by the context (Salais, 2008). They can clearly play a negative role, too.

From the normative point of view of criteria for justice, the CA also has the advantage of offering a way out of the merit trap: it does not take for granted what is really the outcome of a complex combination highly inter-dependent on structural factors, resources, institutional rules, individual factors and social norms. Seen from this perspective, institutions are funda-mental for dealing with and reducing the inequalities concerning young people's education and their access to work, since they attack the causes and not the effects.

This is a further indication that resources alone – whether public or private – are no solution. Consequently, in an age when public budgets are subject to very strict constraints, private resources are precious but certainly do not replace prerogatives and functions of a purely institutional nature. If support, coordination and an institutional framework are not available, interventions such as those analysed risk remaining very limited and not promoting capa-citating processes while, on the contrary, reproducing persistent conditions and pre-existing situations.

## Conclusions

Ferreras (2008) has underscored Sen's merit in providing elements for unravelling the descriptive and normative tangle in social life that connects the individual to the collectivity. At a normative level, the CA suggests strategies for enabling individuals without necessarily dismantling the social dimension.

It is comprehensible that perspectives such as the CA can be considered too demanding and unrealistic at the present time. But policies cannot hope to deal with the problems of work and the future of young people unless they are demanding.

If we wish to consider the matter from a purely instrumental point of view, it should be emphasized that the competitive advantages of quality production (in the terms implied by the knowledge economy) are all the greater, the more investments and policies for education, as well as being of considerable size, are oriented towards increasing opportunities for autonomy and capabilities and not only technical competences in the strict sense.

In any case, the disproportion between structural problems and indivi-dual prerogatives is now so great and affects young people so brutally that it has become crystal clear that talking about activation – or connected issues – by appealing exclusively to personal responsibilities is, at the very least, an underestimation. This is what, *a contrario*, is demonstrated by the good performances of social investment in countries where more has been invested not only in human capital but also in people's rights and social justice.

## Notes

1  http://ec.europa.eu/eurostat/documents/2995521/6581668/3-30012015-AP-EN.pdf/
   9d4fbadd-d7ae-48f8-b071-672f3c4767dd
2  http://ec.europa.eu/eurostat/statistics-explained/index.php/School_enrolment_and_
   early_leavers_from_education_and_training. The Europe 2020 strategy established
   that early school leaving rates should fall below 10 per cent by 2020.
3  http://appsso.eurostat.ec.europa.eu/nui/show.do?dataset=yth_empl_150&lang=en
4  http://www.eurofound.europa.eu/publications/htmlfiles/ef1392.htm
5  http://eur-lex.europa.eu/LexUriServ/LexUriServ.do?uri=SEC:2011:0097:FIN:EN:
   PDF

# 8 Care and choice: The position of the recipients

In a context of social change that has highlighted lack of self-sufficiency and the reconciling of care-work as important areas of 'new' social risks, the spread of mechanisms of regulation centring on marketization since the 1990s has greatly reduced national differences in response to the need for care (Daly, 2012; Simonazzi, 2009). The policies adopted by European countries in this field tend to converge towards a model that combines public responsibility, market provision and family involvement (Simonazzi, 2009). A related trend is the shift from residential care to home care (Daly, 2012). Particularly where the provision of services is mainly in the hands of for-profit enterprises, the relations between public and private give priority to a logic based on the vendor–purchaser model. As well as this, the commodification of care has developed significantly in the form of remuneration for informal caregivers. Rather than copying an authentic market model, in these cases the relationship between the provider and the receiver of care takes the form of a 'between gift and market' contract (Ungerson, 1997), combining the logic of commodification with the actual relational aspects of care, that is, being involved 'in meeting the physical and emotional requirements' of dependent people (Daly and Newman, 2000, p. 283).

According to the established perspective in the political area of neoliberalism, the quasi-markets of care are supposed to create conditions of pluralism, bringing the monopoly of the public authority to an end, both as the direct manager of services, and as financer of suppliers operating on protected markets. Along with the assumption that competition brings down costs and encourages a better quality of offer, one driving force of marketization is the idea of freedom of choice. As well as ensuring that the beneficiary has the possibility of exercising his 'sovereign' right as a consumer (Andersson and Kvist, 2015), this principle of free choice is supposed to encourage the provision of individualized, tailor-made services. Amongst the declared objectives is also that of promoting employment on the social markets by supporting private demand using instruments such as vouchers and tax incentives. More limited, but still significant, is the link to work-care-life strategies, for example in France (Bode, Gardin and Nyssens, 2011).

The market is the main blueprint for freedom of choice but not the one and only option in this field. First, despite the intensification of marketization, non-competitive regulatory formulas, such as partnership, may bear considerable weight in structuring contractual relations between public actors and care providers, particularly (but not necessarily) if third-sector organizations are involved. Second, in the set of instruments used, choice may combine differing points of reference, such as consumer freedom, autonomy and independence.

On this scenario a number of questions still remain to be answered, mainly concerning the various positions adopted by beneficiaries in the case of interventions that are theoretically aimed at ensuring or increasing their 'freedom of choice'. This chapter sets out to analyse these questions with specific reference to interventions based on economic benefits that have the purpose of increasing the independence of recipients.

## Freedom of choice and its instruments

As regards the public authority, the downsizing of its role as provider is compensated for by an increase in its function as regulator of fees, approval of the workers involved and quality of services provided. The last are inflected in different ways, in connection with the contexts in which they are institutionalized: public regulation is stricter in central and northern Europe and more easy-going in the Mediterranean area. In all cases, coherently with the logic of NPM, the regulation of competition and quality of care services is associated everywhere with the application of a vast assortment of tools for monitoring and standardization (Meagher and Szebehely, eds, 2013). It should be stressed that the shift in the public role from monopolist decision-maker and provider to that of regulator does not necessarily imply less coverage. The number of elderly people receiving care has increased over the past years in Germany, France and the Netherlands (Pavolini and Ranci, 2008). In the UK the number of beneficiaries has decreased but the number of hours of care provided has grown (Bode, Gardin and Nyssens, 2011).

The dynamics triggered as regards the mix between public, private for-profit and non-profit differ according to the context. In Scandinavian welfare, the role of private for-profit providers remains limited (Petersen and Hjelmar, 2014). In Denmark and Sweden they only account for less than 20 per cent of the market of eldercare and childcare while in the UK the share of private providers is around 70–80 per cent (Brennan et al., 2012; Meagher and Szebehely, eds, 2013). Nonetheless, starting from the tendency to reinforce the formal care provided by professionalized organizations, in general private for-profit providers are on the increase and in some cases have overtaken the non-profit sector. In Germany, for example, the organizations in the non-profit sector cover less than half the market. Informal care remains significant, however, and a large portion of care benefits is used to remunerate a family member (woman) (Bode, Gardin and Nyssens, 2011).

Although they are probably the most famous, vouchers are not the only instruments[1] used for achieving freedom of choice as the principle for reorganizing care. In the UK, a pioneer in the marketization of care, in the last ten years direct payments and cash measures have provided a strong impulse, to the benefit of all social care service users (Glendinning, 2008). In 2008, with the objective of integrating intervention and making it more transparent, the individual budget was introduced, which was supposed to direct and pool resources and financing made available by different providers and institutions (local authorities, the Department for Work and Pensions, the Independent Living Fund for disabled people, etc.). The budget can be used to pay informal caregivers directly or to purchase services from local authorities (Bode, Gardin and Nyssens, 2011).

In Germany the main instrument for many years has been a long-term care insurance leaving ample room to for-profit providers (Pavolini and Ranci, 2008). In France, a prepaid system of vouchers and tax incentives regulates and supports the supply of formal home care. A care allowance introduced in 2002 allows beneficiaries to hire private employees and has considerably increased the presence of for-profit providers on the market (Bode, Gardin and Nyssens, 2011).

Once they had spread throughout the neoliberal context in the UK, the marketization of care and mechanisms of free choice also established themselves in Scandinavian countries, in spite of their historically rooted public-universalistic ethos. In 2009 in Sweden the Act on System of Choice in the Public Sector was approved. The principle of consumer choice plays an important role in the discourse legitimizing marketization in the country and specific legislation and tax incentives have been used to put it into practice. Choice is not obligatory, however, and a 'non choice' option is guaranteed (Meagher and Szebehely, eds, 2013).

It is in relation to the role of the recipients that the changes induced by marketization reveal themselves in the most incisive and yet most elusive ways. In general this role tends to reinforce the coordination functions implicit in providing care that are carried out by family caregivers (Bode, Gardin and Nyssens, 2011). The cash and direct payment modes nonetheless cause a strongly consumerist inflection to prevail in terms of the ways in which the choice is defined and put into practice (Newman and Tonkens, 2011). Other instruments, such as personal budgets, accompany this inflection with an orientation towards reinforcing the prerogative of the recipients' independence and control over their own lives (ibid.).

One point on which there is almost unanimous agreement regards the problems the choice encounters once it has been put into practice. The frailty of those who benefit from these measures makes the actual practice of the formally recognized freedom particularly difficult. Given the asymmetrical nature of the information provided, which is typical of market relations, choosing means having a good deal of time and resources to invest in collecting information and making comparisons. In conditions of vulnerability this can result in a burden that is extremely wearing (Glendinning, 2008). Moreover, in the context of care relations, dimensions such as trust and continuity over time count heavily and are often appreciated more than the opportunity to choose (Meagher and Szebehely, eds, 2013). In any case, not everyone can take advantage to the same extent of the opportunity for choice on offer. The result can thus be an increase in inequality 'in terms of who gets to choose, and who tends to be chosen by providers' (Newman and Tonkens, 2011, p. 194). In fact, in some cases the empirical evidence reveals that the gap between those who have more resources and those who have fewer is actually aggravated instead of being reduced (Meagher and Szebehely, eds, 2013). As Bode, Gardin and Nyssens (2011) note, redistributional issues matter. The instruments adopted are not neutral here. Tax incentives supporting demand adopted in France, for example, tend to reward high-income households. Where access to measures is conditioned by income, a person may prove to be excluded from the choice of a quasi-market provider even when she/he does not have sufficient resources to access the free market (ibid.).

From a gender perspective more types of inequality are to be noted. Cash-for-care measures are frequently associated with a high level of involvement of families, which basically means less freedom of choice for women compared to a work-care-life balance. Another connected issue is the spread of less qualified forms of employment which affect women in particular in their role as care employees (ibid.).

As we have mentioned several times, freedom can assume different inflections. Andersson and Kvist (2015) have reconstructed the public debate accompanying the introduction of freedom of choice in Sweden, stressing how freedom was interpreted in this context as being the opposite of paternalism. But from a report by the Swedish National Board of Health and Welfare we can see that users may not be aware of, or not even remember, having chosen a care provider. Moreover, regarding cost efficiency and quality, there is no empirical evidence to suggest that the expectations of reformers have been fulfilled (Meagher and Szebehely, eds, 2013).

The idea of freedom of choice warmly affirmed in public discourse to justify marketization ends up by ratifying the model of the market player: a rational and calculating actor, without the relations of interdependence intrinsic in care relations, particularly in conditions of vulnerability (Andersson and Kvist, 2015). This combines with a perspective that conceives of choice not as a process in which decisions can be redefined and negotiated but as a one-off action that the individual takes without need of any support (Glendinning, 2008).

Basically, the problem is that the principle of freedom of choice is encapsulated, as it were, in the market model. Nonetheless, the choice does not necessarily have to remain a prerogative of marketization or fail to be accompanied by paths of empowerment leading to greater autonomy and independence. As Newman and Tonkens (2011) observe, to understand the variety of logic and implications involved in choice, the focus must be shifted to the political context in which it takes place, and the relationship between public administrations, providers and recipients.

## Instruments in action

To look at a cross-section of this variety in greater detail, we shall examine two care instruments in two regional contexts in Italy: Lombardy and Campania, respectively in the north and in the south of the country.[2] In Italy the importance of the Regions in regulation and decision-making is linked to the characteristics of the national welfare system, which combines weak social rights with a high incidence of institutional fragmentation and territorial differentiation (Paci, 1989; Ferrera 1998; Mingione, 2000; Bifulco, 2014). The process of decentralization initiated in the 1970s culminated in a federalist reform launched in the name of devolution in 2001, which granted the Regions legislative competence in social services.[3] The territorial areas under analysis have witnessed the implementation of socio-medical care based on economic transfers: vouchers in Lombardy and the health care budget in Campania. These instruments, while falling into the same category of care intervention marked by personalization, autonomy and freedom of choice, reveal significant differences both in terms of their institutional and regulative system and in terms of the specific content of the services to which they provide access. Whilst vouchers in Lombardy are part of the regulatory mechanisms of the quasi-market, the care budgets refer to contractual relations typical of collaborative partnership (Chapter 3). Thus, they trigger different dynamics of relations, both between public and private parties, and between organizations and users. The position of the latter is the privileged focus of the analysis that follows.

For both contractual devices, the organizational field comprises five 'organizational populations' (Powell, 1991): (1) the region, (2) the local health authority, (3) the provider, (4) the municipality, and (5) the beneficiary and her/his family. On the methodological front, interviews were organized both with selected witnesses in public administration and in the third sector, and with beneficiaries. In addition, official documents and reports commissioned by the Regions were analysed.

### *The socio-medical care voucher in the Region of Lombardy*

The Lombard context is characterized by a firm tradition in the field of social policies, as shown by the medium-high level of per-capita regional social spending. However, at the same time this tradition entails a tendency to absorb social care into health policies. Moreover, the idea of self-regulation is central in this Region, which has had a stable central-right government ever since 1995. More precisely there are two reference points: the market and subsidiarity. On the one hand, the regional actor is committed to ensuring conditions for development and the institutionalization of commercialization.

On the other hand, thanks to the emphasis placed on the social dynamics of self-organization, the subsidiarity principle plays a decisive role in blending reference to the market with reference to the family and the local community (Bifulco and Vitale, 2006).

In a national political-administrative framework that has made devolution its main evolutionary axis, Lombardy is the Region that stands out in Italy for the conviction with which it invested in vouchers in socio-medical care through a rather complex path of experimentation launched in 1999 and concluding in 2003 with the extension of social and health vouchers to the whole of Lombardy.

The socio-medical care voucher is part of the reorganization of the integrated home-based care service; it aims to 'avoid or delay the institutionalization of non self-sufficient individuals' (institutionalization in health residences). It can be used exclusively to purchase integrated home-based socio-medical services from an accredited organization, public or private, profit or non-profit, provided by professional caregivers. Users may use it to pay for rehabilitation and nursing services.[10] The voucher is received by each frail person who can be assisted at home, without limits of age or income. In order to obtain it, the person or his/her family must refer to their GP, who may then request the authorization of the local health authority upon his own judgement and at his own discretion. Three levels of intensity are foreseen: the first is a basic profile, with the recipient receiving a voucher equivalent to €362 each month; the second is for a complex patient profile (€464); and the third is for a terminal patient profile (€619). This measure is consistent with that already applied in Lombardy in the health sector since the early 1990s, characterized by situations of competition *within* the market and not *for* the market, and by a system having a pre-established tariff but without a fixed volume of maximum expenditure.

Thus, in the field of health care a competitive type of regulation has established itself between providers, leaving little room for interaction in decision-making between public and private organizations: public agencies establish standards according to the pre-selected providers, with providers making their own arrangements. The Region has a regulatory role in the system above all in contracting and defining resources, remuneration for each service, authorization-accreditation and consumer-satisfaction assessment.

The introduction of the voucher represents the de facto consolidation of a process of externalization, coming from afar, of integrated home-based services in favour of accredited private providers. A separation between purchasers and providers of services was introduced by assigning the exclusive role of planning, purchasing and control to the local health authorities, with the consequent closure of directly managed services. Thus, a quasi-market was created in which the providers of socio-medical services compete on the basis of a pre-established fixed rate (*yardstick competition*) and attempt to attract patients. The recipients are free to choose their preferred provider based on their 'health demand'.

Following a more or less identical approach, in this region social vouchers were later introduced. These, too, regarded mainly home care for elderly or disabled people and, less frequently, for minors, sometimes including services providing food or transport. The Region has obliged the municipalities to convert social care intervention from services into economic transfers. In fact, for some years after 2002 the regional government bound municipalities to spend in 'cash' (vouchers and care cheques) 70 per cent of the funds coming from the National Fund for Social Policies.

The consolidation of vouchers has for a long time been one of the priorities of the Lombardy Region regarding this sector, not only because these instruments are considered the most coherent way to put into practice the guiding principle of freedom of choice, but also because, by supporting the demand for services, they promise to develop interesting market potential.

Vouchers meet with a fair degree of appreciation from the beneficiaries, in particular with regard to the longer hours of assistance covered by the service and the possibility of differentiating the services provided. Appreciation of the freedom of choice is more limited: in fact this kind of freedom is considered by many as an added burden (Bifulco, 2011b).

Its limited appeal to citizens and/or families (of no secondary importance for a tool that places its main emphasis on freedom of choice) is not the only problem. Studies carried out on this measure confirm the limits pointed out in the literature previously quoted: the skimming away of the less remunerative interventions; the asymmetrical nature of the information exchanged between suppliers and citizens/consumers; the difficulty of exercising freedom of choice when the people in question are in a condition of need and fragility (ibid.; de Leonardis, 2011b). These problems are all the more evident when the function of coordination carried out by the local public authority is weak. The important point to notice here is that in the regulatory model implied by vouchers in Lombardy the sole task of the local public administration is to watch over a private transaction: this is clearly the situation theoretically corresponding to the market-type contract. This regulation mode in fact assumes consumers' 'freedom of choice' as a premise, a precondition, a *datum*.

One specific issue regards the practical impact of freedom of choice in situations where the options on offer are predefined and it is not possible to contribute to defining, discussing or modifying them. As established by regional directives, the beneficiaries and/or families limit themselves to signing the project for assistance pre-established by the services, although they do have the right to change provider. The citizen is a consumer, and is thus formally free to make a choice, but his or her 'freedom of choice' is a negative freedom, it is a freedom '*from*' (Berlin, 1969). According to Hirschman's well-known typology, the citizen-consumer has the freedom of *exit* but not of *voice*: he or she can change provider but cannot contribute directly to co-defining the services received. Therefore, his or her choice is a *private* choice, supported by private networks. It is also a *lonely* choice, if the consumer is alone, especially without family or neighbourhood support. In addition to this, the position of the citizen-consumer is asymmetrical to that of the provider. There is a strong disparity of power grounded in the consumer's condition of hardship, urgent need, or deprivation. Thus, the citizen-consumer is conditioned by the provider and he or she is obliged to accept services which are predetermined and which are not individualized but fixed beforehand and standardized. Consumer preferences can only adapt to the context of constraints and the opportunities offered. In more abstract terms, this poses questions as to what the citizen's real prerogatives are, once his or her central role is reduced to the central role of the demand function, destined to encourage the development of a market for services.

### Health care budgets in the Region of Campania

Despite being characterized by a long history of residual welfare, very poor in resources (per-capita spending remains one of the lowest in Italy), the Region of Campania promoted some interesting innovations – both in method and in content – in social policies during the political season when it was governed by the centre-left (2000–2010), at the same time pursuing the objective of reinforcing local autonomies and developing the territorial social service system. In certain areas of this region, the municipalities make a true effort to act, even with different external actors, as the new institutional subjects for the political synthesis of local governance, with visible results in the activation and organization of the territory's potential for cooperative interaction. One immediate effect concerns the third sector and the tendency to overcome the two most critical situations which have long had a widespread presence in this region: on the one hand, oligopolistic situations, with very few third-sector organizations controlling the decisive areas of influence and action for taking possession of the territory's resources; and on the other hand, situations of fragmentation, with segmentation and conflict among the various organizations, condemning them to a marginal role. In fact, the adoption of more rigorous criteria of regulation with regard to the supply of services has favoured the entry of new organizations onto the social market. Besides, the local authorities have directly or indirectly supported the creation of formalized networks for the coordination of the third sector (Bifulco and Vitale, 2006; Bifulco and Centemeri, 2008).

The care budget was introduced as an experiment in 2006 in a limited area of the regional territory. Despite referring to the same sphere of individualized care and also addressing people in a condition of frailty, there are many differences compared to the voucher system in Lombardy. The aim of the budget is to progressively reduce the numbers of people in residential care. More precisely, it aims to develop 'actions and resources directed towards the maintenance, building or rebuilding of family, community, educational and social well-being', for people affected by social disabilities deriving from psycho-organic illnesses or socio-environmental marginality. The core concept is to convert the public expenditure for residential structures into individual budgets to be spent on sustaining the beneficiaries in relation to three basic functions: housing, work, and socialization. With this aim, the measure decisively points towards integration between social and health care, and between public subjects (local health authorities and municipalities) and non-profit organizations (mainly cooperatives). Thus, the health care budget presupposes a profound transformation in institutional and organizational logics and practices. In fact, this measure requires municipalities and Local Health Authorities to rethink their own system of offer in a perspective promoting a gradual decrease in confinement to residential structures of people who are not self-sufficient. The application for enabling a care budget may be formulated either by the social services of the municipality or by the health services; a local health authority committee examines this application. If accepted, the public agent who made the request draws up an initial hypothesis for the personalized rehabilitation project, together with the beneficiary and his or her family. In this way, the families and beneficiaries themselves also become part of an active rehabilitation process. On the basis of this first project, a cooperative capable of providing services relating to the three areas is identified for the beneficiary.

Should the selected organization accept the conditions of the project, a mixed team is formed composed of social workers from the local health authority (with health competence), from the recipient's municipality of residence (with social competence), and from the non-profit organization, with a view to refining the details and scope of the individual project, and to further verify the private organization's compliance therewith.

As regards the relationship between the user, the public service (local health authority/municipality) and the private partner, care budgets are regulated by a contract that is stipulated on the basis of a customized project, formulated by the operators responsible, the user, and his or her family. The overall procedure of the individualized project is monitored and evaluated by the Integrated Evaluation Unit, which must be activated for each case, and which consists of operators from the corresponding service (from the local health authority and the municipality of residence), family members, and the recipient of the budget. Although the operators of the non-profit organizations are involved in the Integrated Evaluation Unit in order to assess the customized projects, final responsibility for the progress assessment regarding the relationship between beneficiary and provider remains in the hands of the public administration, and of the local health authority in particular.

The maximum duration of a care budget contract is two years. The aim of the project engaging the various parties is the transition from higher levels to lower levels of medical aid, via processes of de-medicalization and social inclusion centring on the three axes already mentioned (housing, work or job training, and socialization). The reduction of the level of medical care is incentivized through a mechanism based on premiums, whereby the care budget is increased by 10 per cent for every step down in the amount of medical care required (consequently supporting the social inclusion of the beneficiary).

In this case promoting freedom of choice means, first and foremost, guaranteeing resources that make it possible to reactivate and sustain the capabilities of the individual and provide the conditions for his or her integration. The path of reactivating capabilities is the basis for involving the person in the project that regards him or her and the exercise of his or her freedom. Second, it means weaving a network of well-structured relations for coordinating public services, the third sector and also families. This constant work of weaving relations implies an innovation in institutional architecture and, at the same time, learning to cooperate with one another.

The contract does not therefore intervene as a device for regulating the encounter between supply and demand, but as a strategy to create a stronger bargaining position for 'frail' individuals, by initiating an active process of change: the beneficiary in this case is not recognized as a consumer, but as an actor in his or her own individualized rehabilitation project, an actor with his or her own social ties and resources.

The position of the recipient is completely different in the case of the voucher and in the case of the care budget. As has been pointed out, in the former the user is a consumer who expresses preferences for competing providers whilst the public administration merely ensures that a regular market transaction takes place. In the case of the care budget in Campania, local authorities 'follow' the citizen in his or her relationship with the provider and take care of problems as soon as they occur. Meanwhile, public administration obliges the private organizations to modify and to raise the level of complexity of their services. The position of the recipient is therefore different because he or she is not alone in contractual relations with the provider, since there is a third party to which he or she can appeal. So, regulation recognizes that the contract is always incomplete, and that renegotiation devices are therefore indispensable. Users and families are called on to participate in the planning of the intervention and to express their voice. Consequently, the demand of the citizen can be defined – and if need be redefined – within an open process, without being entirely predetermined by the services supplied, but modifying the intervention over time. This is at once a sort of guarantee and a moving force for the care budget to support and develop the recipient's capabilities. More importantly, the bargaining competence (and power) of the citizen is not considered as a starting point, but as the purpose of the intervention. The idea is to support the ability of the frail or needy citizen to make a choice with regard to the project he or she is involved in, yet without requiring that this capability should be fully developed right from the beginning.

The 'health-care budget' therefore requires joint management on the part of the public and private actors, avoiding mechanisms of delegation or 'burdening' with responsibility, whilst encouraging innovative methods of work within the services. The result of this is the emergence of practices which consolidate and promote the specific characteristics of the various participating actors: the public subject firmly maintains the responsibility for the service; private social actors, on the other hand, are assigned the task of fostering and expanding social networks in the context of the life of the user, based on the idea that the production of sociality is, so to speak, 'therapeutic'.

## Conclusions

In the cases of both vouchers and care budgets a recipient role marked by the prerogative of choice, freedom and an active position is entailed. Yet there are differences in the ways in which this role actually develops. They may be summed up as follows:

- In the case of vouchers in Lombardy freedom is inflected as freedom of exit and the conditions that make it possible (more in general the conditions for independence) are considered a prerequisite. The context in which recipients and/or their families make their choices does not foresee either relations of interdependence or processes of renegotiation. The beneficiary's individuality is mainly defined by a state of isolation typical of the market consumer.
- Care budgets occur in a context that does not assume that conditions for freedom of choice and independence already exist but aims, instead, to build them up or reinforce them. As well as being a dynamic context, it is rich in social relations. In addition, and as a result, it is assumed as an active terrain: it is not a given fact but can be modified and redefined. The beneficiary is an active participant in this redefinition of the context, which increases social relations of interdependence.

With regard to these differences, it is important to stress that in both cases the public subject has the authority to mediate and establish the institutional frameworks of decision-making processes and regulations, yet the objectives, logic, and effects with respect to the recipient citizens are all different. On the one hand we find a public authority that limits itself to regulating market transactions, on the other the public authority uses resources and powers to increase people's autonomy. This confirms what has already been reported in Chapter 6 as to the implications of the different roles and different types of responsibility that an enabling public actor can assume on the scenario of a public–private mix. It makes a significant difference whether the public administration merely checks on the conditions of a private transaction, or whether it takes part in all the processes, even without directly providing services but nonetheless taking care of the quality of organizational arrangements that support the contractual devices.

To sum up, the two cases show that instruments hinging on freedom of choice can have very different implications for recipient agency and that, in order to gain a better understanding of these differences, a profound analysis is required of all the institutional, normative and social factors influencing the relationship between choice and care. Be this as it may, possibilities of agency simultaneously invoke the activation of a social dimension and the exercise of a specific institutional role.

## Notes

1  The range of instruments is very wide: childcare vouchers in the United Kingdom, individual or personal budgets in Norway, socio-medical vouchers in Italy, *chèques emploi service universel* (CESU) in France, *titres-services pour les services et emplois de proximité* in Belgium.
2  I refer here to studies carried out between 2005 and 2010 in collaboration with other colleagues taking part in the Research Center 'Sui Generis', at the University of Milano Bicocca, coordinated by Ota de Leonardis.
3  With the exception of the definition of LIVEAS, i.e. essential levels of social services, to be guaranteed across the entire national territory

# 9    Inclusion and the city

Europe's cities are leading actors in the territorial order traced by rescaling processes. Their leading role is affected by different sorts of pressure which nonetheless converge in some senses. The constraints deriving from globalization have obliged the institutions of city government to adopt strategies of partnership with economic actors in order to increase the territory's attractiveness and competitiveness. The process of devolution has widened urban decision-making areas and powers. In this way new forms of local governance have been designed, backed by instruments for action and collective decision, aiming to reconcile different interests (Le Galès, 2002). At the same time, ever since the 1970s cities have felt the most critical effects of restructuring and the economic crises. A growing combination of problems, fruit of the 2007/2008 crisis, weighs on the present-day scenario. Economic competition between cities only acts in the interests of those able to operate as strategic links in the relations between the economy and politics (Rossi and Vanolo, 2010). Processes of financialization of the economy transform the urban structure and the living conditions of its inhabitants profoundly. The growth of economic and socio-spatial inequality fuels dynamics of fragmentization and polarization (Cassiers and Kesteloot, 2012). The State fiscal crisis, which returned as a key issue from 2008 onwards, induced rentrenchment strategies that have harsh consequences for balances and local powers. Despite all this, cities are considered 'the economic engines of the European economy'[1] and the places in which new strategies of economic and social development can be set up. According to the EU: 'Cities are the places where social and/or economic problems become most manifest, but cities are also the places where innovative solutions are found more rapidly'.[2] Initiatives in cities take place in a framework of constraints and opportunities in which frames, financial incentives and models for action are assembled, whose negotiation originates with the EU, the States and the subnational governments but also the transnational networks that connect cities directly, for example *Eurocities*. As Uitermark (2005, p. 149; cited in Blakeley, 2010) maintains, this results in the impression that cities are subject to a general strategy conceived by a central government (national or European). Nonetheless, similar global trends are incorporated everywhere, according to different dynamics (ibid.).

The processes of territorialization and localization of welfare already discussed in Chapter 3 have increased the importance of the city as a privileged space for policies of social inclusion, at the same time encouraging a stronger link between urban and social policies. In this chapter we shall look at how, starting from here, a relationship takes shape between cities and social inclusion, and the questions it raises.

## The agenda of the inclusive city in Europe

In the time span between the Lisbon summit and today, public and scientific debate have given impetus to the relationship between the city and inclusion, pinning it to two main axes. The first of these hinges on territorialized public action and inclusive development. Along this axis cities become important actors as promoters of strategies capable of combining growth and cohesion, in line with the objectives and guiding concepts approved from Lisbon onwards. Although social Europe, which was fuelled by these concepts, seems to have faded (Chapter 2), this role is no less important. If anything, it has been reinforced and redefined by the perspective of 'smart, green inclusive growth'. The reform of the EU's Regional Policy has allocated half the investments of the European Regional Development Fund for 2014–2020 to urban areas. For the same period the European Commission has asked the Member States to draw up an urban agenda involving local governments in the elaboration of trajectories of development that are coherent with the Europe 2020 strategy. This agenda is supposed 'to guide action, to bring coherence to a diversity of initiatives and policies' (EU 2014),[3] related to matters including urban renovation, transport and sustainable mobility, climate and energy, work and welfare. The view according to which unequal motivations, interests and capacities should recompose and find a planning dimension corresponds to that of cities as places:

> where the opportunities and threats to sustainable development come together … Cities are places of innovation, drivers of our economy, where wealth and jobs are created. They are dynamic places where change can happen on a larger scale and at a more rapid pace.[4]

This axis not only emphasizes the potential of cities as engines of growth but also places the odds on their 'political' dimension, on their capacity to assume the role of a collective actor mobilizing instruments and models of governance equipped to mediate and produce a synthesis of a number of different interests. It also involves the capacity for multi-scalar action. The scale architecture the EU is encouraging is classical multilevel governance, therefore the intention is to valorize the territorialized dimension of government, not in order to set up new structures of government but to identify 'a modality by which the various levels of government can cooperate'.[5]

The public agenda of the inclusive city planned in this way certainly owes a debt to research studies on social cohesion which point to the elements of frailty and crisis linked to the precarious nature of work (with a consequent increase in dualization on the labour market), the increase in migrant flows (and consequent pluralization of ethnic groups), re-commodification in the housing sector (and consequent socio-spatial segregation), changing family structures (and consequent increase in the need to reconcile care/work: Ranci, Brandsen and Sabatinelli, eds, 2014). As is now unanimously acknowledged, these problems and the way in which they accumulate in the city call for a range of coordinated responses.

More problematic and controversial is the relationship with the debate on the approaches to development. From the latter, policy framing has drawn an interpretative grid centring on the need to move beyond the economistic stamp of orthodox models. This is where the importance of the relationship between cohesion and growth originates, as well as the opening towards integrated approaches that take the local level and reference to the territory as pillars for a trajectory of development and pre-conditions for the mobilization of local resources, the integration between policy agendas, the construction of networks of collaboration, the promotion of the active role of the beneficiaries in defining their needs and respective responses (Moulaert et al., 2005). The debate on these themes has helped to open up a political window of attention to growth models and the issue of social and environmental sustainability. However, the conditions have been lacking for deriving a real change of political prospects from all this: competitiveness has managed to impose itself as an obligatory choice with no alternative and cohesion has been conceived of as a corollary of it (Maloutas and Malouta, 2004; Ache et al., eds, 2008). Briefly, in the EU context the axis of inclusive development has been affected by two types of dynamics which have operated jointly, reinforcing one another: desocialization, which has diminished the social impact of the issues, and depoliticization, which has reduced the space for discussion and public debate. In this context the strategies launched to promote the smart, sustainable and inclusive city may have the effect of normalizing market-oriented governance (Fainstein, 2015), as an approach especially if they rely on what Brenner and Schmid (2015) define as 'technoscientific urbanism', an approach in which 'information technology corporations are aggressively marketing new modes of spatial monitoring, information processing and data visualization to embattled municipal and metropolitan governments around the world as a technical "fix" for intractable governance problems' (ibid., p. 157). Since, as we know, instruments, regulation and representations have extraordinary performative power, the empirical reality of the inclusive city risks being desocialized and depoliticized – despite declaration of the urgent need to deal with the knotty issues that coagulate in cities damaging social cohesion.

This refers us directly to the second axis, centring on the spatial dimension of exclusion/inclusion, which sees the city in the light of the changes that have affected mechanisms historically connected to the origin of 'the social question'.

If these changes are read according to the category of 'the urban question', as Donzelot (2006) does, it brings into the limelight the specific dynamics whereby the urban space acts as a reagent in the mixture of increasingly precarious employment, housing problems, lack of security, poor integration between native and immigrant populations (Agustoni, Alietti and Cucca, 2015). Whilst last century the social question coincided with the social conflict, i.e. mobilization and collective demands for equality, today the question is the city as a receptacle and engine of separation: social conflict is absent but the distances between social groups increase and the latter withdraw defensively into delimited physical and social spaces, sometimes self-segregating. What is at stake, then, is the city's capacity to build society (Donzelot, 2006), a capacity that European cities owe at least partially to their spatial structures, small but densely filled, with many differences confronting one another in limited spaces (Cassiers and Kesteloot, 2012). This has caused the urban space to operate as a mediating factor between 'everyday social experiences and confrontations' (ibid), or as a theatre (Donzelot and Jaillet, 1997, quoted in Cassiers and Kesteloot, 2012).

This prospect, introduced in public debate in France ever since the 1990s, is connected to a reinterpretation of social exclusion, which on the one hand emphasizes the spatial dimension and on the other challenges conventional scientific categories. For Castel (1995, 2009), who was the first to propose the reformulation, the concept of social exclusion is limited by its referring back to a contrast between states, between included and excluded, neglecting the processes by which these states are produced: the destabilization of salaries as an effect of the decomposition of the salaried society. Vulnerability and 'disaffiliation' mark phenomena of profound relational frailty and true social isolation associated with the metamorphosis in work and the 'advance of uncertainty' linked to it.

Apart from the primacy given to 'the social question' or to 'the urban question' as a category of explanation, the evidence assumed by the societal impact of urban problems and phenomena explains the renewed interest catalysed by the socio-spatial dynamics of concentration and segregation.[6] Although less marked than in American cities, these dynamics are nonetheless present in Europe (Kazepov, 2005) where they accompanied processes of urbanization and the construction of public buildings for the working class in the post-war period, giving rise to authentic enclaves. 'Neighbourhood effect' is the term used to indicate the negative and cumulative consequences deriving from living in urban areas that are homogeneous in terms of the socio-economic position of the inhabitants or their membership of ethnic groups and characterized by lack of opportunities and services, social stigma or frail social ties (Bolt, Phillips and van Kempen, 2010).

The policies against social exclusion promoted in Europe in the 1990s are strongly marked by this spatial approach. However, the strength of the link between exclusion and urban space and the effects that this link produces are controversial matters that are hotly debated. Several research studies, for example, question the fact that the main factor for creating marginalization is residence in deprived neighbourhoods (Agustoni, Alietti and Cucca, 2015). In other words, the spatial concentration of poverty is supposed to be a mere reflection of economic and structural inequality from which processes of impoverishment also derive (ibid.).

In any case, the issue of disadvantaged neighbourhoods or those experiencing crisis (a considerable number of which are neighbourhoods characterized by a high rate of public housing) has come to weigh more heavily in European, national and local policy-framing. The identification of the neighbourhood as a target reflects and at the same time reinforces a territorialized attitude to public action, which brings into the limelight the capacity for carrying out integrated intervention which targets the physical, social and economic aspects of problems at one and the same time.

The evolutionary lines along which intervention to contrast social exclusion develops converge and partly overlap. They have been influenced by the often unsuccessful results of traditional methodologies with a sectorial basis. Even the central importance that the notion of social exclusion has assumed since the 1990s in Europe signals a shift towards an interpretative and normative framework which places the emphasis on the characteristics of multidimensionality and the cumulative effect of social issues (Negri and Saraceno, 2000). Though in a more confused manner, the theme of vulnerability has also made its appearance in European discourse – proof of a closer focus on the processes that led to marginal states.

If we look at the European scale, we see that the two axes intersected and overlapped considerably in the period in which social Europe reached its peak. This is obvious, if we consider that both the drive to combine cohesion and growth in the city and the tendency to assume urban areas as the target for contrasting poverty and exclusion imply a weakening of the confines between traditionally distinct programmes. As well as intersecting, in the most fortunate of cases the measures and relative financing have also interacted to create synergy.

It is here that urban governance meets one of its main challenges, as well as an important source of legitimacy. Over the past two decades, European cities have tried out several multi-actor and multilevel programmes in the context of this orientation towards integrated intervention valorizing the relationship between urban space and inclusive development. Only part of them are linked to European financing and regulations but their common characteristic is the tangible fruit of dynamics of Europeanization based on the spread of distinct models and instruments of intervention.

## Diversity, participation, social innovation

Urban strategies for social inclusion obviously question local welfare systems, i.e. the specific configuration of needs, resources and arrangements that contribute to creating both the problems and the solutions that accumulate in the relationship between city and inclusion. The multitude of ways in which the challenges are managed is proof of the importance of contexts but also, as previously mentioned, of the availability of certain margins of freedom. It should not be forgotten that these margins are in turn affected by complicated geometries of powers and responsibilities traced by the relations between the local, national and supra-national levels.

The range of instruments includes programmes with a decidedly territorialized vocation, such as urban regeneration, or sectorial policies, for example on housing, employment, education, assistance, which are nevertheless encouraged to coordinate.

Diversity, participation and social innovation are the three guiding strategies in policies that take into account the city as a privileged space for social inclusion. We shall now look at this in greater detail.

### Diversity

As Fainstein (2005) points out, diversity has become the new orthodoxy of city planning. The term indicates mainly mixes of uses and subjects of the city and has taken root as a reaction against the urban landscape created by segregation in homogeneous districts, such as working-class public housing areas, immigration neighbourhoods, deindustrialized inner-city districts.

In the European framework associating cities and inclusive development, diversity is conceived of as a creative force for urban well-being. More precisely, urban diversity and creativity 'work together to power innovation and economic growth' (European Commission, 2011, p. 34). In the path opened up by the valorization of the city's innovative potential as a crucible of creativity and space for tolerance,[7] the vision of the diverse city proposed at a European level takes into account the need to acknowledge the wide range of differences – anagraphical, socio-economic, cultural, ethnic, spatial – as propellers of growth and a basis for social links (ibid., p. 86): 'We need to work on strategies for mutual knowledge between all cultures present in the city: European and non-European cultures, middle-class and working-class culture … 'high' and 'low' culture, and especially specific youth cultures'. The diverse city organizes and reorganizes its spaces so as to make the most of differences as a resource, thus contrasting separation and segregation. 'In the diverse city, there are no ghettos or gated communities, and there is no strict delimitation of territories according to different cultural or ethnic origins' (ibid.). Consequently, the space generates a variety of interactions, from informal ones to formal discussions on public choices:

> In a diverse city, public spaces become meeting places in the broadest sense: from just observing each other to physical meetings, interaction and communication and further, to forums where questions affecting the

way the city spends its budget can be discussed openly, as people have
their say in public budgeting exercises.

(ibid.)

From this perspective, the spaces and exchanges that develop in the city sustain
the expression of forms of grassroots solidarity 'facilitating and stimulating
common projects for urban dwellers' (ibid.).

In terms of contrasting urban exclusion, diversity is brought into play as an
anti-segregational factor in policies aiming to create a social mix through
mixed neighbourhoods.[8] Policy makers who agree with this orientation are
convinced that the social mix can contribute to reducing the more problematic
outcomes of spatial concentration. Embryonic forms of policies oriented towards
producing this social mix were already to be seen in the post-war period, for
example in Great Britain. Since the mid 1990s, however, neighbourhood-scale
social mix has become a policy imperative (Bridge et al., 2014). In operational
terms, strategies mainly concentrate on diversification of housing, e.g. by offering
different types of accommodation, and balancing the social and ethnic make-
up of neighbourhoods, e.g. by reviewing the criteria for assigning public
housing (Bricocoli and Cucca, 2012; Agustoni, Alietti and Cucca, 2015). The
advantages of mixing are supposed to derive mainly from the poor emulating
middle-class codes of conduct. Moreover, the physical proximity of residents
from different social classes or cultures is supposed to increase social capital
and social cohesion.

The approaches of mixed-neighbourhood policies have raised a clamour of
critical voices. Lees (2008) has spoken of cosmetic policies that are inadequate
for dealing with the problems of concentrations of poor people in cities. The
absence of empirical evidence is challenged in very strong terms. Cheshire
(2009) argues that a mixed communities policy is essentially a faith-based
policy since there is no proof of its benefits in developing interaction between
social groups, the creation of mixed networks and inclusive communities and
the reduction of poverty and class segmentation. Another type of criticism,
already mentioned, points out the limits of a perspective that spatializes social
problems without considering the mechanisms – operating in the economy –
that lie at their origin (Bacqué et al., 2014). This is equivalent to treating the
symptoms and not the causes of the problems, which in this way may, instead,
become even more invisible and remote. As Tissot (2007) emphasizes, the
effect of the 'spatialization' of social problems may be to make invisible
everything that happens in poorer neighbourhoods because of what goes on
in 'good neighbourhoods'.

Another line of criticism that is just as important has highlighted the problematic consequences of gentrification processes encouraged by the social mix.
The middle-class or better-off inhabitants often assume the role 'of providing a
social framework for the poor' (Rose et al., 2013, p. 445), establishing role
models and rules regarding the commitment that should be devoted to the
neighbourhood as a community. Not infrequently, social mix programmes

require lower-income inhabitants to give proof of their independence from social assistance, in other words to demonstrate their compatibility with the better-off newcomers (ibid.). More in general, studies of gentrification have shown that diversity can be managed to the advantage of privileged groups and inhabitants through strategies that activate a mix of spatial inclusion and exclusion, so as to have 'a limited and controlled proportion of 'others' in their residential area' (Tissot, 2014, p. 1195). Thus diversity and segregation can both act in favour of a new kind of social distinction 'which does not rely on segregation between homogeneous residential areas, but on strict control of spatial mixing within residential areas' (ibid.).

One paradoxical aspect is that, in certain circumstances, instead of promoting conditions for social cohesion, the insistence on social mix contributes to excluding those social groups that are most at a disadvantage in terms of access to housing. As Bricocoli and Cucca (2012) observe, it has to be admitted that, where the mix is interpreted and naturalized as an instrument that is assumed to be purely technical, there is the risk that the conditions are lacking for acknowledging, discussing and dealing with the complexity of social issues that coagulate in marginality in the city and in housing. This complexity calls for an exchange of views and mediation between many possible options, i.e. the political sphere.

### Participation

It is not only in Europe that the city and the neighbourhood have become a laboratory for experimental policies based on participation. Well-known experiments have been carried out in Brazil (Avritzer, 2006) but significant initiatives have also taken place elsewhere.

We shall remain in Europe. Some degree of involvement of the inhabitants is contemplated, and is sometimes obligatory, in most of the integrated development programmes and interventions against social exclusion that take the city or parts of the city as their target and scale of intervention. *Contratti di Quartiere* (Neighbourhood Contracts) in Italy are an interesting case and foresee the regeneration of urban public housing areas through formal agreements signed by public administrations, private subjects and associations. The restructuring of buildings is normally accompanied by the construction of infrastructures and the recovery of collective spaces for social and cultural life, commercial activity and business enterprise. The financers (the State and the Regions) have identified the participation of the inhabitants in defining the objectives of intervention as one of the conditions for assigning resources (Bifulco, 2014). A very similar approach is that of the earlier French *Contrats de Ville*, which, however, operate on a wider scale with broader objectives.

Some general issues relating to the weaknesses of participation have already been mentioned in Chapter 5. Amongst the variables to be considered when weighing up the specific inclusive impact of cities and their policies, scale is certainly a central issue. When participation fails to reach beyond the boundaries of the neighbourhood, in other words when it does not manage to affect the city as a whole, the inclusive effects are limited. One related problem is the relationship between the powers of the city and other powers. Blakeley's (2010) comparison between Manchester and Barcelona sheds light on this problem helping to clarify it. In the UK context, the progressive disempowering of the local government with respect to central government has favoured the entry of economic interests in local politics and closer links between administrations and private actors (Blakeley 2010; Geddes, 2010). In the 1980s right up to the early 1990s the key actors in local political life were mainly the municipal administration and private entrepreneurs. Subsequently, with the change in national government, participation gained more space and programmes of an inclusive nature were launched, such as City Challenge and the Single Regeneration Budget. The urban development programmes launched by New Labour (including the New Deal for Communities) have nonetheless had a very limited impact on the mechanisms of economic inequality (Geddes, 2010). As regards Manchester, some initiatives signal an attempt to achieve an organic, inclusive policy extending to the whole city. The Local Government Act of 1999, for example, foresaw citizens being consulted on the development of services and intervention in the neighbourhoods. In 2000, a system of district committees was set up, where the inhabitants have a voice and formulate proposals on local problems (Blakeley, 2010). Institutional initiatives have often been demanded and accompanied by the protest of citizens. The involvement of the citizens of Manchester, however, is mainly related to initiatives on urban regeneration undertaken in specific areas of the city. The New Deal for Communities, launched in 1998 in two neighbourhoods, brought into being a multitude of work groups on issues such as crime, housing, education, youth, the environment, applying innovative methodologies such as neighbourhood planning and door-to-door consultations. Barcelona is a different context, thanks to the post-Franco democraticization which facilitated considerable devolution. Here again, though, the financial weakness of local governments has been a decisive factor in opening up the decision-making processes to economic actors and citizens. Barcelona can boast both a combination of inclusive instruments and measures operating all over the city and also a fair amount of success in attracting economic actors and investments. A considerable part of the resources and services are managed directly by the districts the city's administration is divided into, which have a great deal of financial autonomy. A complex architecture of councils, at district and city level, allows the voice of citizens, inhabitants and associations to weigh in the decisions taken by the city council, which is obliged to inform citizens if and how their proposals are accepted (ibid.).

The distribution of power between institutional levels counts a lot. In Italy the process of devolution and the local electoral reform of the 1990s have made far more space for subnational governments. The case of the city of Turin is an example of how this architecture can interact with the characteristics of a specific context. The *Progetto Speciale Periferia* (Special Project for the

Suburbs), which came into being as an experiment in 1997, resulted in setting up a municipal structure with the task of promoting local development and the participation of the inhabitants in the city suburbs. The methodologies applied in the different urban development actions (for example the Plan of Social Support) have become an important reference point for those operating in this field, not only within the city confines.

Therefore, there is empirical documentation of (at least partially) inclusive cities. Of course these are not always stable experiences. The fact is that a dual challenge is faced by the inclusive city in terms of participation: inclusion in social life and inclusion in decision-making – i.e., redistribution of resources and redistribution of powers. Inevitably the weaknesses of the instruments available are exasperated, as they are frequently characterized by a volunteer register. Of a particularly frail nature are those instruments that overestimate the virtue of debate and communication, to the detriment of the substance of the issues at stake, which includes structural inequality and hierarchies of power (Fainstein, 2010). Tissot's (2007) analysis of the French *politique de la ville* makes it clear how the overwhelming role assigned to dialogue can go hand in hand with the depoliticization of the issues. The institutionalization of an interpretative grid for urban problems based on responsibilization of the inhabitants and the mobilization of their sense of civic responsibility has led to the devaluation of conflictuality and claims of a more political nature. In Tissot's view, the *politique de la ville* has thus ended by discrediting the protest and making room for rationalized public action, legitimized by the production of statistics and the competences of professional experts on urban social development.

### Social innovation

In the basic meaning of the term, social innovation refers to innovation and the ways in which it responds to the social needs of a community, by means of new products, services, organizational structures or activities. In the EU context, the term is used to indicate:

> innovations that are social both as to their ends and their means and in particular those which relate to the development and implementation of new ideas (concerning products, services and models), that simultaneously meet social needs and create new social relationships or collaborations, thereby benefiting society and boosting its capacity to act.[9]

Defined in this way, social innovation is linked to an extremely close bond between the social economy and social entrepreneurship: 'Social enterprises can act as engines of social change by offering innovative solutions, promoting inclusive labour markets and social services accessible to all'.[10]

In a more profound sense, the concept involves new ways of defining and facing situations of social exclusion, ways that 'imply social innovation because they aim to acknowledge and satisfy needs that have not found an answer and are therefore oriented towards building new social relations between individuals and groups both in the neighbourhood and on a higher territorial scale' (Moulaert and Vicari Haddock, 2009, p. 54). Moulaert, Martinelli and González (2007) were amongst the first to tackle the formulation of an interpretative grid on social innovation in connection with integrated approaches of development and the fight against exclusion. They particularly stress three interdependent dimensions:

> the satisfaction of human needs (content dimension); changes in social relations, especially with regard to governance, that increase the level of participation of all but especially deprived groups (process dimension); and an increase in the socio-political capability and access to resources (empowerment dimension).
>
> (Gerometta, Hussermann and Longo, 2005, p. 2007)

On this basis, the research carried out by Evers et al. (eds, 2013, p. 13) distinguished between: 'innovation in terms of (i) different conceptions of users, (ii) different types of services and (iii) different ways to provide a service'. In any case, social innovations do not affect just the organizational dimension of services but can focus on or affect regulatory structures and the decision-making arenas of governance (ibid.).

Thus, innovation is social in that it feeds on the social – relations, networks, capacity for collective action – fuelling it in turn (in this perspective, social enterprises are a paradigmatic case of social innovation: de Leonardis et al., 1994). It is not sufficient for an action to be promoted by explicitly pro-social subjects, such as third-sector organizations, for the effects of social innovation to be produced, since the social consists in what may be produced and is not an intrinsic attribute of an actor (ibid.). For the same reasons, it is not the field of intervention – a problem area of social need – that qualifies social innovation as such.

It does not need to be something entirely new. The re-proposal of 'old' instruments (for example the extension of the field for exercising a social right) produces social innovation when it contributes to contrasting and inverting mechanisms of social exclusion by opening up the way for building new social relations (Moulaert and Vicari Haddock, 2009).

The bond between the city and social innovation can be understood in relation to the perspective that sees cities both as places of crisis and as places of change in governance relations and primary arenas of 'civil society social experiments' (Gerometta et al., 2005). This has given credit to urban policies as fields of social innovation and inclusion, alongside and/or coordinated with social policies and welfare in the strict sense. A certain number of initiatives, which can be interpreted according to the category of social innovation, have confirmed the importance of urban planning and the innovatory value of new connections between urban transformation and social intervention, and between the competences and knowledge implied in this (Evers et al., eds, 2013). Social Innovation Europe (SIE), a platform that came into being in 2011 for initiatives relating to the General Division for Growth, is investing a good deal in spreading ideas and experiences of social innovation in cities – 'a great landscape for social innovation'.

The spectrum of activities is wide, given the extension that tends to affect the fields of action. The *Singocom* research (MacCallum et al., eds, 2009; Moulaert et al., eds, 2010), which analysed some initiatives of social innovation set in motion in nine European cities (Vienna, Berlin, Lille, Cardiff, Newcastle, Antwerp, Brussels, Milan, Naples), examined a rather heterogeneous constellation of practices according to three main frames. Where social inclusion is associated mainly with involvement in decision-making processes, both as a requirement of the political system to open up channels for citizens' participation in making choices, and as a demand coming from local communities, the interventions rely on setting up open spaces for citizens. Economic development is the main focus of approaches that give priority to the aim of creating opportunities for employment, often through the promotion of social markets. A third frame has culture as its nucleus and valorizes the city as a space for producing and consuming culture by caring for the aesthetic quality of places, the building of new infrastructures, the valorization of the city's artistic and architectural heritage, and support for local artistic communities (Vicari Haddock, 2009; Bifulco, 2009). In any case there is a frequent tendency to cause a coordinated spectrum of actions to converge in a specific context, as well as the attempt to use the space as a lever to reactivate processes of inclusion and development, as well as urban cohabitation. This may be done by building a brand new structure but also by transforming existing structures and places. Whether they are converted or reconverted, spaces assume central importance since they are conceived of not as containers for action but as resources for generating new significances and possibilities for action. Thus, the processes whereby spaces open up for a whole range of different uses, users and experiences are of fundamental importance (ibid.).

By shedding light on the inclusive and generative potential of urban contexts, a close look at actual practices reveals an open scenario, which translates what at the level of European policy-making appears mainly as a set of constraints into opportunities for innovation that nurture the social and give it renewed vigour.

We should be careful to note that the point is not to identify a recipe for innovation in the resources of action and social organization. The picture here is heterogeneous. The literature has shown that initiatives of social innovation have different origins (Moulaert, Martinelli and González, 2007; Bifulco, 2009): they may arise spontaneously or be the fruit of intentional planning by the political-administrative actors or, again, they may coincide with variable mixes of social self-organization and institutional investments. In any case, it is true that even the most formalized initiatives, recognized as part of a strict institutional context, exist thanks to local capacity for action and mobilization that they themselves contribute to organizing. In this sense, the potential for action and social action available or that can be activated locally is important, as well as the social practices of self-organization through which the local communities negotiate perspectives and strategies regarding problems and their solutions. However, the institutional framework – regulatory and normative – in which the social actors develop their initiatives is just as important. This framework can obviously have negative effects or, also, positive ones. In some cases the mobilization practices may be supported and reinforced differently and the local administrations themselves assume the task of making sure that capacities that would otherwise be wasted or lose their impetus blend into a network of action able to fuel itself. In other cases, factors of frailty or discontinuity arise out of them. For their part, the initiatives that arise spontaneously are constantly challenged by the need to find an appropriate counterpart in the form of institutional actors able to deal with resources and practices of self-organization and sustain them without allowing them to crystallize.

Thus the ways of social innovation are multiple. Nonetheless, there are certain focuses that must be taken into account.

First, the chosen space for social innovation to take root in is the city but it will fade if it fails to extend beyond local confines and mobilize different scales in order to bring into being new institutional arrangements arising out of local action (Cassiers and Kesteloot, 2012). Despite the hopes aroused by its potential for inclusion – in the dual sense that the term inclusion assumes in this context – the local level in itself does not have any great impact on the mechanisms underlying the inequality of resources and power (Dreier, Mollenkopf and Swanstrom, 2004). The main problem regarding the local context, as mentioned in Chapter 3, consists in the tendency to overestimate its democratic virtues.

Second, social innovation appeals to the community's capacity for self-organization but is not simply the self-organized community itself, since it encourages and calls upon institutional devices, resources and capacities. In varying geographical and political contexts the use of the concept of community tends to correspond to an approach that takes social virtues for granted, often in contrast to the State and the limits attributed to it, from which it is assumed the community can and must free itself (de Leonardis, 1998). Yet, the community in itself is no guarantee of robust social links, and divisions and laceration are frequent experiences, as well as cooperative impulses. As pointed out in Chapter 6, the vision of a community that is intrinsically supportive is based on a regime of justification that reduces social relations to a moral virtue (ibid.). In a context of this nature, the definitions of problems and solutions give priority to categories of a subjective or moral, rather than a social and political nature. This moralization of social bonds is connected to the success recorded by organic visions of communities, which depict them as irenic worlds, capable of including individuals as a whole, without friction, distances, institutional mediation or conflicts. In addition, this combines with a 'socio-spatial dualism' (Amin, 2005), which crystalizes the separation between poor and rich areas: what is in store for the former is the obligation to improve, rebuild and recover the local community, whilst in the case of rich areas company models are supported that are based on transnational concessions, spatial mobility and cosmopolitism.

Third, social innovation affects – and should place under pressure – processes of reorganization of the powers that actually fuel it. Generally, however, the more optimistic visions of cohesion and territorial development tend to ignore thorny issues, such as 'power relations, territorial fragmentation and access to social rights' (Eizaguirre et al., 2013, p. 2012). This has the effect of neutralizing the broadly political value of initiatives, even those that are the fruit of mobilization by the citizens, aiming 'not only to obtain material or immaterial resources for the excluded, but also to redefine norms and values at the root of exclusion' (ibid.).

Fourth, the tendency to define as social innovation experiences that mainly make use of short-term forms of support and informal responses to social needs and problems legitimizes the fact that issues linked to social rights fade into the background. This means amplifying one of the main factors on which the worsening situations of vulnerability and their downwards trajectory into real exclusion depend. In this sense there is the risk of confirming a further subtraction of resources and powers from those who already possess very few – a risk that the responses already formulated to deal with the crisis only help to emphasize.

## Conclusions

The key strategies running though the policies of the inclusive city converge to raise certain interwoven questions. The first is that spatialization may obscure the mechanisms that determine the appearance of social problems (a sort of short-sightedness). The second is that in order to avoid localism, local action must interconnect with other levels and other wider networks. The third is that the questions at stake have a political dimension that is not always explicit but often translated and neutralized as a technical dimension. The fourth is that behind the label 'social' practices may develop that weaken the social value of the issues. This pessimism is somewhat relieved, if we place the inclusive effects that the actual initiatives can generate in the forefront, in particular participation and social innovation. In all events, faced with growing social problems, the city's capacity for acting as a laboratory of inclusion is not an option but a necessity (Mingione and Vicari, 2015).

## Notes

1  http://ec.europa.eu/regional_policy/sources/conferences/urban2014/doc/report_cities_of_tomorrow_2014.pdf
2  http://ec.europa.eu/regional_policy/sources/conferences/urban2014/doc/report_cities_of_tomorrow_2014.pdf

3 http://ec.europa.eu/regional_policy/en/conferences/urban2014/
4 http://ec.europa.eu/regional_policy/sources/conferences/urban2014/doc/issues_paper_final.pdf
5 http://ec.europa.eu/regional_policy/sources/conferences/urban2014/doc/issues_paper_final.pdf
6 The theme of social segregation has been tackled by the social sciences ever since the 1920s.
7 The relationship between social diversity and urban growth is at the centre of Florida's (2002) perspective on the creative class.
8 According to Cassiers and Kesteloot (2012), there are three main types of policies against segregation: the social mix strategies; policies that aim to reduce the effects of segregation without, however, intervening in the spatial dimension; and programmes of a more global nature regarding disadvantaged or crisis areas.
9 European Union Programme for Employment and Social Innovation (EaSI).
10 European Union Programme for Employment and Social Innovation (EaSI).

# Part IV
# Conclusions

# 10 Back to the 'social'?

Although the initial Lisbon theory was less one-sided than Lisbon practice (Vandenbroucke and Vleminckx, 2011), the imbalance between the economic and the social is an original characteristic of social Europe that has become more evident in connection with the evolutionary dynamics of neoliberalism. In the relationship between growth and social cohesion that stood at the centre of the Lisbon agenda, competition has gained increasingly evident supremacy and has been taken as a benchmark for social policies and intervention. This has given rise to a reversal between goals and means (Maloutas and Malouta, 2004): social cohesion is not a goal in itself but has gained legitimacy due to being necessary to economic development. This perspective is part of the building blocks of social Europe, despite empirical evidence contradicting the existence of a strong relationship between cohesion and economic growth. In fact, problems of cohesion are recorded both in highly competitive contexts and in those with a depressed economy (Ranci, Brandse and Sabatinelli, eds, 2014). The thread running through social Europe from the Delors presidency to our own times and passing though instruments like the Structural Funds and Social Investment programmes is thus the frailty of the social dimension. One critical thesis that effectively sums up this point is that 'the emphasis in 'social investment' is too much on the 'investment' and too little on the 'social' (Beckfield, 2012, p. 3).

The results of the previous analyses confirm this thesis and at the same time suggest that it should be elaborated by tackling a specific issue: what sort of social are we talking about? Undoubtedly, the hegemony of the economic and the free market model involves the ability to shape social issues and the very idea of society. It has been pointed out, for example, that neoliberal approaches to labour policies tend to neutralize the social dimension of the employment issue and its nature in terms of a social relationship structured by power imbalances (Beckfield, 2012; Borghi, 2011). Yet there is the risk that defending the social may appeal to perspectives that paradoxically contribute to rob of depth and energy instead of invigorating it, i.e. give more impetus to dynamics of desocialization.

The fact is that, as pointed to by analyses developed in this volume, the social dimension tends to broaden, at the same time becoming vague and indeterminate. Thus, a change comes about in the confines and meanings of that specific way of conceiving and dealing with the social that had its roots in the historical experience of the welfare state and was fuelled by it. In terms of this experience, 'social' refers to the processes through which social ties are mediated by institutionalized support and public responsibilities. At the same time, it indicates the measures for social protection and forms of social organization that these measures contribute to support. In this sense, social policies are implicated not only for the goods and resources they ensure but also for the social weight they have in contributing to 'building society' (Donzelot et al., 2003). Besides, we should bear in mind that ever since Marshall (1950) 'social' has been connected to a range of rights 'from the right to a modicum of economic welfare and security to the right to share to the full in the social heritage and to live the life of a civilized being according to the standards prevailing in the society' (p. 11).

Regardless of how improper the extensive and yet at the same time generic use of the term 'social' is today, it is significant due to what it reveals in terms of the dynamics of change. The analysis carried out in the previous chapters has identified certain processes of desocialization, or levelling down and neutralization of the social, in which we observe the reflection on the one hand of a devaluation of the institutionally mediated dimension of social life – the celebration of immediacy, the DIY (or 'do-it-yourself') myth, the moralization of the social bond, the idealized search for mutual belonging based on similarity, and on the other hand the advance of processes of commodification. Nevertheless, some (albeit few) possibilities have also emerged for generating the 'social' and these should be emphasized.

This scenario is complicated by multiple causal mechanisms. In the current features of the social we see the coagulation of radical changes in the traditional integration mechanisms at work in salaried society, based on employment and on social/family networks (Castel, 2009). Problems of social realm can thus be interpreted by focusing on the interaction between dynamics of a structural nature and policies.

It is, however, as well to briefly take up what has emerged in the previous chapters as to how social policies contribute to the metamorphoses that are occurring today in the social realm.

## Individualization

These metamorphoses have deep and complex social roots. An essential root can easily be detected in the culture of the new capitalism (Boltanski and Chiapello, 1999; Sennett, 2006) and in the specific dynamics of individualization that form one of its central axes. We have already seen (Chapter 4) how these dynamics come into play in social policies, giving rise to the binomial negative freedom/punitive responsibilization. This is not to say that the Fordist social order was free of problems. Organized modernity, as Wagner (1994) defined it, has been a remarkable concentration of tension between 'liberty and discipline', the ambivalence that constitutes this same modernity. This dual nature is reflected in the structure of a social realm that on the one hand has implied some degree of cohesion, whilst on the other limiting ambitions towards freedom. Moreover, disparity and lack of symmetry have been widespread and recurrent, as is demonstrated by the way in which gender relations have been implicitly or explicitly managed. However, the limiting side of modernity is the other face of those social processes which, mediated by public institutions and welfare, have ended up producing an individual who is both socialized and at the same time autonomous (Dubet, 2002). Be this as it may, it is in the context of present-day capitalism that we are witnessing the erosion of the social basis of individuality so that, as Castel (1995) would say, what individuals share is precisely their condition as de-socialized individuals, which is itself the fruit of a precise social order whose development is deeply affected by changes in social protection and regulations on employment.

The investigation of the relationship between public action and social models of agency carried out in Chapter 4 helps us understand just how individualization works in policies and what its side effects are. The Janus-faced nature of policies of activation may be a source of growth for freedom but also a reduction in freedom: 'both emancipatory and disciplining, inclusionary and exclusionary' (Newman and Tonkens, 2009, p. 230). The ambivalence is linked to the way the relationship between the individual and society comes into play. As we have already noted, particularly where the neoliberal matrix is stronger, society becomes blurred – a mere background against which the active, responsible individual, the entrepreneur of him/herself with prerogatives and skills that are largely taken for granted, dominates the scene. On this type of scenario, agency also is weakened. In fact, an undue burden of responsibility is the other face of this individuality, whose value is measured in terms of the capacity for adapting to the labour market instead of the power to plan personal paths of training or work reflectively.

With regard to care (Chapter 8), we have come across other de-socializing aspects of individualization which refer more closely to processes of commodification. They emerge out of devices aiming at freedom of choice, such as vouchers, assigning to beneficiaries the role of consumers, a role that makes the web of interdependence constituting relations of care unimportant. In this case agency is the sort that is typical of the market player, isolated and with the sole power to exit. Besides, the different forms of marketization and commodification that operate in the sphere of social reproduction – the realm where care is situated – may have the effect of naturalizing the social relations (relations between genders and generations) that underlie them. Where care is regulated and codified in terms of a market service, there are no longer the conditions for taking into account the asymmetry, sources of conflict and inequalities that constitute elements of tension intrinsic in these relations.

## Between market and the self-organized community

The model of individualization prevalent in policies does not mean that social issues become less important but rather that they are redefined. In the case of

EU policy framing on social cohesion, it is evident that this redefinition is the fruit of an encounter between two factors: subordination to the market and the community declination. What might seem an improbable pair is, from other points of view, the demonstration of the considerable resilience of the policy perspective.

Actually, since social cohesion has established its place in the European agenda as the trademark of social Europe (Maloutas and Malouta, 2004), its capacity for problematization – which is something it is marked by as a scientific category in sociological theory from Durkheim onwards – has considerably diminished. As Lafaye (2010) observes, this notion mobilizes the representations that a society creates of itself in relation to a concern with moral and social order, posing the question of 'the modes according to which one envisages what constitutes a society' (ibid., p. 2). The main modes through which the debate has answered this question incorporate two dimensions that are analytically distinct: the first regards reduction of inequality and social exclusion; the second concerns social bonds and social capital (Berger-Schmitt, 2000). The concept thus brings together two different spirits: one emphasizes asymmetry and differences, the other stresses relations. Since it has become a political category in the area of European policy, cohesion has tended to privilege the relational spirit and focus on the objective of integration. But this logic is the outcome of the encounter between options relating to problems set in motion by cohesion, not initial data or an intrinsic aspect of the issue. In other words, in the same way as other building blocks of social Europe, activation for example, 'the content of social cohesion is an issue at stake and not a situation that can be unambiguously predefined' (Maloutas and Malouta, 2004, p. 452).

The modes by which several areas of policies on social cohesion (i.e. community initiatives, social investment and social innovation programmes) have been institutionalized can be interpreted as a gradual leaning or inflection of this relational spirit towards a model of the community type, which values community living mainly at a local level and based on relation 'that appears less 'remote', more 'direct', one which occurs not in the 'artificial' political space of society but in matrices of affinity that appear more natural' (Rose, 1996, p. 334). This cohesive community is rich in social capital and sheltered from conflict (Eizaguirre et al., 2012). The tendency to make social ties coincide with community ties is quite clearly reflected in the success of consensual models of governance which, as we have already seen in Chapters 3 and 7, tend to overestimate the social capacities of cooperation. This interpretation of social cohesion validates the commonsensical concepts that imagine the community 'as something natural, not artificial or agreed by contract' (Bagnasco, 2003, p 8). Community forms of cohesion, seen from a perspective that removes the conflict and inequalities, are assumed as a model to be applied to society. In this perspective, which reflects the grafting of Anglo-American communitarianism onto the bases of European socio-political cultures,[1] the true societal dimension of cohesion becomes weaker. Besides, the vocabulary of policy accentuates the communitarian inflection of themes such as belonging and co-responsibility and relaxes its relationship with the issues of citizenship, social justice and social rights (Eizaguirre et al., 2012; Evers and Guillemard, 2013), i.e. with issues which are the starting points from which the way of living in society was historically reorganized in welfare states.

The community inflection cohabitates with the affirmation of the labour market as the principal means of cohesion. One aspect related to this is that interventions of social inclusion based on the extension of rights are hard put to it to find space in European trends. On the contrary, the association of inclusion, community and work is overwhelming. The idea of active social inclusion is mainly construed as active inclusion in the labour market (Reyneri, 2015; Chapter 4 in this book). The result is that the unpaid work of caring is devalued and situations of poverty and disadvantage that do not correspond to the implicit and explicit dictates of employability are neglected. As many have found, the EU's weak social objectives have resulted in an involution of European policies against poverty (Reyneri, 2015; Saraceno 2015).

As a consequence, the combination of market and community is by no means an exceptional occurrence in the policy frame and regulation, confirming a normative core capable of drawing on different reference points. Here, it is highly significant to observe what is going on in terms of the public–private mix (Chapter 6), where the processes of marketization and commodification tend to expand their perimeters and parameters of action: social is the adjective that qualifies both the objectives of solidarity and inclusion of third sector organizations and the market sectors of the more entrepreneurial forms, as well as the attractive aspects that new potential areas of profit can offer in the eyes of economic and financial actors. Examined in the framework of the public–private mix, the combination of market and community reveals the emergence of a dual front where the social may possibly vanish. One front points a finger at the processes of financialization and at the connected erosion of a model of society that originally aimed at a socially embedded economy.[2] As Dowling and Harvie (2014) emphasize, what is going on is a type of commodification within which 'society is not a separate entity to take from or give back to, but a source of wealth to be harnessed' (p. 881). The second front is linked to perspectives that consider the self-organized community to be the way out of the restrictions of welfare, emphasizing characteristics such as proximity and immediacy of support. This can be the equivalent of denying the intrinsically artificial, constructed and mediated nature of the social bond. Besides, in the absence of collective rights and regulations, it risks bringing back to life the traditional logic of help based on membership of a community, personal dependence and paternalism (Castel, 2009).

In the urban policies on inclusion, examined in Chapter 9, we again found some traces of this assembly of free market and community values. We also underlined some problems that may result from it: approaches and strategies of social mix that enhance urban separations and concentrations, participatory practices that do not take into account the inequalities between citizens and thus end up by strengthening them, and social innovations that embrace ways of thinking and behaving that weaken the social.

What has been pointed out up to here is, in many respects, the confirmation of the extraordinary resilience of neoliberal ideas. From the point of view of social policies it can be seen how the denial of the social in the 1980s – well expressed by the Thatcherian motto 'There is no such thing as society' – has made room for a positive posture, so to speak, thanks to which reorganization of the social has been undertaken. The seemingly contradictory assembly of the market and the community is, in fact, the expression of 'the ability to change while maintaining key elements' (Schmidt and Thatcher, 2013, p. 14), which increases the hegemony of a certain way of understanding the social and allows it to be translated into different contexts. In fact the contexts count a great deal, as I have repeated several times in previous chapters. However, it is true that ideas circulate and policy instruments are effective vehicles for ways of seeing problems and solutions. A strongly familiar air can thus be felt between this picture and the philosophy of the Big Society launched by Cameron's Conservative government in the UK, according to which the functions of the community are mainly social control and the voluntary provision of services (Levitas, 2012).[3]

## Depoliticization

The relationship between the metamorphoses of the 'social' and processes of depoliticization is one of the threads running through the whole of this volume. The time has come now to take up this thread once again and untangle a few knots.

Referring to the institutional sphere of policies and their governance, 'depoliticisation is not about less politics, but about a displaced and submerged politics' (Hay, 2014, p. 302; Burnham, 2014). The situations in which the power of public institutions is delegated to non-public and non-accountable entities can reinforce this logic (Mény, 2015). We have glimpsed something like this in the structures of marketized governance which result in the problem of blurring institutional responsibility.

However, it is important to stress that there are more subtle and less evident modes of depoliticization 'both from within and outside the state' (Wood and Flinders, 2014, p. 156). Societal depoliticization implies the displacement of an issue from the public (not necessarily the State) sphere to the private, so that it becomes a matter of private choice (Hay, 2007; Wood and Flinders, 2014). From this point of view, societal depoliticization is intertwined to a great extent with the risks and tendencies towards the privatization of the social discussed in Chapter 6. Policies dealing with the issue of unemployment as though it were a matter of individual responsibility (Hay, 2007) or care as though it were a private, family problem are examples of this mode, which clearly reveal overlapping and mingling between the removal of the social dimension of the issues, the deactivation of their public valence and the neutralization of their political scope.

Another, connected mode of depoliticization consists in denying the existence of alternative choices on a social issue or political option: it is 'the logic of no alternative', thanks to which the issues shift 'to the "realm of necessity" in which "things just happen" and contingency is absent' (Wood and Flinders, 2014, p. 165). By contrast, this mode can be understood by referring to a way of understanding 'the political' that emphasizes 'the possibility that society can be constituted differently' (ibid., p. 162). Briefly, the political conceived as 'the opposite of fatalism and denial' (p. 162), which opens up the realm of the possible by feeding on pluralism and conflict. In Mouffe's (2005) words, the political is not based on the logic of consensus but values the confrontation between antagonistic perspectives, causing them to result in agonism, i.e. in a conflictuality that recognizes the fundamental principles of democratic living and contributes to reinforcing them precisely where it challenges their application.

In this valorization of conflict we can hear an echo of the role Fraser (2011) attributes to the dynamics of 'emancipation' in the civil, public sphere, taken as 'the missing third that mediates every conflict between marketization and social protection' (ibid., p. 140). With their corollary of disputes and contestation, they make the normative fabric of social protection explicit and expose it to criticism. This fabric, it must be remembered, calls into question institutional arrangements but also the norms widespread in society regarding 'understandings not only of danger and safety, but also of family, community, and belonging; of personhood, dignity and desertion; of dependency, contribution, and work; hence, of gender, nationality and race' (ibid., p. 147). This is how the processes of emancipation 'transform taken-for-granted doxa into an object of political contestation' (ibid.).

Therefore, the political and the public are shown to be made up of a similar social substance: disputes, voice and criticism. From this substance dynamics can be nurtured thanks to which social issues are saved from being private issues or a matter of necessity.

Moreover, taken in this sense, the political and the public are both immersed in a social structure of relationships characterized by inequality, domination, power balances and exclusion. This confirms both the need to avoid making a myth out of the social, and the validity of the process perspective mentioned in the introduction: society's civil, public and democratic leanings must not be taken for granted and what is, in the end, the result of processes that involve many actors and levels must not be taken as a premise.

As can be seen, there are many significant intersections between social, political and public domains. Distinguishing the concepts is thus less important at this point than concentrating on what these overlaps help to clarify in terms not only of the problems, but also of the possibilities open to the social sphere. Let us examine them immediately.

## Possibilities of the 'social'

It is certainly true that the crisis has aggravated the processes of de-socialization in different ways:

- by eroding conditions of well-being and social cohesion;
- by fuelling the strategies of entrenchment that have gained ground, in some countries more than others, under the pressure of the politics of austerity;
- by reinforcing the tendency of the market to expand and penetrate into the social sphere to identify new areas of commodification.

The social sphere is thus under pressure but not necessarily disarmed. Between 2010 and 2012, in Denmark there were cuts in education and child benefits but the ceiling on social assistance was abolished and there were increases in interventions for health and the education of vulnerable members of the community. In some countries the social has even grown, though in the directions typical of social investment (Vis, van Kersbergen and Hylands, 2011). In the same period Germany upped the ceiling for child-related tax allowances, invested 12 billion euros in education and research and increased allowances for university students from low-income families (ibid.).

Elsewhere things are different. Dynamics of re-commodification of the social are quite evident in the UK, where the strategy for dealing with the crisis has mainly been to cut taxes and spending on welfare (ibid.). Different logics of erosion of the social realm are to be found in the Mediterranean area, where countries with a traditionally familistic welfare have witnessed weakening of both the family and care policies (Léon and Pavolini, 2014).

Here, then, we once again come across some consequences of the logic of dualization in social Europe that were already found in Chapter 2. The remarkable fact is that in the more de-socialized contexts greater emphasis is also placed on the cooperative capacities inherent in society as a resource for facing the crisis, or as potentials that the crisis itself makes it possible to use, clearly showing the paradox of presupposing precisely what should be created or reconstituted. This is clear in the rhetoric of the Big Society that has established itself in the UK but also emerges elsewhere, for example in the several local programmes for social inclusion set up in Italy.

However, the possibilities do exist, nesting in the multiple regulations that trace social policies and which, despite the growing rigidity of relations along the European-national-subnational axis, have not been eliminated.

From the cross-sections viewed in this volume several indications emerge. Chapters 4, 7 and 8 discuss the possibility of social policies promoting the independence of frail individuals or young people by developing their capabilities and thus reinforcing the relationship between individual agency and the social resources that sustain it.

Compared to the practices of participation investigated in Chapter 5, Appadurai's notion of capacity to aspire suggests observing whether or not there are the conditions for voice and collective agency to mobilize new social meanings and perspectives for the future. From this perspective cities are still vital actors and resources for inclusion and innovation. To put it differently, they are the main laboratory for recreating the social and infusing it with new energy, in the different ways that social innovation strategies are putting into practice, though not without their problems, as already pointed out in Chapter 9. The fact is that this role of cities incorporates and expresses the relationship between changing social and rescaling processes. As Clarke et al. (2015) suggest, the space and scale which the social refers to 'are contingent, complex and constructed' (p. 11). While the European dimension of social shows its weaknesses, the localized social triggers generative potentials but also risks increasing social fragmentation and giving strength to particularistic and exclusive dynamics. However, recognizing the frailty of the inclusive city certainly does not mean condemning it to failure; on the contrary, it means taking steps to safeguard and fuel its possibilities. Indeed, it is heartening to see that urban welfare systems in Europe have become experts in redefining problems and solutions, to a greater extent than the constrictions of national financing would allow us to hope. Yet this expertise clashes more and more harshly with constraints linked to the fiscal crisis. Moreover, if it is not incorporated into a broader capacity to make the 'realm of the possible' accessible to the city and its inhabitants – a capacity that involves both the public and the political – the empirical reality of the inclusive city cannot do much to infuse new life into the social realm.

There are possibilities but certainly not an abundance of them. Cultivating the myth of social self-organization is one way of reducing them still further, not of increasing them. Indeed, we came across clear traces of this myth when discussing participation and social innovation. Believing that the community and its relational capital are 'the solution' really means reifying the social dimension of community or loading onto its weary shoulders the burden of guaranteeing 'that everyone belongs to the same society' (Castel, 2009, p. 554). Social investment, too, reveals reifying implications in as much as it is taken for granted that the social to invest in is a society freed 'from social class and traditional bonds and transformed into a place where everyone has the opportunity to be the master of their own fate' (Cantillon and Van Lancker, 2013, p. 561).

A third way somewhere between commodification and making a myth out of social activation should thus be pursued or reinforced. As far as we are able to see, this third way cannot work unless it combines social protection with investment in social resources and capabilities, at the same time tackling individual frailties and ruptures in social bonds. In Chapter 6 I tried to describe both what role this implies for public institutions and, more in general, what sort of public is needed. The fact that the local communities and their organizations are involved in these policies is a circumstance which, far from contradicting it, may even validate the role of institutions able to exercise their nature as third parties fuelling social and public life, social justice and democracy.

I leave it up to my readers to examine these brief suggestions in greater depth and return to the analyses that have been carried out.

There are some very important axes of analysis that have remained hidden but which, having reached our conclusion, need at the very least to be pointed out and stressed. First and foremost, changes in the welfare states should be seen in connection with the transformations affecting the economy due to the pressure to find new areas for profit-making. A theme that is meeting with growing interest is that of the sharing economy: its evolutions should be carefully followed, in order to understand if and how the relationship between market mechanisms and cooperative mechanisms are reshuffled. Second, since fiscal stability occupies a fundamental place in the public agenda of retrenchment, we should gain a better understanding of how it comes into play in the relationships between the European and national levels of decision-making.

From a normative perspective, we should be better equipped in order to favour the possibilities of the social. This need appeals directly to the role of those who, like myself, carry out research on these issues. The fact that knowledge is a decisive factor in desocialization and resocialization will not have passed unobserved. The datification mentioned in Chapter 6 is an example of the former. Integrated approaches to development are an example of the latter. Let us therefore return to one of the issues we started out from – knowledge and public decisions – to stress, first and foremost, that infusing new life into the social necessitates opening up the black box of policies, which are even blacker when the factual becomes the prevailing code into which choices and options are translated.

Second, the social sciences can make a substantial contribution to opening the black box. In this respect it would be useful to support the appeal made by Burawoy (2005) to the scientific community arguing the importance of a public sociology 'in which the sociologist works in close contact with a visible, dense, local and often antagonistic public' (ibid., p. 263). The position taken by knowledge in this case is not instrumental but pragmatic and reflective, so that the dialogue linking the sociologist to his or her public is a learning process for both, through which 'the invisible can be made visible and the public private' (ibid., p. 264).

The objection may be made that it is difficult to extend this position outside the domain of sociology. Nevertheless, we can all share the more general point of view it can be traced back to. More precisely, as Crouch (2013 p. 148) states: 'it is essential, in the general struggle against neoliberal hegemony, that we assert that many things that cannot be marketed do have a real value to our lives, and we will fight to protect them'. Knowledge is one of these things.

# Notes

1  More precisely, French republicanism, Scandinavian reformism and German corporatism (Maloutas and Malouta, 2004).
2  I am obviously referring here to Karl Polanyi's category of embeddedness.
3  This resonates with what, according to Corbett and Walker (2012), stands at the root of the philosophy of the big society: conservative communitarianism and libertarian paternalism, that 'together (they) underlay the long-term vision of integrating the free market with a theory of social solidarity based on conservative communitarian values' (p. 488).

# References

Abers, R., 1998. From clientelism to cooperation: Local government, participatory policy and civic organizing in Porto Alegre, Brazil. *Politics and Society*, 26(4), pp. 511–537.

Ache, P., Andersen, H. T., Maloutas, Th., Raco, M. and Tasan-Kok, T., eds, 2008. *Cities between Competitiveness and Cohesion: Discourses, Realities and Implementation*. Dordrecht: Springer.

Agustoni, A., Alietti, A. and Cucca, R., 2015. Neoliberalismo, migrazioni e segregazione spaziale. *Sociologia Urbana e Rurale*, 106, pp. 118–136.

Alber, J., 1982. *Vom Armenhaus zum Wohlfahrtsstaat*. Frankfurt am Main: Campus Verlag.

Alber, J., 2010. What the European and American welfare states have in common and where they differ: Facts and fiction in comparisons of the European social model and the United States. *Journal of European Social Policy*, 20(2), pp. 102–125.

Allen, J. and Cochrane, A., 2010. Assemblages of state power: Topological shifts in the organization of government and politics. *Antipode*, 42, pp. 1071–1089.

Almond, G. A. and Verba, S., 1963. *The Civic Culture: Political Attitudes and Democracy in Five Nations*. Princeton, NJ: Princeton University Press.

Ambrosini, M., 2005. *Scelte solidali*. Bologna: Il Mulino.

Amin, A., 2005. Local community on trial. *Economy and Society*, 34(4), pp. 612–633.

Andersson, K. and Kvist, E., 2015. The neoliberal turn and the marketization of care: The transformation of eldercare in Sweden. *European Journal of Women's Studies*, 4, pp. 1–14.

Andreotti, A., Mingione, E. and Polizzi, E., 2012. Local welfare systems: A challenge for social cohesion. *Urban Studies*, 49(9), pp. 1925–1940.

Appadurai, A., 1996. *Modernity at Large: Cultural Dimensions of Globalization*. University of Minneapolis-London: Minnesota Press.

Appadurai, A., 2002. Deep democracy: Urban governmentality and the horizon of politics. *Public Culture*, 14(1), pp. 21–47.

Appadurai, A., 2004. The Capacity to Aspire: Culture and the Terms of Recognition. In V. Rao and M. Walton, eds, *Culture and Public Action*, Palo Alto, CA: Stanford University Press, pp. 59–84.

Appadurai, A., 2013. *The Future as Cultural Fact: Essays on the Global Condition*. London andNew York: Verso.

Arendt, H., 1958. *The Human Condition*. Chicago: University of Chicago Press.

Arnstein, S. R., 1969. A ladder of citizen participation. *Journal of the American Planning Association*, 35(4), pp. 216–224.

Ascoli, U. and Ranci, C., eds, 2002. *Dilemmas of the Welfare Mix*. New York: Plenum.

Atzmüller, R., 2012. Dynamics of educational regimes and capability-oriented research. *Social Work & Society*, 10(1), pp. 1–15.

Avritzer, L., 2006. New public spheres in Brazil. *International Journal of Urban and Regional Research*, 30(3), pp. 623–637.

Bäck, H., Heinelt, H. and Magnier, A., 2006. *The European Mayor: Political Leaders in the Changing Context of Local Democracy*. Wiesbaden: Vs Verlag.

Bacqué, M. H., Rey, H. and Sintomer, Y., eds, 2005. *Gestion de proximité et démocratie participative*. Paris: La Découverte.

Bacqué, M. H., Fijalkow, Y., Launay, L. and Vermeersch, S., 2011. Social mix policies in Paris: Discourses, policies and social effects. *International Journal of Urban and Regional Research*, 35, pp. 256–273.

Bacqué, M. H., Charmes, E. and Vermeersch, S., 2014. The middle class 'at home among the poor': How social mix is lived in Parisian suburbs: between local attachment and metropolitan practices. *International Journal of Urban and Regional Research*, 38, pp. 1211–1233.

Bagnasco, A., 2003. *Città fuori squadra*. Bologna: Il Mulino.

Bagnasco, A. and Le Galès, P., 1997. Introduction. In A. Bagnasco and P. Le Galès, eds, *Villes en Europe*. Paris: La Découverte, pp. 7–43.

Barber, B. R., 2007. *Consumed: How Markets Corrupt Children, Infantilize Adults, and Swallow Citizens Whole*. New York: W.W. Norton.

Barbier, J.-C., 2005. Attivazione. *La Rivista delle Politiche Sociali*, 1, pp. 257–290.

Barbier, J.-C. and Colomb, F., 2012. EU Law as Janus bifrons, a Sociological Approach to 'Social Europe'. In J.-C. Barbier, ed., *EU Law, Governance and Social Policy*, European Integration online Papers (EIoP), Special Mini-Issue 1, vol. 16, Article 2. http://eiop.or.at/eiop/texte/2012-002a.htm, pp. 1–25.

Barbier, J.-C. and Colomb, F., 2014. The Janus faces of European policy. *Transfer*, 20 (1), pp. 23–36.

Bauböck, R. and Guiraudon, V., 2009. Introduction: Realignments of citizenship, *Citizenship Studies*, 13(5), pp. 439–450.

Bauman, Z., 1999. *In Search of Politics*. Cambridge: Polity Press.

Bauman, Z., 2000. *Liquid Modernity*. Cambridge: Polity Press.

Bauman, Z., 2009. *Living on Borrowed Time: Conversations with Citlali Rovirosa-Madrazo*. Cambridge: Polity Press.

Beaumont, J. and Nicholls, W., 2008. Plural governance, participation and democracy in cities. *International Journal of Urban and Regional Research*, 32(1), pp. 87–94.

Beck, U., 1992. *Risk Society*. London: Sage.

Beckfield, J., 2012. Comment on Anton Hemerijck/3. More Europe, not less: Reversing the long, slow decline of the European social Model. *Sociologica*, 1, doi: 10.2383/36890.

Béland, D. and Cox, R. H., eds. 2011. *Ideas and Politics in Social Science Research*. Oxford: Oxford University Press.

Berger-Schmitt, R., 2000. Social cohesion as an aspect of the quality of societies: Concept and measurement. *EuReporting Working Paper*, 14, pp.1–31.

Berlin, I., 1969. *Four Essays on Liberty*. Oxford: Oxford University Press.

Berthet, T. and Simon, V., 2012. Regional policies and individual capabilities: Drawing lessons from two experimental programs fighting early school leaving in France. *Social Work & Society*, 10(1), pp. 1–19.

Bieling, H. J., 2012. EU facing the crisis: Social and employment policies in times of tight budgets. *Transfer*, 18(3), pp. 255–271.

Bifulco, L., 2008. *Gabbie di vetro*. Milan:Bruno Mondadori.

Bifulco, L., 2009. Pratiche organizzative per l'innovazione sociale. In S. Vicari Haddock and F. Moulaert, eds, *Rigenerare la città*. Bologna: Il Mulino, pp. 75–122.

Bifulco, L., 2011a. Old and new organizational cages: What about autonomy and Freedom?. *Public Organization Review*, 11(3), pp. 283–295.

Bifulco, L., 2011b. Quasi-mercato e sussidiarietà come pilastri del modello lombardo di welfare. In G. Carabelli and C. Facchini, eds, *Il modello lombardo di welfare*, Milan:Franco Angeli, pp. 39–58.

Bifulco, L., 2011c. Becoming public: Notes on governance and local welfare in Italy. *Administration and Society*, 4, pp. 301–318.

Bifulco, L., 2013. Citizen participation, agency and voice. *European Journal of Social Theory*, 16(2), pp.174–187.

Bifulco, L., 2014. Citizenship and governance at a time of territorialisation. *European, Urban and Regional Studies*. doi: 10.1177/0969776414531969.

Bifulco, L. and de Leonardis, O., 2003. Partnership o partecipazione. Una conversazione sul tema. In F. Karrer and S. Arnofi, eds, *Lo spazio europeo fra pianificazione e governance*, Firenze: Alinea, pp. 67–85.

Bifulco, L. and de Leonardis, O., 2005. Sulle tracce dell'azione pubblica. In L. Bifulco, ed., *Le politiche sociali. Temi e prospettive emergenti*. Rome:Carocci, pp. 193–221.

Bifulco, L. and Vitale, T., 2006. Contracting for welfare services in Italy. *Journal of Social Policy*, 35(3), pp. 1–19.

Bifulco, L. and Centemeri, L., 2008. Governance and participation in local welfare: The case of the Italian 'Piani di Zona' (area plans). *Social Policy & Administration*, 3, pp. 211–227.

Bifulco, L. and Mozzana, C., 2011. La dimensione sociale delle capacità: fattori di conversione, istituzioni e azione pubblica. *Rassegna italiana di sociologia*, 3, pp. 399–415.

Bifulco, L. and Facchini, C., eds, 2013. *Partecipazione sociale e competenze*. Milan: Franco Angeli.

Bifulco, L., Monteleone, R. and Mozzana, C., 2012. Capabilities without rights? The trespassing project in Naples. *Social Work & Society*, 10(1), pp. 1–15.

Bishop, P. and Davis, G., 2002. Mapping public participation in policy choices. *Australian Journal of Public Administration*, 61(1), pp. 14–29.

Blakeley, G., 2010. Governing ourselves: Citizen participation and governance in Barcelona and Manchester. *International Journal of Urban and Regional Research*, 34, pp. 130–145.

Blakeley, G. and Evans, B., 2009. Who participates, how and why in urban regeneration projects? The case of the new 'City' of East Manchester. *Social Policy & Administration*, 43(1), pp. 15–32.

Blondiaux, L., Sintomer, Y., 2002. L'impératif délibératif, *Politix*, 15, pp. 17–35.

Boarelli, M., 2010. L'inganno della meritocrazia, *Lo Straniero*, 118, pp. 118–120.

Bobbio, L., 2006. Le politiche contrattualizzate. In C. Donolo, ed., *Il futuro delle politiche pubbliche*. Milan: Bruno Mondadori, pp. 59–79.

Bobbio, L., 2000. Produzione di politiche a mezzi di contratti nella pubblica amministrazione italiana, *Stato e Mercato*, 1, pp. 111–141.

Bode, I., Gardin, L. and Nyssens, M., 2011. Quasi-marketisation in domiciliary care: Varied patterns, similar problems?. *International Journal of Sociology and Social Policy*, 31(3/4), pp. 222–235.

Bolt, G., Phillips, D. A. and van Kempen, R., 2010. Housing policy, (de)segregation and social mixing: An international perspective. *Housing Studies*, 25, pp.129–135.

Boltanski, L. and Thévenot, L., 1991. *De la justification*. Paris: Gallimard.

Boltanski, L. and Chiapello, E., 1999. *Le nouvel esprit du capitalisme*. Paris: Gallimard.

Bonetti, M. and Villa, M., 2014. In the shadow of legalism: Understanding community participation in an overly-bureaucratic context. *Critical Policy Studies*, 8(4), pp. 447–464.

Bonvin, J. M. and Farvaque, N., 2003. Towards a Capability-Friendly Social Policy: The Role of Implementing Local Agencies. Paper presented at the Third Conference on the Capability Approach, 7–9 September, University of Pavia.

Bonvin, J. M. and Thelen, L., 2003. Deliberative Democracy and Capabilities. The Impact and Significance of Capability for Voice. Paper presented at the Third Conference on the Capability Approach, 7–9 September, University of Pavia.

Bonvin, J. M. and Moachon, E., 2014. Right to Work and Individual Responsibility in Contemporary Welfare States. A Capability Approach to Activation Policies for the Unemployed. In E. Dermine and Dumont, D., eds, *Activation Policies for the Unemployed: The Right to Work and the Duty to Work*. Brussels: P.I.E. Peter Lang, pp. 179–205.

Borghi, V., 2005. Il lavoro dell'attivazione: lo statuto sociale del legame tra welfare e lavoro nelle politiche di attivazione. In L. Bifulco, ed., *Le politiche sociali*. Rome: Carocci, pp. 39–60.

Borghi, V., 2006. Tra cittadini e istituzioni. Riflessioni sull'introduzione di dispositivi partecipativi nelle pra-tiche istituzionali locali. *La Rivista delle Politiche Sociali*, 2, pp. 147–182.

Borghi, V., 2011. One-way Europe ?. *European Journal of Social Theory*, 14(3), pp. 321–341.

Borghi, V., 2014. Le basi sociali della cooperazione: ri-politicizzare le forme del legame sociale. *Scienza & Politica. Per una storia delle dottrine*, 50, pp. 9–25.

Borghi, V. and van Berkel, R., 2007. New modes of governance in Italy and the Netherlands: The case of activation policies. *Public Administration*, 85, pp. 83–101.

Brennan, D., Cass, B., Himmelweit, S. and Szebehely, M., 2012. The marketisation of care: Rationales and consequences in Nordic and liberal care regimes. *Journal of European Social Policy* 22(4), pp. 377–391.

Brenner, N., 2004. *New States Spaces: Urban Governance and the Rescaling of Statehood*. London andNew York: Oxford University Press.

Brenner, N., 2009. Open questions on state rescaling. *Cambridge Journal of Regions, Economy and Society*, 2, pp. 123–139.

Brenner, N. and Schmid, C., 2015. Towards a new epistemology of the urban?. *CITY*, 19(2–3), pp. 151–182.

Brenner, N., Peck, J. and Theodore, N., 2010. After neoliberalization?. *Globalizations*, 7(3), pp. 327–345.

Bricocoli, M. and Cucca, R., 2012. Mix sociale: da categoria analitica a strumento delle politiche? Una riflessione a partire dal caso milanese. *Archivio di Studi Urbani e Regionali*, 105(3), pp. 143–152.

Bridge, G., Butler, T. and Le Galès, P., 2014. Power relations and social mix in metropolitan neighbourhoods in North America and Europe: Moving beyond gentrification?. *International Journal of Urban and Regional Research*, 38, pp. 1133–1141.

Bryan, D. and Rafferty, M., 2014. Financial derivatives as social policy beyond the crisis. *Sociology*, 48(5), pp. 887–903.

Burawoy, M., 2005. For public sociology. *American Sociological Review*, 70(1), pp. 4–28.
Burnham, P., 2014. Depoliticisation: Economic crisis and political management. *Policy and Politics*, 42(2), pp. 189–206.
Bussi, M., 2014. Going beyond work-first and human capital approaches to employability: The added-value of the capability approach. *Social Work & Society*, 12(2), pp. 1–15.
Cantillon, B., 2011. The paradox of the social investment state: Growth, employment and poverty in the Lisbon era. *Journal of European Social Policy*, 21(5), 432–449.
Cantillon, B. and van Lancker, W., 2013. Three shortcomings of the social investment perspective. *Social Policy and Society*, 12(4), pp. 553–564.
Capano, G., 2003. Administrative traditions and policy change: When policy paradigms matter. *Public Administration*, 81(4), pp. 781–801.
Carabelli, G. and Facchini, C., eds, 2011. *Il modello lombardo di welfare*. Milan: Franco Angeli.
Carter, I., 2012. Equality. In A. Besussi, ed., *A Companion to Political Philosophy: Methods, Tools, Topics*, Farnham: Ashgate, pp. 161–170.
Cassiers, T. and Kesteloot, C., 2012. Socio-spatial inequalities and social cohesion in European cities. *Urban Studies*, 4(9), 1909–1924.
Castel, R., 1995. *Les méthamorphoses de la question sociale. Une chronique du salariat.* Paris: Fayard.
Castel, R., 2003. *L'insécurité sociale. Qu'est-ce qu'être protégé?*Paris: Seuil.
Castel, R., 2005. Devenir de l'Etat providence et travail social. In J. Ion, ed., *Le travail social en débat(s)*. Paris: La Découverte, pp. 27–49.
Castel, R., 2009. *La montée des incertitudes. Travail, protection, statut des individus.* Paris: Seuil.
Castel, R. and Haroche, C., 2001. *Propriété privée, propriétés sociale, propriété de soi. Entretiens sur la construction de l'individu modern.* Paris: Fayard.
Castells, M., 1996. *The Networked Society.* Oxford: Blackwell.
Cefaï, D., 2002. Qu'est-ce qu'une arène publique?. In D. Cefaï and I. Joseph, eds, *L'héritage du pragmatisme. Conflits d'urbanité et épreuves de civisme*, Paris: Editions de l'Aube, pp. 51–82.
Cheshire, P., 2009. Policies for mixed communities: Faith-based displacement activity?. *International Regional Science Review*, 3, pp. 343–375.
Chiappello, E., 2013. Why so much interest in measuring social impact?http://www. confrontations.org/en/publications-en/articles-and-interventions/1925-why-so-m uch-interest-in-measuring-social-impact
Clarke, J., 2004. Dissolving the public realm?. *Journal of Social Policy*, 33(1), pp. 27–48.
Clarke, J., 2008. Governing the local?. *Social Work & Society*, 6(1), pp. 15–20.
Clarke, J. and Newman, J., 1997. *The Managerial State.* London: Sage.
Clarke, J., Coll, K., Dagnino, E. and Neveu, C., 2014. *Disputing Citizenship.* Bristol: Policy Press.
Clarke, J., Bainton, D., Lendvai, N. and Stubbs, P., 2015. *Making Policy Move: Towards a Politics of Translation and Assemblage.* Bristol: Policy Press.
Corbett, S. and Walker, A., 2012. The big society: Back to the future. *The Political Quarterly*, 83, pp. 487–493.
Corcoran, M., 2006. The challenge of urban regeneration in deprived European neighbourhoods. *The Economic and Social Review*, 37(3), pp. 399–422.
Council of the European Union, 2011. Council Recommendation on Policies to Reduce Early School Leavers, 10544/11 EDUC 100 SOC 424. http://ec.europa.eu/ education/school-education/doc/earlyrec_en.pdf

Crouch, C., 1999. *Social Change in Western Europe*. Oxford: Oxford University Press.

Crouch, C., 2004. *Post-Democracy*. Cambridge: Polity Press.

Crouch, C., 2009. Privatised Keynesianism: An unacknowledged policy regime. *The British Journal of Politics & International Relations*, 11, pp. 382–399.

Crouch, C., 2011. *The Strange Non-Death of Neoliberalism*. Cambridge: Polity Press.

Crouch, C., 2013. *Making Capitalism Fit for Society*. Cambridge: Polity Press.

Crouch, C., Eder, K. and Tambini, D., eds, 2001. *Citizenship, Markets and the State*. Oxford: Oxford University Press.

d'Albergo, E., 2012. Fra governance e partecipazione. In E. d'Albergo and R. Segatori, eds, *Governance e partecipazione politica*. Milan:Franco Angeli, pp. 67–92.

d'Albergo, E. and Segatori, R., 2012. Introduzione. In E. d'Albergo and R. Segatori, eds, *Governance e partecipazione politica*. Milan:Franco Angeli, pp. 7–22.

Daly, M., 2011. What adult worker model? A critical look at recent social policy reform in Europe from a gender and family perspective. *Social Politics*, 18(1), pp. 1–23.

Daly, M., 2012. Making policy for care: Experience in Europe and its implications in Asia. *International Journal of Sociology and Social Policy*, 32(11/12), pp. 623–635.

Daly, M., 2014. Paradigms in EU social policy: A critical account of Europe 2020. *Transfer*, 18(3), pp. 273–284.

Daly, M. and Lewis, J., 2000. The concept of social care and the analysis of contemporary welfare states. *British Journal of Sociology*, 51(2), pp. 281–298.

Dean, H., Bonvin, J.-M., Vielle, P. and Farvaque, N., 2005. Developing capabilities and rights in welfare-to-work policies. *European Societies*, 7(1), pp. 3–26.

Degryse, C., 2012. The New European Economic Governance. *ETUI working paper series*, 12/14. Brussels: ETUI.

Dekker, P. and van den Broek, A., 1998. Civil society in comparative perspective. *Voluntas* 8(1), pp. 11–38.

Delanty, G., 2014. Introduction: Perspectives on crisis and critique in Europe today. *European Journal of Social Theory*, 17(3), pp. 207–218.

De la Porte, C. and Jacobsson, C., 2011. Social Investment or Recommodification? Assessing the Employment Policies of the EU Member States. In N. Morel, B. Palier and J. Palme, eds, *Towards a Social Investment Welfare State?* Bristol: Policy Press, pp. 117–152.

de Leonardis, O., 1993. Le capacità fondamentali: soggetti, diritti e risorse della riproduzione sociale. In A. Carbonaro and C. Facchini, eds, *Capacità, vincoli e risorse nella vita quotidiana*, Milan:Franco Angeli, pp. 13–28.

de Leonardis, O., 1997. Declino della sfera pubblica e privatismo. *Rassegna Italiana di Sociologia*, 38(2), pp. 169–193.

de Leonardis, O., 1998. *In un diverso welfare*. Milan:Feltrinelli.

de Leonardis, O., 2000. Quel povero abile povero. Il tema della povertà e la questione della giustizia. *Filosofia e questioni pubbliche*, 2, pp. 117–136.

de Leonardis, O., 2002. Principi, culture e pratiche di giustizia sociale. In A. Montebugnoli (ed.), *Questioni di welfare*. Milan: Franco Angeli, pp. 73–84.

de Leonardis, O., 2009. Conoscenza e democrazia nelle scelte di giustizia: un'introduzione. *La Rivista delle Politiche Sociale*, 3, pp. 73–84.

de Leonardis, O., 2011a. E se parlassimo un po' di politica? In A. Appadurai, *Le aspirazioni nutrono la democrazia*, Milan: Et. Al., pp. ix–xxxix.

de Leonardis, O., 2011b. Dividing or Combining Citizens. The Politics of Active Citizenship in Italy. In J. Newman and E. Tonkens, eds, *Active Citizenship and the Modernisation of Social Welfare*, Amsterdam: Amsterdam University Press, pp. 127–146.

de Leonardis, O. and Deriu, M., 2012. Introduzione. La capacità di aspirare come ponte tra quotidiano e futuro. In O. de Leonardis and M. Deriu, eds, *Il futuro nel quotidiano*. Milan: Egea, pp. xi–xx.

de Leonardis, O. and Negrelli, S., 2012. A New Perspective on Welfare Policies: Why and How the Capability for Voice Matters. In O. De Leonardis, S. Negrelli and R. Salais, eds, *Democracy and Capabilites for Voice*, Brussels: Peter Lang, pp. 11–36.

de Leonardis, O. and Giorgi, A., 2013. Sulle tracce della depoliticizzazione nel governo della città. In V. Borghi, O. de Leonardis and G. Procacci, eds, *La ragion pratica*. Naples: Liguori, pp. 135–168.

de Leonardis, O., Mauri, D. and Rotelli, F., 1994. *L'impresa sociale*. Milan: Anabasi.

de Leonardis, O., Negrelli, S. and Salais, R., eds, 2012. *Democracy and Capabilites for Voice*. Brussels: Peter Lang.

della Porta, D., 2008. La partecipazione nelle istituzioni: concettualizzare gli esperimenti di democrazia deliberativa e partecipativa. *Partecipazione e Conflitto*, 0, pp. 15–42.

de Munck, J., 2008. Qu'est-ce Qu'une Capacité?. In J. De Munck and B. Zimmermann, eds, *La liberté au prisme des capacités. Amartya Sen au-delà du libéralisme*, Raisons pratiques, vol. 18, Paris: Editions de l'Ehess, pp. 21–49.

de Munck, J. and Zimmermann, B., eds, 2008. *La liberté au prisme des capacités. Amartya Sen au-delà du libéralisme*. Raisons pratiques, vol. 18. Paris: Editions de l'Ehess.

Dewey, J., 1927. *The Public and its Problems*. New York: Henry Holt.

Diani, M., 2008. Modelli di azione collettiva: quale specificità per i movimenti sociali?. *Partecipazione e Conflitto*, 0, pp. 43–66.

Dimoulas, C., 2014. Exploring the impact of employment policy measures in the context of crisis: The case of Greece. *International Social Security Review*, 67(2), pp. 49–65.

Dingeldey, I., 2007. Between workfare and enablement – the different paths to transformation of the welfare state: A comparative analysis of activating labour market policies. *European Journal of Political Research*, 46, pp. 823–885.

Donolo, C., 1997. *L'intelligenza delle istituzioni*. Milan: Feltrinelli.

Donolo, C., 2005. Dalle politiche pubbliche alle pratiche sociali nella produzione di beni pubblici?. *Stato e Mercato*, 73(1), pp. 33–65.

Donzelot, J., 1984. *L'Invention du Social*. Paris: Fayard.

Donzelot, J., 2006. *Quand la ville se défait : quelle politique face à la crise des banlieues?*. Paris: Seuil.

Donzelot, J. and Jaillet, M. C., 1997. *Deprived Urban Areas: Summary Report of the Pilot Study*. Brussels: NATO.

Donzelot, J., Mével, C. and Wyvekens, A., 2003. *Faire société. La politique de la ville aux Etats-Unis et en France*. Paris: Seuil.

Dowling, E. and Harvie, D., 2014. Harnessing the social: State, society and (big) society. *Sociology*, 48(5), pp. 869–886.

Dreier, P. J., Mollenkopf, J. H. and Swanstrom, T., 2004. *Place Matters: Metropolitics for the Twenty-First Century*. Lawrence, KS: University Press of Kansas.

Dubet, F., 2002. *Le déclin de l'institution*. Paris: Éd. du Seuil.

Dubet, F., 2005. Pour une conception dialogique de l'individu – L'individu comme machine à poser et à résoudre des problèmes sociologiques. *EspacesTemps.net*, 21 June. http://www.espacestemps.net/document1438.html

Düker, J. and Ley, T., 2012. Establishing caseness, institutional selves and 'realistic perspectives': A German case study on the transition from school to work. *Social Work & Society*, 10(1), pp. 1–17.

Dumont, L., 1984. *Essais sur l'individualisme: une perspective anthropologique sur l'idéologie modern*. Paris: Seuil.

Eder, K., 2014. The EU in search of its people: The birth of a society out of the crisis of Europe. *European Journal of Social Theory*, 17(3), pp. 219–237.

Ehrenberg, A., 1998. *La fatigue d'être soi. Dépression et société*. Paris: Odile Jacob.

Eizaguirre, S., Pradel, M., Terrones, A., Martinez-Celorrio, X. and García, M., 2012. Multilevel governance and social cohesion. *Urban Studies*, 4(9), pp. 1999–2016.

Ellison, M. and van Berkel, R., 2014. Introduction: Innovative social and labour market policies in Europe in times of crisis. *International Social Security Review*, 67(2), pp. 1–9.

Espeland, W. N. and Sauder, M., 2007. Rankings and reactivity: How public measures recreate social worlds. *American Journal of Sociology*, 113(1), pp. 1–40.

Esping-Andersen, G., 1999. *Social Foundations of Post-industrial Economies*. Oxford: Oxford University Press.

Esping-Andersen, G., Gallie, D., Hemerijck, A. and Myles, J., 2002. *Why We Need a New Welfare State*. Oxford: Oxford University Press.

Estèbe, P., 2005. Les quartiers, une affaire d'État. In P. Lascoumes and P. Le Galès, eds, *Gouverner par les instruments*. Paris: Presses de Sciences-Po, pp. 47–70.

Eurofound, 2014. *Mapping Youth Transitions in Europe*. Luxembourg: Publications Office of the European Union.

European Commission, 2011. *Cities of Tomorrow: Challenges, Visions, Ways Forward*. Brussels. http://ec.europa.eu/regional_policy/archive/conferences/citiesoftom orrow/index_en.cfm

European Commission, 2014. *'CITIES – Cities of Tomorrow: Investing in Europe' forum summary report*, Brussels, 17–18 February. http://ec.europa.eu/regional_ policy/en/conferences/urban2014/

European Union, Committee of the Regions, 2009. *The White Paper on multi-level governance*.

Evers, A. and Guillemard, A. M., 2013. Reconfiguring Welfare and Reshaping Citizenship. In A. Evers and A. M. Guillemard, eds, 2013. *Social Policy and Citizenship: The Changing Landscape*. New York: Oxford University Press, pp. 359–386.

Evers, A. and Guillemard, A. M., eds, 2013. *Social Policy and Citizenship: The Changing Landscape*. New York: Oxford University Press.

Evers, A., Ewert, B., and Brandsen, T., eds, 2014. *Social Innovations for Social Cohesion: Transnational Patterns and Approaches from 20 European Cities*. Liege: EMES European Research Network, WILCO project. http://www.wilcoproject.eu/downloa ds/WILCO-project-eReader.pdf

Fainstein, S. S., 2005. Cities and diversity: Should we want it? Can we plan for it?. *Urban Affairs Review*, 41(1), pp. 3–19.

Fainstein, S. S., 2010. *The Just City*. Ithaca, NY: Cornell University Press.

Fainstein, S. S., 2015. Resilience and justice. *International Journal of Urban and Regional Research*, 39, pp. 157–167.

Faucher, F. and Le Galès, P., 2010. *Les Gouvernements New Labour: Le bilan de Tony Blair et Gordon Brown*. Paris: Presses de Sciences Po.

Ferrarese, M. R., 2011. La governance e la democrazia postmoderna. In A. Pizzorno, ed., *La democrazia di fronte allo Stato*. Milan:Feltrinelli, pp. 61–109.

Ferrera, M., 1993. *Modelli di solidarietà*. Bologna: Il Mulino.

Ferrera, M., 1998. *Le trappole del welfare*. Bologna: Il Mulino.

Ferrera, M., 2005. *The Boundaries of Welfare: European Integration and the New Spatial Politics of Social Protection*. Oxford: Oxford University Press.

Ferrera, M., 2013. Neowelfarismo liberale: nuove prospettive per lo stato sociale in Europa. *Stato e Mercato*, 97, pp. 3–35.

Ferreras, I., 2008. De la dimension collective de la liberté individuelle. In J. De Munck and B. Zimmermann, eds, *La liberté au prisme des capacités. Amartya Sen au-delà du libéralisme*, Raisons pratiques, vol. 18, Paris: Editions de l'Ehess, pp. 281–296.

Florida, R., 2002. *The Rise of the Creative Class.* New York: Basic Books.

Fondazione Giovanni Agnelli, 2010. *Rapporto sulla scuola in Italia 2010.* Roma-Bari: Laterza.

Fraser, N., 1997. *Justice Interruptus: Critical Reflections on the 'Postsocialist' Condition.* New York: Routledge.

Fraser, N., 2011. Marketization, Social Protection, Emancipation. In C. Calhoun and G. Derluguian, eds, *Business as Usual: The Roots of the Global Financial Meltdown.* New York: N.Y.U. Press, pp. 137–158.

Fraser, N., 2013. A triple movement?. *New Left Review*, May–June, pp. 119–132.

Freedland, M., 2001. The Marketization of Public Services. In C. Crouch, K. Eder and D. Tambini, eds, *Citizenship, Markets and the State.* Oxford: Oxford University Press, pp. 90–110.

Fung, A., 2006. Varieties of participation in complex governance. *Public Administration Review*, 66(1), pp. 66–75.

Fung, A. and Wright, E. O., 2003. Thinking about Empowered Participatory Governance. In A. Fung and E. O. Wright, eds, *Deepening Democracy.* London and New York: Verso, pp. 4–45.

Gallino, L., 2011. *Finanzcapitalismo. La civiltà del denaro in crisi.* Torino: Einaudi.

García, M., 2006. Citizenship practices and urban governance in European cities. *Urban Studies*, 43(4), pp. 745–765.

Garsten, C. and Jacobsson, K., 2013. Soft power and post-political visions in global governance. *Critical Sociology*, 39(3), pp. 421–437.

Geddes, M., 2000. Tackling social exclusion in the European Union? The limits to the new orthodoxy of local partnership. *International Journal of Urban and Regional Research*, 24(4), pp. 782–800.

Geddes, M., 2010. Building and contesting neoliberalism at the local level. *International Journal of Urban and Regional Research*, 34(1), pp. 163–173.

Geddes, M. and Benington, J., eds, 2001. *Local Partnerships and Social Exclusion in the European Union.* London: Routledge.

Geddes, M. and Le Galès, P., 2001. Local Partnerships, Welfare Regimes and Local Governance. In M. Geddes and J. Benington, eds, *Local Partnerships and Social Exclusion in the European Union.* London: Routledge, pp. 220–241.

Gerometta, J., Hussermann, H. and Longo, G., 2005. Social innovation and civil society in urban governance: Strategies for an inclusive city. *Urban Studies*, 42(11), 2007–2021.

Gilligan, C., 1982. *In a Different Voice.* Harvard: Harvard University Press.

Glendinning, C., 2008. Increasing choice and control for older and disabled people: A critical review of new developments in England. *Social Policy and Administration*, 42(5), pp. 451–469.

Governa, F. and Salone, C., 2004. Territories in action, territories for action: The territorial dimension of Italian local development policies. *International Journal of Urban and Regional Research*, 28(4), pp. 796–818.

Granaglia, E., 2011. Il welfare mancante. Crisi economica, domande sociali inevase, rischi emergenti. *La Rivista delle Politiche Sociali*, 2, pp. 13–31.

Greve, B., 2014. Introduction: Small European welfare states – impact of the fiscal crisis. *Social Policy & Administration*, 48, pp. 391–393.

Habermas, J., 1989. *The Structural Transformation of the Public Sphere: An Inquiry into a Category of Bourgeois Society*. Cambridge, MA: MIT Press.

Hadjimichalis, C. and Hudson, R., 2007. Rethinking local and regional development: Implications for radical political practice in Europe. *European Urban and Regional Studies*, 14, pp. 99–113.

Haidinger, B. and Kasper, R., 2012. Learning to work: Young people's social and labour-market integration through supra-company apprenticeship training in Austria. *Social Work & Society*, 10(1), pp. 1–16.

Hall, P. A., 1993. Policy paradigms, social learning, and the state: The case of economic policymaking in Britain. *Comparative Politics*, 25, pp. 275–296.

Hall, P. A., 2014. Varieties of capitalism and the euro crisis. *West European Politics*, 37(6), pp. 1223–1243.

Hall, P. A. and Taylor, R. C. R., 1996. Political science and the three new institutionalisms. *Political Studies*, 44, pp. 936–957.

Handler, J. F., 2003. Social citizenship and workfare in the US and Western Europe: From status to contract. *Journal of European Social Policy*, 3, pp. 229–243.

Hansen, H. K., 2015. Numerical operations, transparency illusions and the datafication of governance. *European Journal of Social Theory*, 18(2), pp. 203–220.

Hay, C., 2007. *Why We Hate Politics*. Cambridge: Polity.

Hay, C., 2014. Depoliticisation as process, governance as practice: What did the 'first wave' get wrong and do we need a 'second wave' to put it right?. *Policy & Politics*, 42(2), pp. 293–311.

Heclo, H., 1981. Towards a New Welfare State?. In P. Flora and A. J. Heidenheimer, eds, *The Development of Welfare States in Europe and Nord America*. New Brunswick: Transaction, pp. 383–406.

Hemerijck, A., 2012. *Changing Welfare States*. Oxford: Oxford University Press.

Hibou, B., 2012. *La bureaucratisation du monde*. Paris: La Découverte.

Hirschman, A. O., 1970. *Exit, Voice and Loyalty*. Cambridge, MA: Harvard University Press.

Hollywood, E., Egdell, V., McQuaid, R. and Michel-Schertges, D., 2012. Methodological issues in operationalising the capability approach in empirical research: An example of cross-country research on youth unemployment in the EU. *Social Work and Society*, 10(1), pp. 1–20.

Honneth, A., 2004. Organized self-realization. Some paradoxes of individualization. *European Journal of Social Theory*, 4(7) pp. 463–478.

Hood, C., 1991. A public management for all seasons?. *Public Administration*, 69(1), pp. 3–19.

Hood, C. and Dixon, R., 2015. What we have to show for 30 years of new public management: Higher costs, more complaints. *Governance*, 28, pp. 265–267.

Hvinden, B., 1999. Activation: A Nordic Perspective. In M. Heikkilä, ed., *Linking Welfare and Work*. Dublin: European Foundation for the Improvement of Living and Working Conditions, pp. 27–42.

Hyman, R., 2011. Trade unions, Lisbon and Europe 2020: From dream to nightmare. *Europe in Question*, Discussion Paper 45. London: London School of Economics and Political Science.

ILO, 2013. *Youth Guarantees: A Response to the Youth Employment Crisis?*. Employment Policy Brief, April. Geneva: ILO. http://www.ilo.org/employment/Whatwedo/Publica tions/WCMS_209468/lang

Imrie, R. and Raco, M., eds, 2003. *Urban Renaissance?: New Labour, Community and Urban Policy*. Bristol: The Policy Press.

Jenson, J., 2010. Diffusing ideas for after neoliberalism: The social investment perspective in Europe and Latin America. *Global Social Policy*, 10(1), pp. 59–84.

Jessop, B., 2013. Finance-Dominated Accumulation and Post-Democratic Capitalism. In S. Fadda and P. Tridico, eds, *Institutions and Economic Development after the Financial Crisis*, London: Routledge, pp.83–105.

Jenson, J., 2012. Redesigning Citizenship Regimes after Neoliberalism. In N. Morel, B. Palier and J. Palme, eds, *Towards a Social Investment Welfare State? Ideas, Policies and Challenges*. Bristol: Policy Press, pp. 61–87.

Kazepov, Y., ed., 2005. *Cities of Europe: Changing Contexts, Local Arrangements, and the Challenge to Urban Cohesion*. Oxford: Blackwell.

Kazepov, Y., 2008. The subsidiarisation of social policies: Actors, processes and impacts. some reflections on the Italian case from a European perspective. *European Societies*, 10(2), pp. 247–273.

Kazepov, Y., ed., 2010. *Rescaling Social Policies: Towards Multilevel Governance in Europe*. Farnham: Ashgate.

Keating, M., 1997. The invention of regions: Political restructuring and territorial government in Western Europe. *Environment and Planning C*, 15(4), pp. 383–398.

Keating, M., 2009. Social citizenship, solidarity and welfare in regionalized and plurinational states. *Citizenship Studies*, 13(5), pp. 501–513.

Kentikelenis, A., Karanikolos, M., Reeves, A., McKee, M. and Stuckle, D., 2014. Greece's health crisis: From austerity to denialism. *The Lancet*, 383(9918), pp. 748–753.

Kjeldsen, C. C., Bonvin, J-M., 2015. The Capability Approach, Education and the Labour Market. In H.-U. Otto, ed., *Facing Trajectories from School to Work: Towards a Capability-Friendly Youth Policy in Europe*. Dordrecht: Springer, pp. 19–34.

Kremakova, M. I., 2013. Too soft for economics, too rigid for sociology, or just right? The productive ambiguities of sen's capability approach. *European Journal of Sociology*, 54, pp. 393–419.

Lafaye, C., 2000. Gouvernance et démocratie: quelles reconfigurations?. In C. Andrew and G. Paquet, eds, *La démocratie à l'épreuve de la gouvernance*, Ottawa: Les Presses de l'Université d'Ottawa, pp. 57–86.

Lafaye, C., 2010. *Cohesion sociale et lien social*. https://hal.archives-ouvertes.fr/ha l-00570010

Laruffa, F., forthcoming. The capability approach as a critical yardstick for the employability paradigm. *Sociologia del Lavoro*, 1.

Lascoumes, P. and Le Galès, P., 2007. Introduction: Understanding public policy through its instruments. *Governance*, 20(1), pp. 1–21.

Lees, L., 2008. Gentrification and social mixing: Towards an inclusive urban renaissance?. *Urban Studies*, 45(12), pp. 2440–2470.

Le Galès, P., 2002. *European Cities: Social Conflicts and Governance*. Oxford: Oxford University Press.

Le Galès, P. and Scott, A., 2008. Une révolution bureaucratique britannique?. *Revue Française de Sociologie*, 2, pp. 231–267.

Le Grand, J. and Bartlett, W., eds, 1993. *Quasi-Markets and Social Policy*. Basingstoke: Palgrave.

Leibfried, S. and Pierson, P., eds, 1995. *European Social Policy.* Washington DC: Brookings.

Leibfried, S. and Pierson, P., 2000. Social Policy: Left to Courts and Markets?. In H. Wallace and W. Wallace, eds, *Policy-Making in the European Union.* Oxford: University Press, pp. 267–292.

León, M. and Pavolini, E., 2014. 'Social investment' or back to 'familism': The impact of the economic crisis on family and care policies in Italy and Spain. *South European Society and Politics,* 19(3), pp. 353–369.

Levitas, R., 2012. The just's umbrella: Austerity and the big society in coalition policy and beyond. *Critical Social Policy,* 32(3), pp. 320–342.

Lewis, J., 2001. The decline of the male breadwinner model: Implications for work and care. *Social Politics,* 8(2), pp. 152–169.

Lewis, J., 2006. Work/family reconciliation, equal opportunities and social policies: The interpretation of policy trajectories at the EU level and the meaning of gender equality. *Journal of European Public Policy,* 13(3), pp. 420–437.

Lister, R., 2003. Investing in the citizen-workers of the future: Transformations in citizenship and the state under New Labour. *Social Policy & Administration,* 37, pp. 427–443.

Lister, R., 2006. Children (but not women) first: New Labour, child welfare and gender. *Critical Social Policy,* 26(2), pp. 315–335.

Lovering, J., 1995. Creating Discourses rather than Jobs. In P. Healey, S. Cameron, S. Davoudi, S. Graham and A. Madanipour, eds, *Managing Cities: The New Urban Context.* London: Wiley, pp. 109–126.

Lowndes, V., Pratchett, L. and Stoker, G., 2006. Local political participation. *Public Administration,* 84(3), pp. 539–561.

Lukes, S., 1973. *Individualism.* New York: Harper & Row.

MacCallum, D., Moulaert, F., Hillier, J. and Vicari, S., eds, 2009. *Social Innovation and Territorial Development.* Aldershot: Ashgate.

McQuaid, R. and Lindsay, C., 2005. The concept of employability. *Urban Studies,* 42(2), pp. 197–219.

Madanipour, A., 1998. Social Exclusion and Space. In A. Madanipour, G. Cars and J. Alles, eds, *Social Exclusion in European Cities,* London: Jessica Kingsley Publishers, pp. 75–94.

Maloutas, T. and Pantelidou Malouta, M., 2004. The glass menagerie of urban governance and social cohesion: Concepts and stakes/concepts as stakes. *International Journal of Urban and Regional Research,* 28, pp. 449–465.

March, J. G. and Olsen, J. P., 1989. *Rediscovering Institutions.* New York: Free Press.

Marshall, T. H., 1950. *Citizenship and Social Class.* Oxford: Oxford University Press.

Mayer, M., 2003. The onward sweep of social capital: Causes and consequences for understanding cities, communities and urban movements. *International Journal of Urban and Regional Research,* 27, pp. 110–132.

Mayer, M., 2008. To what end do we theorize sociospatial relations?. *Environment and Planning D,* 26(3), pp. 414–441.

Mazzucato, M., 2011. *The Entrepreneurial State.* London: Demos.

Meagher, G. and Szebehely, M., eds, 2013. *Marketisation in Nordic Eldercare.* Studies in Social Work 30. Stockholm: University of Stockholm.

Mény, Y., 2015. 'It's politics, stupid!': The hollowing out of politics in Europe – and its return, with a vengeance. *Stato e Mercato,* 103, pp. 4–28.

Mény, Y. and Wright, V., 1985. General Introduction. In Y. Meny and W. Wright, eds, *Centre-Periphery Relations in Western Europe,* London: George Allen & Unwin.

Mingione, E., 2000. Modello sud europeo di welfare, forme di povertà e politiche contro l'esclusione sociale. *Sociologia e politiche sociali*, 1, pp. 87–112.

Mingione, E. and Vicari, S., 2015. Politiche urbane e innovazione sociale. In A. Calafati (ed), *Città tra sviluppo e declino: un'agenda urbana per l'Italia*. Rome: Donzelli, pp. 97–108.

Moini, G., 2012. *Teoria critica della partecipazione*. Milan: Franco Angeli.

Moini, G., ed., 2013. *Neoliberismi e azione pubblica*. Rome: Ediesse.

Monteleone, R., ed., 2007. *La contrattualizzazione delle politiche sociali: forme ed effetti*. Rome: Officina.

Morel, N., Palier, B. and Palme, J., eds, 2012. *Towards a Social Investment State? Ideas, Policies and Challenges*. Bristol: Policy Press.

Morlicchio, E., 2012. *Sociologia della povertà*. Bologna: Il Mulino.

Mouffe, C., 2005. *On the Political*. Abingdon: Routledge.

Moulaert, F. and Vicari Haddock, S., 2009. Innovazione sociale e sviluppo integrato del territorio. In S. Vicari Haddock and F. Moulaert, eds, *Rigenerare la città*, Bologna: Il Mulino, pp. 56–75.

Moulaert, F., Martinelli, F., Swyngedouw, E. and González, S., 2005. Towards alternative model(s) of local innovation. *Urban Studies*, 42(11), pp. 1969–1990.

Moulaert, F., Martinelli, F. and González, S., 2007. Social innovation and governance in European cities: Urban developments between the path dependency and radical innovation. *European Urban and Regional Studies*, 14(3), pp. 195–209.

Moulaert, F., Swyngedouw, E., Martinelli, F. and Gonzalez, S., eds, 2010. *Can Neighbourhoods Save the City? Community Development and Social Innovation*. Abingdon: Routledge.

Muller, P., 1995. Les politiques publiques comme construction d'un rapport au monde. In A. Faure, G. Pollet and P. Warin, eds, *La construction du sens dans les politiques publiques – Débats autour de la notion de référentiel*. Paris: L'Harmattan, pp. 153–179.

Muller, P., 2000. L'analyse cognitive des politiques publiques: vers une sociologie politique de l'action publique. *Revue française de science politique*, 50(2), pp. 189–208.

Natali, D., 2012. Future Prospects – Has the European Social Model Really Gone?. In *Social Developments in the EU, 2011*, Brussels: European Trade Union Institute, pp. 237–249.

Negri, N. and Saraceno, C., 2000. Povertà, disoccupazione ed esclusione sociale. *Stato e Mercato*, 2, pp. 175–210.

Neri, S., 2009. Convergenza e divergenza nell'evoluzione recente dei servizi sanitari nazionali. Un confronto tra Regno Unito e Italia. *Stato e Mercato*, 87, pp. 357–386.

Neveu, C., 2011. Just Being an Active Citizen?. In J. Newman and E. Tonkens, eds, *Participation, Responsibility and Choice*, Amsterdam: Amsterdam University Press, pp. 147–160.

Newman, J., 2005. *Remaking Governance: Peoples, Politics and the Public Sphere*. Bristol: Policy Press.

Newman, J. and Clarke, J., 2009. *Publics, Politics and Power: Remaking the Public in Public Services*. London: Sage.

Newman, J. and Tonkens, E., 2011. Active Citizenship. In J. Newman and E. Tonkens, eds, *Participation, Responsibility and Choice*, Amsterdam: Amsterdam University Press, pp. 179–200.

Nussbaum, M., 2000. *Women and Human Development: The Capabilities Approach*. Cambridge: Cambridge University Press.

O'Connor, J., 2005. Employment-anchored social policy, gender mainstreaming and the open method of policy coordination in the European Union. *European Societies*, 7(1), pp. 27–52.

OECD, 2011. *Divided We Stand: Why Inequality Keeps Rising*. Paris: OECD Publishing.

OECD, 2013. *Education at a Glance 2013: OECD Indicators*. Paris: OECD Publishing. http://dx.doi.org/10.1787/eag-2013-en

OECD, 2014a. *Local Implementation of Youth Guarantees: Emerging Lessons from European Experiences*. OECD Working Papers. Paris: OECD Publishing.

OECD, 2014b. *Society at a Glance 2014: OECD Social Indicators*. Paris: OECD Publishing. http://dx.doi.org/10.1787/soc_glance-2014-en

Ostrom, E., 1990. *Governing the Commons: The Evolution of Institutions for Collective Action*. Cambridge: Cambridge University Press.

Ostrom, E., 1999. Institutional Rational Choice: An Assessment of the Institutional Analysis and Development Framework. In P. Sabatier, ed., *Theories of the Policy Process*, Boulder, CO: Westview Press, pp. 35–72.

Ostrom, E., 2005. *Understanding Institutional Diversity*. Princeton, NJ: Princeton University Press.

Otto, H.-U., Atzmüller, R., Berthet, T., Bifulco, L., Bonvin, J.-M., Chiappero-Martinetti, E., Egdell, V., Halleröd, B., Kjeldsen, C. C., Kwiek, M., Schröer, R., Vero, J. and Zielenska, M., eds, 2015. *Facing Trajectories from School to Work: Towards a Capability-Friendly Youth Policy in Europe*. Dordrecht: Springer.

Paci, M., 1989. *Pubblico e privato nei moderni sistemi di welfare*. Naples: Liguori.

Paci, M., 2005. *Nuovi lavori, nuovo welfare*. Bologna: Il Mulino.

Paci, M., ed., 2008. *Welfare locale e democrazia partecipativa*. Bologna: Il Mulino.

Paci, M., 2011. Le politiche di emancipazione sociale e promozione delle capacità. In M. Paci and E. Pugliese, eds, *Welfare promozione delle capacità*. Bologna: Il Mulino, pp. 17–50.

Paci, M. and Pugliese, E., eds, 2011. *Wellfare e promozione delle capacità*. Bologna: Il Mulino.

Palier, B., 2013. Social policy paradigms, welfare state reforms and the crisis. *Stato e mercato*, 97, pp. 37–66.

Palier, B. and Surel, Y., 2005. Les 'trois I' et l'analyse de l'État en action. *Revue française de science politique*, 55(1), pp. 7–32.

Palier, B., Rovny, A. E. and Rovny, J., 2015. The Dualization of Europe. Paper presented at the Conference Party Competition and Voter Alignments in Times of Welfare State Transformation, 18–19 June, European University Institute, Florence.

Papadopoulos, Y., 2000. Governance, coordination and legitimacy in public policies. *International Journal of Urban and Regional Research*, 24(1), pp. 210–223.

Papadopoulos, Y. and Warin, P., 2007. Are innovative, participatory and deliberative procedures in policy making democratic and effective?. *European Journal of Political Research*, 46, pp. 445–472.

Pavolini, E., 2003. *Le nuove politiche sociali. I sistemi di welfare tra istituzioni e società civile*. Bologna: Il Mulino.

Pavolini, E. and Ranci, C., 2008. Restructuring the welfare state: Reforms in long-term care in Western European countries. *Journal of European Social Policy*, 18(3), pp. 246–259.

Peck, J. and Tickell, A., 2002. Neoliberalizing space. *Antipode*, 34, pp. 380–404.

Petersen, O. H. and Hjelmar, U., 2014. Marketization of welfare services in Scandinavia: A review of Swedish and Danish experiences. *Scandinavian Journal of Public Administration*, 17(4), pp. 3–20.

Pitch, T., 2007. *La società della prevenzione*. Rome: Carocci.

Pizzorno, A., 2001. Natura della disuguaglianza, potere politico e potere privato nella società in via di globalizzazione. *Stato e mercato*, 2, pp. 201–236.

Pochet, P. and Degryse, C., 2012. The programmed dismantling of the European social model. *Intereconomics*, 47(4), pp. 200–229.

Poggi, G., 2013. *La burocrazia. Natura e patologie*. Roma-Bari: Laterza.

Pollitt, C. and Bouckaert, G., 2000. *Public Management Reform: A Comparative Analysis*. Oxford: Oxford University Press.

Polizzi, E., 2008. Costruire le politiche sociali con la società civile. Piani di zona e partecipazione nella Provincia di Milano. *Autonomie locali e servizi sociali*, 3, pp. 437–456.

Powell, W. W., 1991. Expanding the scope of institutional analysis. In W. W. Powell and P. J. DiMaggio, (eds), *The New Institutionalism in Organisational Analysis*, Chicago: University of Chicago Press, pp. 183–203.

Power, M., 1997. *The Audit Society: Rituals of Verification*. Oxford: Oxford University Press.

Purcell, M., 2006. Urban democracy and the local trap. *Urban Studies*, 43(11), pp. 1921–1941.

Raco, M., 2006. Rethinking urban competitiveness, cohesion and governance. *Public Administration*, 84, pp. 513–515.

Raco, M., Parker, G. and Doak, J., 2006. Reshaping spaces of local governance? Community strategies and the modernisation of local government in England. *Environment and Planning* C., 24(4), pp. 475–496.

Raffestin, C., 2012. Space, territory, and territoriality. *Environment and PlanningD*, 30(1), pp. 121–141.

Ranci, C., Brandsen, T. and Sabatinelli, S., eds, 2014. *Social Vulnerability in European Cities: The Role of Local Welfare in Times of Crisis*. Basingstoke: Palgrave Macmillan.

Rein, M. and Schön, D., 1996. Knowledge and policy. *The International Journal of Knowledge Transfer and Utilization*, 9(1), pp. 85–104.

Reyneri, E., 2011. *Sociologia del mercato del lavoro*. Bologna: Il Mulino.

Reyneri, E., 2015. Anti-poverty policies and the (decreasing) social cohesion in Europe: A comment. *Stato e Mercato*, 103, pp. 97–103.

Rhodes, R. A. W., 1996. The new governance: Governing without government. *Political Studies*, 44, pp. 652–667.

Rhodes, R. A. W., 2000. New Labour's civil service: Summing-up, joining-up. *Political Quarterly*, 71(2), pp. 151–166.

Rhodes, R. A. W., 2007. Understanding governance: Ten years on. *Organization Studies*, 28, pp. 1243–1264.

Rose, D., Germain, A., Bacqué, M.-H., Bridge, G., Fijalkow, Y. and Slater, T., 2013. 'Social mix' and neighbourhood revitalization in a transatlantic perspective: Comparing local policy discourses and expectations in Paris (France), Bristol (UK) and Montréal (Canada). *International Journal of Urban and Regional Research*, 37, pp. 430–450.

Rose, N., 1996. The death of the social?. *Economy and Society*, 25(3), pp. 327–356.

Rossi, U. and Vanolo, A., 2010. *Geografia politica urbana*. Bari-Rome: Laterza.

Sabatier, P. A. and Jenkins-Smith, H. C., 1993. The Advocacy Coalition Framework. In P. Sabatier and H. C. Jenkins-Smith, eds, *Policy Change and Learning: An Advocacy Coalition Approach*. Boulder, CO: Westview Press, pp. 211–235.

Sabel, C. and Dorf, M., 2006. *A Constitution of Democratic Experimentalism*. Cambridge, MA: Harvard University Press.

Sabel, C. F., 2012. Individualised Service Provision and the New Welfare State: Are there Lessons from Northern Europe for Developing Countries? In C. L. de Mello and M. A. Dutz, eds, *Promoting Inclusive Growth: Challenges and Policies*, Paris: OECD Publishing. http://dx.doi.org/10.1787/9789264168305-5-en

Sacchi, S., 2008. Il metodo aperto di coordinamento delle politiche sociali. In M. Ferrera and M. Giuliani, eds, *Governance e politiche nell'Unione europea*, Bologna: Il Mulino, pp. 269–301.

Salais, R., 2006. Reforming the European Social Model and the Politics of indicators: From the Unemployment Rate to the Employment Rate in the European Employment Strategy. In M. Jepsen and A. Serrano, eds, *Unwrapping the European Social Model*, Bristol: The Policy Press, pp. 189–212.

Salais, R., 2008. Capacités, base informationnelle et démocratie délibérative. Le (contre)-exemple de l'action publique européenne. In J. de Munck and B. Zimmermann eds, *La liberté au prisme des capacités. Amartya Sen au-delà du libéralisme*, Raisons pratiques, vol. 18, Paris: Editions de l'Ehess, pp. 297–326.

Salais, R., 2009. Deliberative Democracy and its Informational Basis: What Lessons from the Capability Approach. SASE (Society for the Advancement of Socio-Economics) Conference, July, Paris.https://halshs.archives-ouvertes.fr/halshs-00429574/document

Saraceno, C., 2002. Deconstructing the myth of welfare dependence. In C. Saraceno, ed., *Social Assistance Dynamics in Europe: National and Local Poverty Regimes*, Bristol: Polity Press.

Saraceno, C., 2009. Genere e cura: vecchie soluzioni per nuovi scenari?. *La Rivista delle Politiche Sociali*, 2, pp. 53–75.

Saraceno, C., 2010. Tra vecchi e nuovi rischi. *La Rivista delle Politiche Sociali*, 4, pp. 31–51.

Saraceno, C., 2013a. Trasformazioni dei welfare state e/o spostamenti discorsivi. *Stato e Mercato*, 97, pp. 67–80.

Saraceno, C., 2013b. *The Undercutting of the European Social Dimension*. LIEPP Working Paper, 7. http://www.sciencespo.fr/liepp/sites/sciencespo.fr.liepp/files/WP7-Saraceno.pdf.

Saraceno, C., 2013c. Three concurrent crises in welfare states in an increasingly asymmetrical European Union. *Stato e Mercato*, 99, pp. 339–358.

Saraceno, C., 2015. The fate of anti-poverty policies between austerity and Europe 2020 targets. *Stato e Mercato*, 1, pp. 29–52.

Sassen, S., 2006. *Territory, Authority, Rights: From Medieval to Global Assemblages*. Princeton, NJ: Princeton University Press.

Savage, M., Bagnall, G. and Longhurst, B., 2005. *Globalization and Belonging*. London: Sage.

Scharpf, F., 2002. The European social model: Coping with the challenges of diversity. *Journal of Common Market Studies*, 40(4), pp. 645–670.

Schmidt, V. A., 2011. Discursive Institutionalism. In F. Fischer and J. Forester, eds, *The Argumentative Turn Revised: Public Policy as Communicative Practice*, Durham, NC: Duke University Press, pp. 85–113.

Schmidt, V. A. and Thatcher, M., 2013. Theorizing Ideational Continuity: The Resilience of Neo-Liberal Ideas in Europe. In V. A. Schmidt and M. Thatcher, M., eds, *Resilient Liberalism: European Political Economy from Boom to Bust*, Cambridge: Cambridge University Press, pp. 1–50.

Schröer, R., 2015. Employability versus Capability: European Strategies for Young People. In H.-U. Otto, ed., *Facing Trajectories from School to Work: Towards a Capability-Friendly Youth Policy in Europe*. Dordrecht: Springer, pp. 361–386.

Sen, A. A., 1990. Justice: Means versus freedom. *Philosophy and Public Affairs*, 19(2), pp. 111–121.

Sen, A. A., 1992. *Inequality Re-Examined*. Oxford: Oxford University Press.

Sen, A. A., 1999. *Development as Freedom*. Oxford: Oxford University Press.

Sennett, R., 2003. *Respect: The Formation of Character in an Age of Inequality*. London: Penguin.

Sennett, R., 2006. *The Culture of the New Capitalism*. New Haven, CT, and London: Yale University Press.

Shahidi, F. V., 2015. Welfare capitalism in crisis: A qualitative comparative analysis of labour market policy responses to the great recession. *Journal of Social Policy*, 44, pp. 659–686.

Shore, C. and Wright, S., 2015. Governing by numbers: Audit culture, rankings and the new world order. *Social Anthropology/Anthropologie Sociale*, 23(1), pp. 22–28.

Silver, H., Scott, A. and Kazepov, Y., 2010. Participation in urban contention and deliberation. *International Journal of Urban and Regional Research*, 34, pp. 453–477.

Simonazzi, A., 2009. Care regimes and national employment models. *Cambridge Journal of Economics*, 33, pp. 211–232.

Smith, G. and Wales, C., 2000. Citizens' juries and deliberative democracy. *Political Studies*, 48, pp. 51–65.

Storey, A., 2008. The ambiguity of resistance: Opposition to neoliberalism in Europe. *Capital and Class*, 96, pp. 55–85.

Streeck, W., 2011. The crises of democratic capitalism. *New Left Review*, 71, pp. 5–29.

Streeck, W., 2013a. *Gekaufte Zeit*. Berlin: Suhrkamp Verlag (Eng. trans., *The Delayed Crisis of Democratic Capitalism*, 2014, Verso).

Streeck, W., 2013b. The construction of a moral duty for the Greek people to repay their national debt. *Socio-Economic Review*, 1, pp. 614–620.

Streeck, W. and Thelen, K., eds, 2005. *Beyond Continuity: Institutional Change in Advanced Political Economies*. Oxford: Oxford University Press.

Suleiman, R., 2005. *Le démantèlement de l'État démocratique*. Paris: Seuil.

Supiot, A., 2005. *Homo Juridicus. Essai sur la fonction anthropologique du Droit*. Paris: Seuil.

Supiot, A., 2010. *L'Esprit de Philadelphie*. Paris: Seuil.

Supiot, A., 2015. *La gouvernance par les nombres*. Paris: Fayard.

Swyngedouw, E., 2000. Authoritarian governance, power and the politics of rescaling. *Environment and Planning D*, 18, pp. 63–76.

Sztandar-Sztanderska, K. and Zieleńska, M., 2012. The development of capabilities of young people with low skills: The case study of a vocational education programme in Poland. *Social & Work Society*, 10(1), pp. 1–15.

Taylor, M., 2007. Community participation in the real World: Opportunities and pitfalls in new governance spaces. *Urban Studies*, 44, pp. 297–317.

Taylor-Gooby, P., 2004. *New Risks, New Welfare: The Transformation of the European Welfare State*. Oxford: Oxford University Press.

Taylor-Gooby, P., 2011. Opportunity and solidarity. *Journal of Social Policy*, 40, pp. 453–470.

Taylor-Gooby, P., 2012. Beveridge overboard?: How the UK government is using the crisis to permanently restructure the welfare state. *Intereconomics: Review of European Economic Policy*, 47(4), pp. 224–229.

Teasdale, S., 2012. What's in a Name? Making Sense of Social Enterprise Discourses. *Public Policy and Administration*, 27(2), pp. 99–119.

Tissot, S., 2007. *L'État et les quartiers. Genèse d'une catégorie de l'action publique.* Paris: Seuil.

Tissot, S., 2014. Loving diversity/controlling diversity: Exploring the ambivalent mobilization of upper-middle-class gentrifiers, South End, Boston. *International Journal of Urban and Regional Research*, 38, pp. 1181–1194.

Titmuss, R. M., 1958. *Essays on 'the Welfare State'.* London: Allen & Unwin.

Titmuss, R. M., 1974. *Social Policy.* London: Allen & Unwin.

Uitermark, J., 2005. The genesis and evolution of urban policy: A confrontation of regulationist and governmentality approaches. *Political Geography*, 24(2), pp. 137–163.

Ungerson, C., 1997. Social politics and the commodification of care. *Social Politics*, 4(3), pp. 362–381.

Unterhalter, E., 2009. What is equity in education? Reflections from the capability approach. *Studies in Philosophy and Education*, 28(5), pp. 415–424.

Urbinati, N., 2008. Il merito e l'uguaglianza. *La Repubblica*, 27 November.

Urbinati, N., 2009. *Individualismo democratico.* Rome: Donzelli.

van Berkel, R. and Hornemann Møller, I., eds, 2002. *Active Social Policies in the EU: Inclusion through Participation?*Bristol: Policy Press.

van Berkel, R. and Valkenburg, B., eds, 2007. *Making it Personal: Individualising Activation Services in the EU.* Bristol: Policy Press.

van der Aa, P. and van Berkel, R., 2014. Innovating job activation by involving employers. *International Social Security Review*, 67(2), pp. 11–27.

van Kersbergen, K., Vis, B. and Hemerijck, A., 2014. The great recession and welfare state restructuring: Is retrenchment the only game left in town? *Social Policy and Administration*, 48(7), pp. 883–904.

Vandenbroucke, F. and Vleminckx, K., 2011. Disappointing poverty trends: Is the social investment state to blame? An exercise in soul-searching for policymakers. *Journal of European Social Policy*, 21(5), pp. 450–471.

Vandenbroucke, F., Hemerijck, A. and Palier, B. 2011. *The EU Needs a Social Investment Pact*. OSE Paper Series, Opinion paper No. 5. Brussels: Observatoire Social Européen.

Vicari Haddock, S., 2004. *La città contemporanea.* Bologna: Il Mulino.

Vicari Haddock, S., 2005. La rigenerazione urbana: frammentazioni e integrazioni. In L. Bifulco, ed., *Le politiche sociali.* Rome: Carocci, pp. 117–134.

Vicari Haddock, S., 2009. La rigenerazione urbana: un concetto da rigenerare. In S. Vicari Haddock and F. Moulaert, eds, *Rigenerare la città.* Bologna: Il Mulino, pp. 19–50.

Vicari Haddock, S. and Moulaert, F., eds, 2009. *Rigenerare la città.* Bologna: Il Mulino.

Vis, B., van Kersbergen, K. and Hylands, T., 2011. To what extent did the financial crisis intensify the pressure to reform the welfare state?. *Social Policy & Administration*, 45, pp. 338–353.

Wagner, P., 1994. *A Sociology of Modernity.* London: Routledge.

Walker, M., 2005. The capability approach and Education. *Educational Action Research*, 13(1), pp. 103–110.

Wolin, S. S., 2008. *Democracy Incorporated*. Princeton, NJ: Princeton University Press.

Wood, M. and Flinders, M., 2014. Rethinking depoliticisation: Beyond the governmental. *Policy & Politics*, 2(2), 151–170.

Young, M., 1958. *The Rise of the Meritocracy, 1870–2033*. London: Thames & Hudson.

Zimmermann, B., 2006. Pragmatism and the capability approach: Challenges in social theory and empirical research. *European Journal of Social Theory*, 9, pp. 467–484.

# Index

Page numbers in *italics* refer to tables.

Printed in the United States
By Bookmasters